Lydia Whitesell

What Do The Prophets Say?

by

C. I. Scofield, D.D.

Author of "Rightly Dividing the Word of Truth." "The New Life in Christ Jesus," The Scofield Correspondence Bible Course, etc., and Editor of the Scofield Reference Bible

The Gospel Hour, Inc., Oliver B. Greene, Director
Box 2024, Greenville, South Carolina 29602

All rights reserved

TO
MY FRIEND
ALWYN BALL, JUNIOR,

whose generous fellowship and constant affection have done so much to make possible such work as I have, by God's grace, been enabled to do, I dedicate this book as a token of gratitude.

C. I. SCOFIELD.

Easter, 1918.
Greyshingles,
Douglaston, Long Island, N.Y.

FOREWORD

THAT the human race is in a supreme crisis is obvious to the dullest intelligence. Nothing like it has ever marked the long life of humanity on the earth. It is impossible to restrain the effort to find the meaning of it all. No one is really either satisfied with or convinced by the easy solutions proposed by a shallow optimism. For thirty years these prophets of peace without righteousness have assured us that great and serious wars were ended forever; and yet we are in the greatest and most serious of all wars. *What does it all mean?*

The Christian believes that somehow, somewhere, the answer is in the writings of the Prophets—writings authenticated by Jesus Christ (Luke 16:31; 24:27, 44), and by hundreds of literal fulfilments. But these writings, plain and explicit in themselves, have been forced into meanings utterly foreign to the language used, in the effort to make them apply to the Church instead of to Israel; or have been the ready resort of unscholarly fanatics.

Surely it is timely that a sane and reasonable interpretation of those writings should be found. This book is a sincere effort to present such an interpretation, after thirty-five years of earnest study.

C. I. Scofield.

Greyshingles, Douglaston, L. I.
  Easter, 1918.

CONTENTS

		PAGE
I.	DOES THE BIBLE THROW LIGHT ON THIS WAR?	9
II.	THE PROPHET	21
III.	THE ETHICAL MESSAGE	27
IV.	THE MESSIAH	37
V.	THE VISION OF THE KINGDOM	53
VI.	THE PROPHETIC MINISTRY OF JESUS CHRIST	75
VII.	THE PROPHETIC MESSAGE OF THE ACTS	99
VIII.	PROPHECY IN THE EPISTLES	111
IX.	THE REVELATION	127
X.	THE LAST SEVEN YEARS OF THE AGE	141
XI.	EARTH'S GOLDEN AGE	159

As a convenience to the reader, almost every passage of Scripture referred to throughout this book is given, in whole or in part, in the footnotes. And the reader will find that, for his further convenience, the same Scripture material is repeated over and over again in these footnotes, so that he may have constantly before him, without having to turn pages or look up references in his Bible, the Word of God on which this book is based.

A Scripture Index at the end of the book will enable one to find the location of every Scripture passage here discussed; the Topical Index locates many details of prophecy on which God's Word throws light.

I. DOES THE BIBLE THROW LIGHT ON THIS WAR?

WHAT significance, if any, has the great war now raging over Europe and the East in the light of prophecy? May it be confidently affirmed that this particular war is mentioned in the prophetic Word? If it be true that "prophecy is history written beforehand" it might well seem a strange thing if a war wholly without parallel in human history should be passed without notice in the Scriptures. With such light as I have, I shall try to meet the question fairly. I hold no new or peculiar theories of prophetic interpretation, nor have I any novel doctrine in the interests of which I might be tempted to force favorable applications of obscure predictions.

Perhaps no other one thing has done so much to bring the study and teaching of prophecy into its present evident neglect as too hasty generalizations. The method is easy; it dispenses with long and arduous study and reflection; and often serves to make a desired point. But it is not convincing, and the conclusions so reached are soon invalidated by the discovery of other passages which can by no means be brought into harmony with them.

All such conclusions are reached in disregard of the great inspired rule governing prophetical interpretation, "Knowing this first, that no prophecy of the Scripture is of its own interpretation" (2 Pet. 1:20, Version of 1911),—that is, no prophecy is to be interpreted "by itself," but in harmony with the whole body of prediction on any given subject. What a safeguard of sanity that is! It is not too much to say that, had Peter's rule been observed we should have had, with some minor disagreements no doubt, a majestic consensus of interpretation of the body of predictive prophecy.

In all fairness, however, it must be said that not the faddists only, but the very men who carefully avoid every savor of fanaticism, and pride themselves on sanity as their honorable characteristic, have been sinners also against Peter's rule. The common misinterpretation of the numerous and explicit predictions of the Lord's return, that he comes for the believer at death, may serve to illustrate this. The most superficial study of the passages would have shown that whatever they mean they cannot mean that.

The first thing which Peter's rule does for us is to send us to the Bible with our questions about the future. We speak sometimes of "far-seeing" men. Apart from inspiration there are no such men. Merely human attempts to forecast the future have always been put to shame by the event. Urquhart has brought together a number of striking illustrations of this. At crises in human affairs the ablest men of the time have spoken with assurance of the outcome. In no instance was the attempt successful. Just now many about us are essaying the never accomplished task. We are told that so shocked is humanity by the carnage and suffering of the present struggle that it will never tolerate another war. We are told that the inevitable outcome of this desperate struggle will be the federation of nations in "the United States of the World." But, even if that come to pass, it will not insure the peace of the peoples. The federation known as the United States of America did not safeguard those States from a long and bloody war. Our question then is to be put to Holy Writ. If there is no answer there, there is no answer anywhere.

But an honest application of Peter's rule sends us to the whole body of revealed truth concerning the future. Not that all prophecy has to do with the political future of the nations of the earth; but all prophecy must be searched that such parts of the whole as bear upon that future may be gathered into our thought. For prophecy, like all revealed truth, is vitally interrelated. Scripture is to be thought of not as an edifice built of separate stones, but as a stately tree, built of interlaced fibers—a growth, not a structure. I propose, therefore, in sub-

DOES THE BIBLE THROW LIGHT ON THIS WAR? 11

sequent chapters, such a survey of the prophetic Word as will put us at the right point of vision for the finding of our answer. Surely such an attempt to see in due and sober proportion what it has pleased God to reveal of the future of our race is well worth our thought at the present tremendous moment.

To say what may be the significance of this unprecedented world-war requires more than a citation of some supposedly applicable text. For prophecy on the great world-scale deals in epochs, and sweeps centuries into its ken. Prophecy has to do with great periods called "ages." We are living to-day in two of these ages; two streams of prophecy have met and flow on together, but do not mingle. These are, the "Times of the Gentiles," and the Church Age.

Of the first, Daniel is the chief prophet; of the second, Christ. And it is to be carefully noted that Christ authenticates Daniel, and sends us to him for information (Matt. 24:15).[1]

It is Christ, moreover, who gives us both the name and the sign of the times of the Gentiles:

"And Jerusalem shall be trodden down of the Gentiles, until the times of the Gentiles be fulfilled" (Luke 21:24).

Obviously the words refer to the political rule of the Gentiles; and the specific sign which marks the presence and continuance of the rule is Gentile domination over Jerusalem. This enables us to fix with certainty the beginning of the "times of the Gentiles." For the first Gentile overlord of Jerusalem was Necco, king of Egypt (2 Chron. 36:3-5).[2] But his authority was short lived and negligible. With the conquest of Jerusalem by

---

[1] When ye therefore shall see the abomination of desolation, spoken of by Daniel the prophet, stand in the holy place, (whoso readeth, let him understand:) —*Matt. 24:15.*

[2] And the king of Egypt put him down at Jerusalem, and condemned the land in a hundred talents of silver and a talent of gold.

And the king of Egypt made Eliakim his brother king over Judah and Jerusalem, and turned his name to 'Jehoiakim. And Necho took Jehoahaz his brother, and carried him to Egypt.

Jehoiakim *was* twenty and five years old when he began to reign, and he reigned eleven years in Jerusalem: and he did *that which was* evil in the sight of the Lord his God.—*2 Chron. 36:3-5.*

WHAT DO THE PROPHETS SAY?

Nebuchadnezzar, 606 B. C., began the period, of more than two thousand five hundred years' duration, in which we are living, and of which the present world-war may be the beginning of the end.

Two things mark in Scripture the beginning of a new dispensation—miracle, and a new prophetic revelation. With the captivity of Judah began the times of the Gentiles, and it was then, at the beginning of the rule of the Gentiles over the earth, that to Daniel was revealed in broad outline the whole course of that epoch, and with minute detail its end (Dan. 2:1-45; 7:1-27; 9:20-27; 11:36 to 12:3).[3]

The outline of Gentile world rule is simple. Four great empires are to dominate the scene; and these are of easy identification to the student of history, first, by the order of their succession, and, secondly, by the characteristics given them in the prophecy. Empires in just the order given by Daniel *have* arisen, *have* possessed the characters ascribed to them by Daniel, and *have* passed away. The event has exactly justified the foreview. The Babylon of Nebuchadnezzar, Medo-Persia, the Greece of Alexander the Great, and Rome have come and gone.

And still not altogether gone. Strange as the statement may at first sight seem, we are not done with the Roman Empire yet.

According to the Danielic foreview the fourth or Roman Empire passes through four distinct phases. These are:

1. The "iron" period (Dan. 2:40; 7:7),[4] fulfilled in the history of Rome during the centuries of growth, union, and conquest.

2. The division into two, symbolized by the two legs

---

[3] This Scripture material is discussed in detail in the later chapters.

[4] And the fourth kingdom shall be strong as iron: forasmuch as iron breaketh in pieces and subdueth all *things:* and as iron that breaketh all these, shall it break in pieces and bruise.—*Dan. 2:40.*

After this I saw in the night visions, and behold a fourth beast, dreadful and terrible, and strong exceedingly; and it had great iron teeth: it devoured and brake in pieces, and stamped the residue with the feet of it: and it *was* diverse from all the beasts that *were* before it; and it had ten horns.—*Dan. 7:7.*

DOES THE BIBLE THROW LIGHT ON THIS WAR? 13

of the Image Vision and fulfilled in the division of the empire into Eastern and Western.

3. The period of further division and of deterioration (2:41, 42)[5] resulting in the present national world-system with the iron of the *imperium* mingled with the "brittle" (not "miry," as in Authorized Version) element of the fluctuant popular will, as in the constitutional monarchies and republics which have come into existence in that which was formerly the great fourth Empire of Rome. Thus, by a necessary historical sequence not at all depending on some arbitrary system of supposed chronology based upon the dates of the decrees of Cyrus or Darius, we are brought down to our own time. The division territorially, and deterioration in respect of power held to obedience to one will, has come to pass. We are living in the day of it, and it is the nations formed out of ancient Rome that are (with the exception of Russia) engaged to-day in the war of wars – which may indeed be the death struggle of the present world system.

For the Prophecy of Daniel, confirmed by our Lord's own testimony, and reinforced by that other great book of the end-time, The Revelation, is clear that what follows the Third Period of the Fourth Empire, the period of division and deterioration, is the kingdom which the God of the heaven sets up, the kingdom which has no successor, but endures forever (2:44, 45).[6]

But it is important to note that the end-time of the

---

[5] And whereas thou sawest the feet and toes, part of potters' clay, and part of iron, the kingdom shall be divided; but there shall be in it of the strength of the iron, forasmuch as thou sawest the iron mixed with miry clay.
And *as* the toes of the feet *were* part of iron, and part of clay, so the kingdom shall be partly strong, and partly broken. —*Dan.* 2:41, 42.

[6] And in the days of these kings shall the God of heaven set up a kingdom, which shall never be destroyed: and the kingdom shall not be left to other people, *but* it shall break in pieces and consume all these kingdoms, and it shall stand for ever.
Forasmuch as thou sawest that the stone was cut out of the mountain without hands, and that it brake in pieces the iron, the brass, the clay, the silver, and the gold; the great God hath made known to the king what shall come to pass hereafter: and the dream *is* certain, and the interpretation thereof sure.—*Dan.* 2:44, 45.

last phase of the history of that which once was Rome, and is now the nations at war, forms a period in itself, of which prophecy gives us a detailed description:

4. The period of the end of the Times of the Gentiles (Dan. 7:8, 19-26; 9:26, 27; 11:36).[7]

The detail will be given in chapters which are to follow. I must be permitted again to lay emphasis upon Peter's rule, and to say once more that it is folly to hope

---

[7] I considered the horns, and, behold, there came up among them another little horn, before whom there were three of the first horns plucked up by the roots: and, behold, in this horn *were* eyes like the eyes of man, and a mouth speaking great things.—*Dan. 7:8.*

Then I would know the truth of the fourth beast, which was diverse from all the others, exceeding dreadful, whose teeth *were of* iron, and his nails *of* brass; *which* devoured, brake in pieces, and stamped the residue with his feet;

And of the ten horns that *were* in his head, and *of* the other which came up, and before whom three fell; even *of* that horn that had eyes, and a mouth that spake very great things, whose look *was* more stout than his fellows.

I beheld, and the same horn made war with the saints, and prevailed against them;

Until the Ancient of days came, and judgment was given to the saints of the Most High; and the time came that the saints possessed the kingdom.

Thus he said, The fourth beast shall be the fourth kingdom upon earth, which shall be diverse from all kingdoms, and shall devour the whole earth, and shall tread it down, and break it in pieces.

And the ten horns out of this kingdom *are* ten kings *that* shall arise: and another shall rise after them; and he shall be diverse from the first, and he shall subdue three kings.

And he shall speak *great* words against the Most High, and shall wear out the saints of the Most High, and think to change times and laws: and they shall be given into his hand until a time and times and the dividing of time.

But the judgment shall sit, and they shall take away his dominion, to consume and to destroy *it* unto the end.—*Dan. 7: 19-26.*

And after threescore and two weeks shall Messiah be cut off, but not for himself: and the people of the prince that shall come shall destroy the city and the sanctuary; and the end thereof *shall be* with a flood, and unto the end of the war desolations are determined.

And he shall confirm the covenant with many for one week: and in the midst of the week he shall cause the sacrifice and the oblation to cease, and for the overspreading of abominations he shall make *it* desolate, even until the consummation, and that determined shall be poured upon the desolate.—*Dan. 9: 26, 27.*

And the king shall do according to his will; and he shall exalt himself, and magnify himself above every god, and shall speak marvellous things against the God of gods, and shall prosper till the indignation be accomplished: for that that is determined shall be done.—*Dan. 11: 36.*

DOES THE BIBLE THROW LIGHT ON THIS WAR? 15

to understand prophecy from the study of fragments. It is only in the field of Bible study that any such false hope is entertained. In no other department of human inquiry is it expected that clear and convincing knowledge may be secured by the method which has been aptly called "grasshopper" study.

I have mentioned, for example, in a preceding paragraph, "the kingdom which the God of heaven sets up" after the Gentile rule over the earth is ended. But, obviously, that raises the whole question of that kingdom—what it will be, and how it will come. The mere statement might well mean a half-dozen different things to as many different readers. There is no short cut to sound results in Bible study any more than in the study of other fields.

It may, however, be helpful to present in outline the prophetic testimony concerning the end-time of Gentile rule over the earth, taking up throughout this book the proof in detail.

1. The age ends in catastrophe. No prophetic voice describes the end of the "times of the Gentiles" in the peaceful terms which uninspired forecasters in pulpits and newspapers have made familiar. Daniel says that the end "shall be with a flood"; and that, "unto the end wars and desolations are determined." The Lord Jesus finds in the Biblical history of the flood, and of the destruction of Sodom and Gomorrah, suited pictures of the end-time of the age. "As it was in the days of Noah." "As it was in the days of Lot." The significance is terrible. The age which ended with the flood was prosperous, busy, famous, wicked, and though warned was unheeding (Dan. 9:26; Luke 17:26-30; Gen. 4:21, 22; 6:4; Matt. 24:37-39).[8] When the astonished disciples

---

[8] And after threescore and two weeks shall Messiah be cut off, but not for himself: and the people of the prince that shall come shall destroy the city and the sanctuary; and the end thereof *shall be* with a flood, and unto the end of the war desolations are determined.—*Dan. 9:26.*

And as it was in the days of Noe, so shall it be also in the days of the Son of man.

They did eat, they drank, they married wives, they were given in marriage, until the day that Noe entered into the ark, and the flood came, and destroyed them all.

Likewise also as it was in the

would know details of place and time, our Lord referred them to Armageddon (Luke 17:37; Rev. 19:17-21).[9]

His foreview of the end of the age includes wars, famines, and pestilences, as the mere "beginning of sorrows" (Matt. 24:6-8),[10] and these deepen into the great tribulation which in turn is brought to a close only by the appearing of Christ in glory and the battle of

---

days of Lot; they did eat, they drank, they bought, they sold, they planted, they builded;

But the same day that Lot went out of Sodom it rained fire and brimstone from heaven, and destroyed *them* all.

Even thus shall it be in the day when the Son of man is revealed.—*Luke 17: 26-30.*

And his brother's name *was* Jubal: he was the father of all such as handle the harp and organ.

And Zillah, she also bare Tubal-cain, an instructor of every artificer in brass and iron: and the sister of Tubal-cain *was* Naamah.—*Gen. 4: 21, 22.*

There were giants in the earth in those days; and also after that, when the sons of God came in unto the daughters of men, and they bare *children* to them, the same *became* mighty men which *were* of old, men of renown.—*Gen. 6: 4.*

But as the days of Noe *were*, so shall also the coming of the Son of man be.

For as in the days that were before the flood they were eating and drinking, marrying, and giving in marriage, until the day that Noe entered into the ark,

And knew not until the flood came, and took them all away; so shall also the coming of the Son of man be.—*Matt. 24: 37-39.*

[9] And they answered and said unto him, Where, Lord? And he said unto them, Wheresoever the body *is*, thither will the eagles be gathered together.—*Luke 17: 37.*

And I saw an angel standing in the sun; and he cried with a loud voice, saying to all the fowls that fly in the midst of heaven, Come and gather yourselves together unto the supper of the great God;

That ye may eat the flesh of kings, and the flesh of captains, and the flesh of mighty men, and the flesh of horses, and of them that sit on them, and the flesh of all *men*, both free and bond, both small and great.

And I saw the beast, and the kings of the earth, and their armies, gathered together to make war against him that sat on the horse, and against his army.

And the beast was taken, and with him the false prophet that wrought miracles before him, with which he deceived them that had received the mark of the beast, and them that worshipped his image. These both were cast alive into a lake of fire burning with brimstone.

And the remnant were slain with the sword of him that sat upon the horse, which *sword* proceeded out of his mouth: and all the fowls were filled with their flesh.—*Rev. 19: 17-21.*

[10] And ye shall hear of wars and rumours of wars: see that ye be not troubled: for all *these things* must come to pass, but the end is not yet.

For nation shall rise against nation, and kingdom against kingdom: and there shall be famines, and pestilences, and earthquakes, in divers places.

All these *are* the beginning of sorrows.—*Matt. 24: 6-8.*

Armageddon (Matt. 24:15-30; Rev. 19:11-21).[11] Then, and not till then, the "Stone cut out without hands" smites upon its feet the image of Nebuchadnezzar's dream—the image in which the whole period of Gentile

[11] When ye therefore shall see the abomination of desolation, spoken of by Daniel the prophet, stand in the holy place, (whoso readeth, let him understand:)

Then let them which be in Judæa flee into the mountains:

Let him which is on the housetop not come down to take any thing out of his house:

Neither let him which is in the field return back to take his clothes.

And woe unto them that are with child, and to them that give suck in those days!

But pray ye that your flight be not in the winter, neither on the sabbath day:

For then shall be great tribulation, such as was not since the beginning of the world to this time, no, nor ever shall be.

And except those days should be shortened, there should no flesh be saved: but for the elect's sake those days shall be shortened.

Then if any man shall say unto you, Lo, here *is* Christ, or there; believe *it* not.

For there shall arise false Christs, and false prophets, and shall shew great signs and wonders: insomuch that, if *it were* possible, they shall deceive the very elect.

Behold, I have told you before.

Wherefore if they shall say unto you, Behold, he is in the desert; go not forth: behold, *he is* in the secret chambers; believe *it* not.

For as the lightning cometh out of the east, and shineth even unto the west; so shall also the coming of the Son of man be.

For wheresoever the carcass is, there will the eagles be gathered together.

Immediately after the tribulation of those days shall the sun be darkened, and the moon shall not give her light, and the stars shall fall from heaven, and the powers of the heavens shall be shaken:

And then shall appear the sign of the Son of man in heaven: and then shall all the tribes of the earth mourn, and they shall see the Son of man coming in the clouds of heaven with power and great glory.—*Matt. 24: 15-30.*

And I saw heaven opened, and behold a white horse; and he that sat upon him *was* called Faithful and True, and in righteousness he doth judge and make war.

His eyes *were* as a flame of fire, and on his head *were* many crowns; and he had a name written, that no man knew, but he himself.

And he *was* clothed with a vesture dipped in blood: and his name is called The Word of God.

And the armies *which were* in heaven followed him upon white horses, clothed in fine linen, white and clean.

And out of his mouth goeth a sharp sword, that with it he should smite the nations; and he shall rule them with a rod of iron: and he treadeth the winepress of the fierceness and wrath of Almighty God.

And he hath on *his* vesture and on his thigh a name written, KING OF KINGS, AND LORD OF LORDS.

And I saw an angel standing in the sun; and he cried with a loud voice, saying to all the fowls that fly in the midst of heaven, Come and gather yourselves together unto the supper of the great God;

world power is set forth (Dan. 2:34, 35)[12]; and then, and not till then, is the kingdom of the "God of heaven" set up. The "Stone" delivers the destructive blow before it becomes a great power, and "fills the whole earth" (Dan. 2:35, 44, 45).[13] In no sense can the destructive blow be said to have fallen at the first advent of Christ, for the smiting is upon the *feet* of the image—the last form of the fourth or Roman empire, and that empire had not entered upon the period of division at the time of the first advent.

2. So far as the prophetic Word has spoken there is not the least warrant for the expectation that the nations engaged in the present gigantic struggle will or can make a permanent peace. It is fondly dreamed that

---

That ye may eat the flesh of kings, and the flesh of captains, and the flesh of mighty men, and the flesh of horses, and of them that sit on them, and the flesh of all *men, both* free and bond, both small and great.

And I saw the beast, and the kings of the earth, and their armies, gathered together to make war against him that sat on the horse, and against his army.

And the beast was taken, and with him the false prophet that wrought miracles before him, with which he deceived them that had received the mark of the beast, and them that worshipped his image. These both were cast alive into a lake of fire burning with brimstone.

And the remnant were slain with the sword of him that sat upon the horse, which *sword* proceeded out of his mouth: and all the fowls were filled with their flesh.—*Rev. 19: 11-21.*

[12] Thou sawest till that a stone was cut out without hands, which smote the image upon his feet *that were* of iron and clay, and brake them to pieces.

Then was the iron, the clay, the brass, the silver, and the gold, broken to pieces together, and became like the chaff of the summer threshingfloors; and the wind carried them away, that no place was found for them: and the stone that smote the image became a great mountain, and filled the whole earth.—*Dan. 2: 34, 35.*

[13] Then was the iron, the clay, the brass, the silver, and the gold broken to pieces together, and became like the chaff of the summer threshingfloors; and the wind carried them away, that no place was found for them: and the stone that smote the image became a great mountain, and filled the whole earth. . . .

And in the days of these kings shall the God of heaven set up a kingdom, which shall never be destroyed: and the kingdom shall not be left to other people, but it shall break in pieces and consume all these kingdoms, and it shall stand for ever.

Forasmuch as thou sawest that the stone was cut out of the mountain without hands, and that it brake in pieces the iron, the brass, the clay, the silver, and the gold; the great God hath made known to the king what shall come to pass hereafter: and the dream *is* certain, and the interpretation thereof sure. —*Dan. 2: 35, 44, 45.*

DOES THE BIBLE THROW LIGHT ON THIS WAR? 19

out of all the suffering and carnage and destruction of this war will be born such a hatred of war as will bring to pass a federation of the nations—the United States of the World—in which will exist but one army, and that an international police, rather than an army.

For once there is some correspondence between a popular dream and the prophetic Word. For that word certainly points to a federated world-empire in the end-time of the age. But that federation is headed up in the "little horn" of Daniel; the "abomination of desolation" of our Lord's great prophetic discourse (Matt. 24: 15)[14]; the "man of sin" of Paul (2 Thess. 2:8-10)[15]; the beast out of the sea of Revelation 13.[16] But the peace which for a little time results is that of universal subjection to earth's last and most hateful despot, and it ends in Armageddon (Rev. 19:11-21).[11]

It is, of course, possible, nay, probable that some temporary truce may end, or suspend for a time, the present world-war, for ten kingdoms will exist at the end-time in the territory once ruled over by Rome. But it will probably be a brief truce, for it is in precisely that state of the old world that the Little Horn comes into the

---

[14] When ye therefore shall see the abomination of desolation, spoken of by Daniel the prophet, stand in the holy place, (whoso readeth, let him understand:)—*Matt. 24: 15.*

[15] And then shall that Wicked be revealed, whom the Lord shall consume with the spirit of his mouth, and shall destroy with the brightness of his coming:
Even him, whose coming is after the working of Satan with all power and signs and lying wonders,
And with all deceivableness of unrighteousness in them that perish; because they received not the love of the truth, that they might be saved.—*2 Thess. 2: 8-10.*

[16] And I stood upon the sand of the sea, and saw a beast rise up out of the sea, having seven heads and ten horns, and upon his horns ten crowns, and upon his heads the name of blasphemy . . . .
And there was given unto him a mouth speaking great things and blasphemies; and power was given unto him to continue forty *and* two months.
And he opened his mouth in blasphemy against God, to blaspheme his name, and his tabernacle, and them that dwell in heaven.
And it was given unto him to make war with the saints, and to overcome them: and power was given him over all kindreds, and tongues, and nations.
And all that dwell upon the earth shall worship him, whose names are not written in the book of life of the Lamb slain from the foundation of the world.—*Rev. 13: 1, 5, 6, 7, 8.*

scene. His appearance rekindles the flames of war, for he swiftly brings under his rule three of the ten kingdoms. He will be the consummate genius of the race of Adam. Of him Antiochus Epiphanes and Napoleon Bonaparte were but adumbrations, and with him on the stage the final tragedy advances with incredible swiftness.

3. But across the awful chasm of a war-cursed earth into which Gentile world-power plunges,—is possibly even now plunging,—rises the blessed vision of the kingdom to be set up by the "God of heaven." And this, and not the story of Gentile tyranny and bloodshed, and of the tragic and pathetic failure of the Gentiles to govern the world in righteousness, forms the great theme of prophecy. When the prophets describe the coming kingdom their pens are dipped in glory. Then—and, oh, how blessedly near it may be!—earth shall have the golden age dreamed of by all the poets, and longed for by all who have loved humanity. Then shall all the ways of God be justified; then shall be born the men and women whose intellects, disenthralled of sin, shall produce a civilization the beauty and power of which we cannot now imagine, for, "the creation itself also shall be delivered from the bondage of corruption into the glorious liberty of the sons of God."

II. THE PROPHET

THE Hebrew prophet is an arresting figure. Lonely, antagonizing kings and priests; austere, seeking no disciples; persecuted, invulnerable alike to bribes and threats; frequently passing on to martyrdom, master through the Spirit of every form of literary expression, a patriot filled with passionate love for Israel,—no men have appeared in human history more lofty in character or of higher courage.

The prophet formed no part of the organized life of the Hebrew Commonwealth. He bore no office which constituted him a prophet. The normal agency for the communication of the Divine will in special emergencies lay in a promise to the priesthood:

"And there I will meet with thee, and I will commune with thee from above the mercy seat, from between the two cherubims which are upon the ark of the testimony, of all things which I will give thee in commandment unto the children of Israel" (Exod. 25:22).

But communion with God is a spiritual act. The High Priest had the *privilege* of that communion as representing the people before God, but that privilege of necessity supposed a High Priest in happy, humble fellowship with God. Even the believer of to-day, who is in possession of the written Word of God, and who is indwelt by the Spirit of God, must himself be spiritual before he can comprehend the deeper meanings and messages of that Word. "He that is spiritual judgeth" (1 Cor. 2:15) is still the inflexible condition. It was, therefore, when the priests became mere performers of a ritual, unspiritual, avaricious, conceiving the religion of Jehovah to lie in external acts and ceremonies, that prophets appeared. *The appearing in Israel of a prophet always meant that Jehovah had a controversy with his people.*

It is most instructive to note the qualifications of a prophet. In the beginning he was called "the man of God" (for example, 1 Sam. 2:27).[1] It was not a divinely bestowed designation; it was the unconscious testimony of the people among whom he lived to his life and character. I have been told that some years ago "Billy" Sunday wrote a letter to the late Major Cole, the evangelist, addressing it, "To the Man of God, Adrian, Michigan." When that letter reached Adrian there was neither delay nor hesitation in its delivery. Within an hour it was in Major Cole's hands. Adrian knew that "a man of God" dwelt in their midst.

Then this man of God came to be called the "seer," the man who could *see* (for example, 2 Sam. 24:11).[2] Like Moses he "endured as seeing him who is invisible." He was a man whose eyes God had opened (Num. 24:3),[3] and God could do that because he was "a man of God." And so, being God's man in Israel, and having for that reason the vision of God, he became a "prophet" —Jehovah's spokesman to Israel.

It has been well said that the Hebrew prophet was not primarily so much a foreteller as a forthteller—a fearless, inspired voice of rebuke, instruction in righteousness, exhortation, and warning. And this part of his ministry concerned not only the individual conscience of the Israelite, but even more the corporate life and conduct of Israel the nation. He was invariably a patriot burning with the conviction that to his nation had been given a priestly and spiritual relation to the Gentile nations as representing the one and only true God, and the blessedness of that people whose God was Jehovah. He knew that while nations rose and fell, the little commonwealth of Israel had but to abide in obedience and

---

[1] And there came a man of God unto Eli, and said unto him, Thus saith the Lord, Did I plainly appear unto the house of thy father, when they were in Egypt in Pharaoh's house?—*1 Sam. 2:27*.

[2] For when David was up in the morning, the word of the Lord came unto the prophet Gad, David's seer.—*2 Sam. 24:11*.

[3] And he took up his parable, and said, Balaam the son of Beor hath said, and the man whose eyes are open hath said.—*Num. 24:3*.

loyalty to her unseen King, to rest secure and invulnerable under his protection (Psa. 89:18 and preceding).[4]

The primary ministry of the prophets, therefore, was patriotic and intensely ethical. They saw peace for Israel only through righteousness (Isa. 32:17, for example).[5] Nothing else would answer. On that high condition and no other would Jehovah throw about the land which he had given to his people the invisible wall of his protection; on that condition and no other should the people be at peace among themselves; on that condition and no other might the individual Israelite be at peace in his own soul. In no part of the Scriptures does the ethical demand rise to greater heights. The Sermon on the Mount is but the ethical teaching of the prophets lifted to its highest potency.

But along with this inflexible demand for righteousness, the prophets revealed attributes and characteristics in God so lovely, so tender, so faithful, that to remain in ignorance of the prophetic writings is to deprive the soul of a vision of God which every soul of man deeply needs.

The patriotic and ethical messages of the prophets fell upon ears grown dull of hearing. The little nation had become rich and ambitious. False prophets abounded, and then as now their message was, "Peace, peace." They were pleasantly optimistic while the true prophets were warning of judgment and captivity. To the sternest and most unsparing of his own prophets Jehovah said, "And, lo, thou art unto them as a very lovely song of one that hath a pleasant voice, and can play well on an instrument: for they hear thy words, but they do them not." The people felt the power of Ezekiel and flocked to hear him, as we do to-day under like circumstances.

It is then, when warnings and pleadings are unheeded, that *predictive* prophecy awakes, and the future is revealed. A familiar and striking illustration of this prin-

---

[4] For the Lord is our defence, and the Holy One of Israel *is* our king.—*Psalm 89:18*.

[5] And the work of righteousness shall be peace; and the effect of righteousness quietness and assurance for ever.—*Isa. 32:17*.

ciple is the great "Immanuel" prediction of Isaiah 7: 10-14.[6]

Under the menace of an impending invasion of Judah by Samaria, leagued with Syria, Isaiah sought to bring King Ahaz back to faith in Jehovah. He was given the unprecedented privilege of himself choosing a sign that might serve as a support to his faith. The king refused even to ask. And then came the burst of predictive prophecy, the supreme "sign," not to the apostate king, but to the "house of David"; the "sign" that made every maiden descendant of David from that time,—for the "sign" has no time-note,—the possible mother of the Messiah.

And these men, thus raised up of God, left to succeeding generations a body of writings unsurpassed if not unequaled in all literature, sacred or secular, in the great qualities of simplicity, directness, striking imagery, biting invective, and lofty splendor of eloquence. Authenticated by Jesus Christ and by the inspired writers of the New Testament; quoted, declared to be in many respects fulfilled, but holding also a far greater body of prediction as yet unfulfilled; called by the Apostle Peter "a light that shineth in a dark place" to which we of this age "do well" that we "take heed"—there is yet a neglect of the prophetic writings which has no parallel in our attitude toward any other great and serious literature.

It is impossible to overstate the loss to spirituality, to comprehension of God in himself and in his immutable purposes toward the earth and the race of men, resulting from this stupid neglect of nearly one-fourth in bulk of the Bible.

The fundamental factors of human life are unchanging, and the apparent changes are superficial. It has

---

[6] Moreover the Lord spake again unto Ahaz, saying,

Ask thee a sign of the Lord thy God; ask it either in the depth, or in the height above.

But Ahaz said, I will not ask, neither will I tempt the Lord.

And he said, Hear ye now, O house of David; *Is it* a small thing for you to weary men, but will ye weary my God also?

Therefore the Lord himself shall give you a sign; Behold, a virgin shall conceive, and bear a son, and shall call his name Immanuel.—*Isa. 7: 10-14.*

been the fond dream of modern optimism that civilization—that civilization which until yesterday we have been accustomed to call "Christian"—had modified primitive human nature. The present world-war has completely undeceived us. Man has not changed, nor has God. What God thought in the times of the prophets he thinks now. Quite apart, therefore, from the predictive element in prophecy, the revelation through the prophets of the mind of God, and of the divine nature and motives has a permanent and altogether inestimable value.

Christians in myriads, and strangest of all, ministers of the Word, thus remain in willing ignorance of this great body of truth.

Of preaching men this statement would be incredible if it were not so patently true. For no greater preachers have appeared among men than the Hebrew prophets. The prophetic writings are for the most part sermons. It is amazing that the teachers of homiletics do not enrich their instructions from these masterly discourses. Surely one would think it might be worth while to set students to the work of a reverent analysis of such sermons as those of Jeremiah *In the Gate of the 'King's House;* or the first sermon of Isaiah to *Backslidden Israel;* or Jeremiah's sermon on *The Broken Covenant.* Is anything in sermonic literature better worth study than Isaiah's discourse on *The Stretched-out Hand?* Might it not be a most rewarding use of a little time for preachers to study the art of Isaiah's sermon on *The Six Woes?* Has anything in the way of sermonic introduction been better done than Isaiah's leading up to his theme in that sermon?

Still more surprising is it that the predictive element in prophecy, so far as this remains unfulfilled, should engage so slight an interest in those whom God would fain take into his confidence. For prophecy, while refusing any satisfaction to mere curiosity, does, nevertheless, give in broad and clear outline the program of the future of the earth and of human life and destiny thereon.

There can be no doubt that the prophetic writings have been wounded in the house of their friends. Sane and thoughtful men have turned in weariness or disgust from the wild interpretations of well-meaning but ill-taught men. To these wild interpreters the most remote analogy between a prophecy and some passing or historical event has been sufficient warrant for declaring a fulfilment. The so-called "historical" interpretation of the Apocalypse, which finds in historic events the fulfilment of explicit predictions having no real likeness to the alleged fulfilment, may serve as illustrating this dogmatic but wholly imaginary kind of prophetic interpretation.

But the evil of so-called "spiritualizing" of prophecies, which came over into Protestantism from Rome, is the greater cause of the neglect of these writings. That interpretation which finds in the Christian Church the fulfilment of the numerous and explicit predictions which the prophets themselves declare relate to Israel, and to the kingdom covenanted to David and his seed, sufficiently explains the common attitude of neglect toward prophecy. For no other writings, Divine or human, are thus interpreted. No one even proposes to interpret a statute, or a contract, or a friendly letter, by a method so grotesque; and the consequence of the attempt seriously to apply that method to prophetic interpretation results, by a law of the human mind, in utter weariness and confusion.

Approach these writings as all other writings are approached; give these great preachers enough reverence to suppose that they were as capable of using language in its ordinary meaning as other preachers and writers; follow Peter's great rule of interpreting every prediction in harmony with all the other predictions on that subject (2 Pet. 1: 19-21)[7]; bring to the study a reverent desire to know, not merely that which is coming to pass, but the mind of God about life, and you will surely find Prophecy a mine of richest spiritual treasure.

---

[7] Knowing this first, that no prophecy of the scripture is of any private interpretation.—2 Pet. 1: 20.

III. THE ETHICAL MESSAGE

ISRAEL failed in not fulfilling the purpose for which she had been set apart. Because of this failure, the prophets were called upon to deliver their ethical message. It will be well for us to have in clear vision the purpose for which God had set apart Israel.

From the creation of man to the call of Abram the race is treated as a unit. Future racial distinctions are indicated in the declarations concerning the sons of Noah (Gen. 9: 25-27),[1] but prior to the call of Abram the covenants of God conditioning human life had a universal application, as had also the divine requirements. The first eleven chapters of Genesis recount three distinct testings of humanity under three specific covenants.

The Edenic Covenant (Gen. 2: 15-17)[2] conditioned the life of man in innocency—unfallen man. Made lord of creation, placed in a perfect environment, given absolute liberty in the use of all things needful for his full development, and such occupation as guarded him from the curse of idleness, one, and only one, prohibition limited his freedom; he must not know evil. He deliberately violated that prohibition (1 Tim. 2: 14),[3] with consequences disastrous to the race of which he was the father

---

[1] And he said, Cursed be Canaan; a servant of servants shall he be unto his brethren.

And he said, Blessed be the Lord God of Shem; and Canaan shall be his servant.

God shall enlarge Japheth, and he shall dwell in the tents of Shem; and Canaan shall be his servant.—*Gen. 9: 25-27.*

[2] And the Lord God took the man, and put him into the garden of Eden to dress it and to keep it.

And the Lord God commanded the man, saying, Of every tree of the garden thou mayest freely eat:

But of the tree of the knowledge of good and evil, thou shalt not eat of it: for in the day that thou eatest thereof thou shalt surely die.—*Gen. 2: 15-17.*

[3] And Adam was not deceived, but the woman being deceived was in the transgression.—*1 Tim. 2: 14.*

and head (Rom. 5:12; Psa. 14:1, 2; 51:5; 1 Cor. 2:14; 15:22).[4]

The Adamic Covenant (Gen. 3:14-19)[5] conditions the life on the earth of a fallen race. Physical death is the end of life. Toil is given as a condition of maintaining life. But upon this dark result of the fall of man shines the great evangelic promise of the Satan-Bruiser— the Seed of the woman. The knowledge of good and evil awoke conscience, and the moral testing of the race under conscience was the requirement that man should do good and not evil. The result after two thousand years was given in the divine declaration: "God saw that the wickedness of man was great in the earth, and that every imagination of the thoughts of his heart was only evil continually" (Gen. 6:5). The judgment of the Flood ended not conscience, indeed, but the testing of man under conscience. This Adamic Covenant, the testing of man under conscience, has still a racial obligation upon

---

[4] Wherefore, as by one man sin entered into the world, and death by sin; and so death passed upon all men, for that all have sinned,—*Rom. 5: 12.*

The fool hath said in his heart, *There is* no God. They are corrupt, they have done abominable works, *there is* none that doeth good.

The Lord looked down from heaven upon the children of men, to see if there were any that did understand, *and* seek God.— *Psalm 14: 1, 2.*

Behold, I was shapen in iniquity; and in sin did my mother conceive me.—*Psalm 51: 5.*

But the natural man receiveth not the things of the Spirit of God: for they are foolishness unto him: neither can he know *them,* because they are spiritually discerned.—*1 Cor. 2: 14.*

For as in Adam all die, even so in Christ shall all be made alive.—*1 Cor. 15: 22.*

[5] And the Lord God said unto the serpent, Because thou hast done this, thou *art* cursed above all cattle, and above every beast of the field; upon thy belly shalt thou go, and dust shalt thou eat all the days of thy life.

And I will put enmity between thee and the woman, and between thy seed and her seed; it shall bruise thy head, and thou shalt bruise his heel.

Unto the woman he said, I will greatly multiply thy sorrow and thy conception; in sorrow thou shalt bring forth children, and thy desire *shall be* to thy husband, and he shall rule over thee.

And unto Adam he said, Because thou hast hearkened unto the voice of thy wife, and hast eaten of the tree, of which I commanded thee, saying, Thou shalt not eat of it: cursed *is* the ground for thy sake; in sorrow shalt thou eat *of* it all the days of thy life,

Thorns also and thistles shall it bring forth to thee, and thou shalt eat the herb of the field;

In the sweat of thy face shalt thou eat bread, till thou return unto the ground; for out of it wast thou taken: for dust thou *art,* and unto dust shalt thou return.—*Gen. 3: 14-19.*

THE ETHICAL MESSAGE

those who know neither the law nor the Gospel, but it brings as in the days of the Flood only condemnation (Rom. 2:12, et seq.).[6]

The Covenant to Noah (Gen. 9:5, 6)[7] established the principle of human government, the rule of man over men. It is still the charter of all civil government; for the right to take, judicially, human life is the highest function of government. Obviously the responsibility was to govern righteously, and the result was Babel and the judgment of the confusion of tongues.

With the migration of the survivors of the Flood and their posterity began the division of humanity into tribes and, ultimately, nations. These, with the single exception of the family of Shem, who had been set apart for a special relation to God in the Noahic Covenant (Gen. 9:26, 27),[8] soon became idolaters, and lost the knowledge of the true God. In Romans 1:21-23[9] the steps of that utter apostasy are traced, and the moving cause disclosed: "They did not like to retain God in their knowledge,"—literally, "did not approve God" (Rom. 1:28).

Hitherto, with one exception (the confusion of tongues, Gen. 11:6-9)[10] the solidarity of the Adamic

---

[6] For as many as have sinned without law shall also perish without law: and as many as have sinned in the law shall be judged by the law.—*Rom. 2:12.*

[7] And surely your blood of your lives will I require; at the hand of every beast will I require it, and at the hand of man; at the hand of every man's brother will I require the life of man.
Whoso sheddeth man's blood, by man shall his blood be shed: for in the image of God made he man.—*Gen. 9:5, 6.*

[8] And he said, Blessed *be* the Lord God of Shem; and Canaan shall be his servant.
God shall enlarge Japheth, and he shall dwell in the tents of Shem; and Canaan shall be his servant.—*Gen. 9:26, 27.*

[9] Because that, when they knew God, they glorified *him* not as God, neither were thankful; but became vain in their imaginations, and their foolish heart was darkened.
Professing themselves to be wise, they became fools,
And changed the glory of the uncorruptible God into an image made like to corruptible man, and to birds, and fourfooted beasts, and creeping things.—*Rom. 1:21-23.*

[10] And the Lord said, Behold, the people *is* one, and they have all one language; and this they begin to do and now nothing will be restrained from them, which they have imagined to do.
Go to, let us go down, and there confound their language, that they may not understand one another's speech.

race had been preserved. But now God begins to act upon the special promise to Shem: "God shall enlarge Japheth, and he shall dwell in the tents of Shem" (Gen. 9:27). One of the Semitic stock, Abram, is called out of Ur in Chaldea that in and through him and his seed the great redemptive purposes of God toward the whole race might be worked out. In Abraham, and in the Abrahamic Covenant (Gen. 12:1-3; 13:15, 16; 15:18 and preceding)[11] the nation which came to be called Israel, after the grandson of Abraham, to whom the Abrahamic Covenant was confirmed (Gen. 28:13 et seq.)[12] was set apart to a special work on behalf of Jehovah with the whole of humanity as the objective. This breadth of the divine intent is the sufficient answer to the charge of partiality in the choice of Israel which is sometimes ignorantly brought (Gen. 12:3; Isa. 2:2-4; 5:26; 9:1, 2; Jer. 16:19; Joel 3:9, 10).[13]

So the Lord scattered them abroad from thence upon the face of all the earth: and they left off to build the city.

Therefore is the name of it called Babel; because the Lord did there confound the language of all the earth; and from thence did the Lord scatter them abroad upon the face of all the earth.—*Gen. 11:6-9.*

[11] Now the Lord had said unto Abram, Get thee out of thy country, and from thy kindred, and from thy father's house, unto a land that I will shew thee:

And I will make of thee a great nation, and I will bless thee, and make thy name great; and thou shalt be a blessing:

And I will bless them that bless thee, and curse him that curseth thee: and in thee shall all families of the earth be blessed.—*Gen. 12:1-3.*

For all the land which thou seest, to thee will I give it, and to thy seed for ever.

And I will make thy seed as the dust of the earth: so that if a man can number the dust of the earth, *then* shall thy seed also be numbered.—*Gen. 13:15, 16.*

In the same day the Lord made a covenant with Abram, saying, Unto thy seed have I given this land, from the river of Egypt unto the great river, the river Euphrates.—*Gen. 15:18.*

[12] And, behold, the Lord stood above it, and said, I *am* the Lord God of Abraham thy father, and the God of Isaac: the land whereon thou liest, to thee will I give it, and to thy seed.—*Gen. 28:13.*

[13] And I will bless them that bless thee, and curse him that curseth thee: and in thee shall all families of the earth be blessed.—*Gen. 12:3.*

And it shall come to pass in the last days, *that* the mountain of the Lord's house shall be established in the top of the mountains, and shall be exalted above the hills; and all nations shall flow unto it.

And many people shall go and say, Come ye, and let us go up to the mountain of the Lord, to the house of the God of Jacob; and he will teach us of his ways,

THE ETHICAL MESSAGE

The nation descended from Abraham was chosen to be:
1. A witness to the unity of God in the midst of universal idolatry (Deut. 6:4; Isa. 43:10, 11.)[14]
2. To illustrate to the nations the blessedness of that people whose God is Jehovah (Deut. 33:26-29.)[15]
3. To receive and transmit the divine revelations. (Rom. 3:1, 2; Deut. 4:5, 6 et seq.)[16]

---

and we will walk in his paths: for out of Zion shall go forth the law, and the word of the Lord from Jerusalem.

And he shall judge among the nations, and shall rebuke many people: and they shall beat their swords into plowshares, and their spears into pruning hooks: nation shall not lift up sword against nation, neither shall they learn war any more.—*Isa. 2: 2-4.*

And he will lift up an ensign to the nations from far, and will hiss unto them from the end of the earth: and, behold, they shall come with speed swiftly.—*Isa. 5: 26.*

Nevertheless the dimness *shall* not *be* such as *was* in her vexation, when at the first he lightly afflicted the land of Zebulun and the land of Naphtali, and afterward did more grievously afflict *her* by the way of the sea, beyond Jordan, in Galilee of the nations.

The people that walked in darkness have seen a great light: they that dwell in the land of the shadow of death, upon them hath the light shined.—*Isa. 9: 1, 2.*

O Lord, my strength, and my fortress, and my refuge in the day of affliction, the Gentiles shall come unto thee from the ends of the earth, and shall say, Surely our fathers have inherited lies, vanity, and *things* wherein *there is* no profit.—*Jer. 16: 19.*

Proclaim ye this among the Gentiles; Prepare war, wake up the mighty men, let all the men of war draw near; let them come up:

Beat your plowshares into swords, and your pruning hooks into spears: let the weak say, I *am* strong.—*Joel 3: 9, 10.*

[14] Hear, O Israel: The Lord our God *is* one Lord.—*Deut. 6: 4.*

Ye *are* my witnesses, saith the Lord, and my servant whom I have chosen: that ye may know and believe me, and understand that I *am* he: before me there was no God formed, neither shall there be after me.

I, *even* I, *am* the Lord; and beside me *there is* no saviour.—*Isa. 43: 10, 11.*

[15] *There is* none like unto the God of Jeshurun, *who* rideth upon the heaven in thy help, and in his excellency on the sky.

The eternal God *is thy* refuge, and underneath *are* the everlasting arms: and he shall thrust out the enemy from before thee; and shall say, Destroy *them.*

Israel then shall dwell in safety alone: the fountain of Jacob *shall be* upon a land of corn and wine; also his heavens shall drop down dew.

Happy *art* thou, O Israel: who *is* like unto thee, O people saved by the Lord, the shield of thy help, and who *is* the sword of thy excellency! and thine enemies shall be found liars unto thee, and thou shalt tread upon their high places.—*Deut. 33: 26-29.*

[16] What advantage then hath the Jew? or what profit *is there* of circumcision?

4. To bring forth the Messiah; Seed of the woman (Gen. 3:15)[17]; seed of Abraham (Gen. 21:3; Matt. 1:1; Gal. 3:16)[18]; son of David (Matt. 1:1)[19]; Son of God (Luke 1:35)[20]; and Son of man (Matt. 16:13).[21]

In the first and second of these trusts committed to the chosen nation there was conspicuous failure. Again and again the people fell into idolatry, thus breaking down in their testimony to the unity and spirituality of God. The immoral and unrighteous conduct so rife in Israel broke down the national testimony to the blessedness of that people whose God is the LORD. Another grave fault was manifested in a constant tendency to depart from the separateness enjoined upon the nation as the subjects of their unseen King, Jehovah. For Israel was a Theocracy. Set between Gentile powers mightier than they, and which were constantly increasing in power, the divine legislation upon which the commonwealth of Israel was organized provided for neither army nor fortress. And, so long as loyalty to Jehovah and the spirit of obedience remained, no hostile foot crossed the fron-

---

Much every way: chiefly, because that unto them were committed the oracles of God.—*Rom. 3:1,2.*

Behold, I have taught you statutes and judgments, even as the Lord my God commanded me, that ye should do so in the land whither ye go to possess it. Keep therefore and do *them;* for this *is* your wisdom and your understanding in the sight of the nations, which shall hear all these statutes, and say, Surely this great nation *is* a wise and understanding people. —*Deut. 4:5,6.*

[17] And I will put enmity between thee and the woman, and between thy seed and her seed; it shall bruise thy head, and thou shalt bruise his heel.—*Gen. 3:15.*

[18] And Abraham called the name of his son that was born unto him, whom Sarah bare to him, Isaac.—*Gen. 21:3.*

The book of the generation of Jesus Christ, the son of David, the son of Abraham.—*Matt. 1:1.*

Now to Abraham and his seed were the promises made. He saith not, And to seeds, as of many, but as of one, And to thy seed, which is Christ.—*Gal. 3:16.*

[19] The book of the generation of Jesus Christ, the son of David, the son of Abraham.—*Matt. 1:1.*

[20] And the angel answered and said unto her, The Holy Ghost shall come upon thee, and the power of the Highest shall overshadow thee: therefore also that holy thing which shall be born of thee shall be called the Son of God.—*Luke 1:35.*

[21] When Jesus came into the coasts of Cæsarea Philippi, he asked his disciples, saying, Whom do men say that I the Son of man am?—*Matt. 16:13.*

tiers of Palestine. An unseen Power guarded Immanuel's land.

These failures constituted the grounds of Jehovah's controversy with Israel—a controversy in which the prophets were the spokesmen for Israel's King. That controversy, which I can but summarize, followed the lines of the great warning passage, Deuteronomy 28: 15-19, et seq.; 29: 24-28,[22]

It is important to bear in mind that, when the greater of the writing prophets appeared, the preliminary and warning chastisements of the disobedient nation foretold in the Deuteronomic passage had already fallen. Already, in Elijah's time, the warning drought had been sent (Deut. 28: 23, 24; 1 Kings 17: 1),[23] and the land had been invaded (Deut. 28: 25; 1 Kings 14: 25, 26).[24] There remained but the alternatives of the re-

---

[22] But it shall come to pass, if thou wilt not hearken unto the voice of the Lord thy God, to observe to do all his commandments and his statutes which I command thee this day; that all these curses shall come upon thee, and overtake thee:

Cursed *shalt* thou *be* in the city, and cursed *shalt* thou *be* in the field.

Cursed *shall be* thy basket and thy store.

Cursed *shall be* the fruit of thy body, and the fruit of thy land, the increase of thy kine, and the flocks of thy sheep.

Cursed *shalt* thou *be* when thou comest in, and cursed *shalt* thou *be* when thou goest out.—*Deut. 28: 15-19.*

Even all nations shall say, Wherefore hath the Lord done thus unto this land? what *meaneth* the heat of this great anger?

Then men shall say, Because they have forsaken the covenant of the Lord God of their fathers, which he made with them when he brought them forth out of the land of Egypt:

For they went and served other gods, and worshipped them, gods whom they knew not, and *whom* he had not given unto them:

And the anger of the Lord was kindled against this land, to bring upon it all the curses that are written in this book:

And the Lord rooted them out of their land in anger, and in wrath, and in great indignation, and cast them into another land, as *it is* this day.—*Deut. 29: 24-28.*

[23] And thy heaven that *is* over thy head shall be brass, and the earth that *is* under thee *shall be* iron.

The Lord shall make the rain of thy land powder and dust: from heaven shall it come down upon thee, until thou be destroyed—*Deut. 28: 23, 24.*

And Elijah the Tishbite, *who was* of the inhabitants of Gilead, said unto Ahab, *As* the Lord God of Israel liveth, before whom I stand, there shall not be dew nor rain these years, but according to my word.—*1 Kings 17: 1.*

[24] The Lord shall cause thee to be smitten before thine enemies: thou shalt go out one way

pentance of the nation or the foretold expulsion from the land. And this was the urgent warning note of the prophetic testimony. Jehovah would no longer stultify his holiness by continuing as his representative among the Gentile nations a people in no sense better than they.

Israel had failed Jehovah, but it should be borne in mind that Israel was disowned and sent into captivity because of *sin*. Jehovah rests his condemnation of the nation upon no narrow ground, no mere tribal failure. "Thou hast made me to serve with thy sins" (Isa. 43:24). "Your iniquities have separated between you and your God, and your sins have hid his face from you, that he will not hear" (Isa. 59:2). "Yea, all Israel have transgressed thy law, even by departing, that they might not obey thy voice; therefore the curse is poured upon us, and the oath that is written in the law of Moses the servant of God, because we have sinned against him" (Dan. 9:11).

No distinction can be made in this respect between the ethical messages of the prophets who prophesied in the northern kingdom and those who were sent to Judah. The broad ground of condemnation in both cases is the same. Both Ephraim and Judah had sinned.

But in these messages of rebuke there is such a disclosure of the mind of God concerning human conduct as invests the prophetic writings with a permanent and intensely vital interest.

The central word of the prophets is righteousness. Israel was a people under law; that is, a people from whom Jehovah demanded righteousness as, under grace, he bestows righteousness through faith (Rom. 3:19-22).[25]

---

against them, and flee seven ways before them: and shalt be removed into all the kingdoms of the earth.—*Deut. 28:25.*

And it came to pass in the fifth year of king Rehoboam, *that* Shishak king of Egypt came up against Jerusalem:

And he took away the treasures of the house of the Lord, and the treasures of the king's house; he even took away all: and he took away all the shields of gold which Solomon had made.—*1 Kings 14:25, 26.*

[25] Now we know that what things soever the law saith, it saith to them who are under the law: that every mouth may be stopped, and all the world may become guilty before God.

Therefore by the deeds of the

THE ETHICAL MESSAGE

But Israel was making righteousness to consist in formal religion instead of in right faith evidenced by right conduct. It is a mistake that millions of formal religionists are making in this day. The refusal of God to accept that substitution is expressed by his prophets with an emphasis that has in it an element of scorn.

It should be remembered that while Israel was substituting religious formalism for righteousness, it was still the religion given at Sinai. It was still a far cry to the day when the Pharisee would be going up to the temple to pray "with himself" (Luke 18:11)[26] and to boast of fasting and tithe-paying. All that came later. The religion that Jehovah would not accept as righteousness was scrupulously according to Leviticus.

The reproach of Jehovah was not that his altars were forsaken, but that the sacrifices were without faith, and offered by unclean hands.

"To what purpose is the multitude of your sacrifices unto me? saith the Lord: I am full of the burnt offerings of rams, and the fat of fed beasts."

"Bring no more vain oblations; incense is an abomination unto me; the new moons and sabbaths, the calling of assemblies, I cannot away with; it is iniquity, even the solemn meeting."

As over against a ritual righteousness, the prophets by the word of the Lord insist on a righteousness of conduct. But this insistence, while absolute and unqualified, is cast in a form of expression which shows how tenderly Jehovah yearned over his people. A lovely illustration of both the insistence and the tenderness is the beautiful parable of the Vineyard of Jehovah (Isa. 5:7, and preceding).[27]

---

law there shall no flesh be justified in his sight: for by the law is the knowledge of sin.

But now the righteousness of God without the law is manifested, being witnessed by the law and the prophets;

Even the righteousness of God *which is* by faith of Jesus Christ unto all and upon all them that believe: for there is no difference.—*Rom. 3: 19-22*.

[26] The Pharisee stood and prayed thus with himself, God, I thank thee, that I am not as other men *are*, extortioners, unjust, adulterers, or even as this publican.—*Luke 18: 11*.

[27] For the vineyard of the Lord of hosts *is* the house of Israel, and the men of Judah his pleasant plant: and he looked for

The words of Micah (6:8) may be taken as a summary of the righteousness demanded, on behalf of Jehovah, by the prophets: "And what doth the Lord require of thee, but to do justly, and to love mercy, and to walk humbly with thy God?" Or, as given through Zechariah (8:16, 17).[28]

Plain honesty in all dealings, chastity, humility, reverence, penitence—these are the qualities which are emphasized as those which, under law, make a people acceptable with God, and for the lack of which the nation, after his long forbearance, must endure the chastisement of captivity and dispersion.

---

judgment, but behold oppression; for righteousness, but behold a cry.—*Isa. 5:7*.

[28] These *are* the things that ye shall do; Speak ye every man the truth to his neighbour; execute the judgment of truth and peace in your gates:

And let none of you imagine evil in your hearts against his neighbour; and love no false oath: for all these *are things* that I hate, saith the Lord.—*Zech. 8:16, 17*.

IV. THE MESSIAH

IN mere bulk the ministry of the Old Testament prophets to their *own* time, the controversy of Jehovah with his people, far exceeds that devoted to prediction. The great predictive messages, indeed, grow out of the condition of Israel at the time when the prophet appears, and are for the instruction and comfort of the nation in view of the coming captivities and dispersion. Typical passages are Isaiah 7: 10-14,[1] where the refusal of the wicked King Ahaz to put God to a test which might have restored his faith brought forth the great Messianic prediction of the Virgin's Son; chapters 60 and 61 [2] of the same book, where predictions of approaching disciplinary judgments are followed by wonderful assur-

---

[1] Moreover the Lord spake again unto Ahaz, saying,

Ask thee a sign of the Lord thy God; ask it either in the depth, or in the height above.

But Ahaz said, I will not ask, neither will I tempt the Lord.

And he said, Hear ye now, O house of David; *Is it* a small thing for you to weary men, but will ye weary my God also?

Therefore the Lord himself shall give you a sign; Behold, a virgin shall conceive, and bear a son, and shall call his name Immanuel.—*Isa. 7:10-14.*

[2] Arise, shine; for thy light is come, and the glory of the Lord is risen upon thee.

For, behold, the darkness shall cover the earth, and gross darkness the people: but the Lord shall arise upon thee, and his glory shall be seen upon thee.

And the Gentiles shall come to thy light, and kings to the brightness of thy rising. Etc.—*Isa. 60.*

The Spirit of the Lord God *is* upon me; because the Lord hath anointed me to preach good tidings unto the meek; he hath sent me to bind up the brokenhearted, to proclaim liberty to the captives, and the opening of the prison to *them that are* bound;

To proclaim the acceptable year of the Lord, and the day of vengeance of our God; to comfort all that mourn;

To appoint unto them that mourn in Zion, to give unto them beauty for ashes, the oil of joy for mourning, the garment of praise for the spirit of heaviness; that they might be called trees of righteousness, the planting of the Lord, that he might be glorified. Etc.—*Isa. 61.*

ances of the perpetuity of the Divine covenants with Israel (for example, 59:20, 21).[3]

The great themes of predictive prophecy are the coming of Messiah; the future restoration of Israel to the land, the national conversion (Jer. 31:6-12)[4]; the exaltation of the nation to be first of the nations; and the blessing of the whole earth in the kingdom of Messiah. Then, overleaping all intervening "times" and "ages," predictive prophecy goes to the end of the present age and gives the detail of all this the "great and dreadful" day of Jehovah; the rise of the man of sin; the great tribulation; the second advent of Christ; the regathering of the elect race, Israel; the judgment of the Gentile nations; and the setting up of the kingdom predicted and described by the Old Testament prophets. The present church age, which fills a parenthesis or gap in

---

[3] And the Redeemer shall come to Zion, and unto them that turn from transgression in Jacob, saith the Lord.

As for me, this *is* my covenant with them, saith the Lord; My spirit that *is* upon thee, and my words which I have put in thy mouth, shall not depart out of thy mouth, nor out of the mouth of thy seed, nor out of the mouth of thy seed's seed, saith the Lord, from henceforth and for ever.—*Isa. 59:20, 21.*

[4] For there shall be a day, *that* the watchmen upon the mount Ephraim shall cry, Arise ye, and let us go up to Zion unto the Lord our God.

For thus saith the Lord; Sing with gladness for Jacob, and shout among the chief of the nations: publish ye, praise ye, and say, O Lord, save thy people, the remnant of Israel.

Behold, I will bring them from the north country, and gather them from the coasts of the earth, *and* with them the blind and the lame, the woman with child and her that travaileth with child together: a great company shall return thither.

They shall come with weeping, and with supplications will I lead them: I will cause them to walk by the rivers of waters in a straight way, wherein they shall not stumble: for I am a father to Israel, and Ephraim *is* my firstborn.

Hear the word of the Lord, O ye nations, and declare *it* in the isles afar off, and say, He that scattered Israel will gather him, and keep him, as a shepherd *doth* his flock.

For the Lord hath redeemed Jacob, and ransomed him from the hand of *him that was* stronger than he.

Therefore they shall come and sing in the height of Zion, and shall flow together to the goodness of the Lord, for wheat, and for wine, and for oil, and for the young of the flock and of the herd: and their soul shall be as a watered garden; and they shall not sorrow any more at all.—*Jer. 31:6-12.*

THE MESSIAH

the Old Testament predicted order of events, was veiled from the Old Testament prophets (Eph. 3:1-11).[5]

It is the Messianic Message which transcends all others in importance, not only because all salvation was to be wrought out by Christ, but also because all the other predicted events have to do with His advents and His authority. It is Christ who regathers Israel; Christ who, by His personal manifestation, converts Israel (Hosea 2:14-17)[6]; Christ who destroys Israel's enemies at Armageddon (Rev. 19:11 et seq.)[7]; Christ who reigns over the earth during the kingdom age (Isa. 9:6, 7; Luke 1:33)[8]; David's Son, Son of God, Son of man, Son of Abraham.

---

[5] For this cause I Paul, the prisoner of Jesus Christ for you Gentiles,

If ye have heard of the dispensation of the grace of God which is given me to you-ward:

How that by revelation he made known unto me the mystery; (as I wrote afore in few words,

Whereby, when ye read, ye may understand my knowledge in the mystery of Christ)

Which in other ages was not made known unto the sons of men, as it is now revealed unto his holy apostles and prophets by the Spirit;

That the Gentiles should be fellowheirs, and of the same body, and partakers of his promise in Christ by the gospel:

Whereof I was made a minister, according to the gift of the grace of God given unto me by the effectual working of his power.

Unto me, who am less than the least of all saints, is this grace given, that I should preach among the Gentiles the unsearchable riches of Christ;

And to make all men see what is the fellowship of the mystery, which from the beginning of the world hath been hid in God, who created all things by Jesus Christ:

To the intent that now unto the principalities and powers in heavenly *places* might be known by the church the manifold wisdom of God,

According to the eternal purpose which he purposed in Christ Jesus our Lord.—*Eph. 3: 1-11.*

[6] Therefore, behold, I will allure her, and bring her into the wilderness, and speak comfortably unto her.

And I will give her her vineyards from thence, and the valley of Achor for a door of hope: and she shall sing there, as in the days of her youth, and as in the day when she came up out of the land of Egypt.

And it shall be at that day, saith the Lord, *that* thou shalt call me Ishi; and shalt call me no more Baali.

For I will take away the names of Baalim out of her mouth, and they shall no more be remembered by their name.—*Hosea 2: 14-17.*

[7] And I saw heaven opened, and behold a white horse; and he that sat upon him *was* called Faithful and True, and in righteousness he doth judge and make war.—*Rev. 19: 11.*

[8] For unto us a child is born, unto us a son is given: and the government shall be upon his shoulder: and his name shall be

The prophetical books are arranged in our Bibles in the order of the fulness of the treatment of the prophetic themes, and not in their chronological order. This has given rise to the division into major, or greater, and minor, or lesser prophets; a division based upon the bulk or volume of the writings. The better division is that based upon the captivities of Israel, and is into prophets before the exile, prophets during the exile, and prophets to the restored remnant (Haggai, Zechariah, Malachi). Taking the prophets in this order the development of the Messianic revelation is progressive and harmonious. It should be remembered that Messianic prophecy did not begin with the Hebrew writing-prophets. They but added detail to a body of revelation concerning a coming One which, in type and testimony, had been growing from the very creation of Adam—nay, from the material creation, for the sun itself is a type of Him. And, to use a figure, the prophets but added to and completed a portrait of the coming Messiah the first lines of which, and many an added touch, had been already put upon the canvas.

The Sun of righteousness (Mal. 4:2)[9]; the second Man (1 Cor. 15:47)[10]; the last Adam (1 Cor. 15:45)[11]; the Seed of the woman (Gen. 3:15; Gal. 4:4)[12]; the

---

called Wonderful, Counsellor, The mighty God, The everlasting Father, The Prince of Peace.

Of the increase of *his* government and peace *there shall be* no end, upon the throne of David, and upon his kingdom, to order it, and to establish it with judgment and with justice from henceforth even for ever. The zeal of the Lord of hosts will perform this.—*Isa. 9:6, 7.*

And he shall reign over the house of Jacob for ever; and of his kingdom there shall be no end.—*Luke 1:33.*

[9] But unto you that fear my name shall the Sun of righteousness arise with healing in his wings; and ye shall go forth, and grow up as calves of the stall.—*Mal. 4:2.*

[10] The first man *is* of the earth, earthy: the second man *is* the Lord from heaven.—*1 Cor. 15:47.*

[11] And so it is written, The first man Adam was made a living soul; the last Adam *was made* a quickening spirit.—*1 Cor. 15:45.*

[12] And I will put enmity between thee and the woman, and between thy seed and her seed; it shall bruise thy head, and thou shalt bruise his heel.—*Gen. 3:15.*

But when the fulness of the time was come, God sent forth his Son, made of a woman, made under the law.—*Gal. 4:4.*

THE MESSIAH

lamb of Abel (Gen. 4:4)[13]; the Son of Abraham (Gen. 12:3)[14]; the Priest after the order of Melchizedek (Gen. 14:18; Heb. 7:11 and preceding)[15]; the Ladder of Jacob (Gen. 28:12, 13; John 1:51)[16]; the Deliverer like Moses (Acts 7:35)[17]; the Prophet like unto Moses (Acts 7:37)[18]; the victorious Captain like Joshua; the Priest after the manner of Aaron, but after the order of Melchizedek; the Mercy seat, shewbread, candlestick, golden altar of incense, and every other object in the tabernacle; Son of Abraham—so, and in like manner, had the Types been telling the story of Messiah. And Baalam had seen the Star out of Jacob; and Jacob had seen Shiloh; and David had seen his great Son; and Job had declared his faith that his Redeemer would stand at the latter day upon the earth. This, and much more, had been painted into the Portrait before the writing prophets took up the brush.

But in the Prophets whatever was vague in the intimations down the ages concerning a coming One becomes definite. Sharpness of outline is a prophetic characteristic. Messiah is to be of the stock of David (Isa. 7:13;

---

[13] And Abel, he also brought of the firstlings of his flock and of the fat thereof. And the Lord had respect unto Abel and to his offering.—*Gen. 4:4.*

[14] And I will bless them that bless thee, and curse him that curseth thee: and in thee shall all the families of the earth be blessed.—*Gen. 12:3.*

[15] And Melchizedek king of Salem brought forth bread and wine; and he *was* the priest of the most high God.—*Gen. 14:18.*

If therefore perfection were by the Levitical priesthood, (for under it the people received the law,) what further need *was there* that another priest should rise after the order of Melchisedec, and not be called after the order of Aaron.—*Heb. 7:11.*

[16] And he dreamed, and behold a ladder set up on the earth, and the top of it reached to heaven: and behold the angels of God ascending and descending on it. And, behold, the Lord stood above it, and said, I *am* the Lord God of Abraham thy father, and the God of Isaac; the land whereon thou liest, to thee will I give it, and to thy seed.—*Gen. 28:12, 13.*

And he saith unto him, Verily, verily, I say unto you, Hereafter ye shall see heaven open, and the angels of God ascending and descending upon the Son of man.—*John 1:51.*

[17] This Moses whom they refused, saying, Who made thee a ruler and a judge? the same did God send *to be* a ruler and a deliverer by the hand of the angel which appeared to him in the bush.—*Acts 7:35.*

[18] This is that Moses, which said unto the children of Israel, A prophet shall the Lord your God raise up unto you of your brethren, like unto me; him shall ye hear.—*Acts 7:37.*

9:7; Jer. 23:5, 6; 33:15-17; Matt. 1:1; Luke 1:32)[19]; He is to be born in the city of David, Bethlehem (Mic. 5:2),[20] of a virgin mother (Isa. 7:13, 14; Luke 1:34, 35).[21] And yet His name is called Wonderful, Counsellor, The mighty God, The Everlasting Father, The Prince of Peace (Isa. 9:6). Still more wonderful, the One of this mighty Name is to be He who will sit "Upon the throne of David, and upon his kingdom, to order it, and to establish it with judgment and with justice from henceforth even for ever" (Isa. 9:7).

These details in the portrait of the Christ, added by the prophets, exclude all possibility of imposture. It is

---

[19] And he said, Hear ye now, O house of David; *Is it* a small thing for you to weary men, but will ye weary my God also?—*Isa. 7:13.*

Of the increase of *his* government and peace *there shall be* no end, upon the throne of David, and upon his kingdom, to order it, and to establish it with judgment and with justice from henceforth even for ever. The zeal of the Lord of hosts will perform this.—*Isa. 9:7.*

Behold, the days come, saith the Lord, that I will raise unto David a righteous Branch, and a King shall reign and prosper, and shall execute judgment and justice in the earth.

In his days Judah shall be saved, and Israel shall dwell safely: and this *is* his name whereby he shall be called, THE LORD OUR RIGHTEOUSNESS.—*Jer. 23:5, 6.*

In those days, and at that time, will I cause the Branch of righteousness to grow up unto David; and he shall execute judgment and righteousness in the land.

In those days shall Judah be saved, and Jerusalem shall dwell safely: and this *is the name* wherewith she shall be called, The Lord our righteousness.

For thus saith the Lord; David shall never want a man to sit upon the throne of the house of Israel.—*Jer. 33:15-17.*

The book of the generation of Jesus Christ, the son of David, the son of Abraham.—*Matt. 1:1.*

He shall be great, and shall be called the son of the Highest: and the Lord God shall give unto him the throne of his father David.—*Luke 1:32.*

[20] But thou, Beth-lehem Ephratah, *though* thou be little among the thousands of Judah, *yet* out of thee shall he come forth unto me *that is* to be ruler in Israel; whose goings forth *have been* from of old, from everlasting.—*Micah 5:2.*

[21] And he said, Hear ye now, O house of David; *Is it* a small thing for you to weary men, but will ye weary my God also?

Therefore the Lord himself shall give you a sign; Behold, a virgin shall conceive, and bear a son, and shall call his name Immanuel.—*Isa. 7:13, 14.*

Then said Mary unto the angel, How shall this be, seeing I know not a man?

And the angel answered and said unto her, The Holy Ghost shall come upon thee, and the power of the Highest shall overshadow thee: therefore also that holy thing which shall be born of thee shall be called the Son of God.—*Luke 1:34, 35.*

open to any man to say, "I am the Christ," but it is not possible for any man to arrange before his birth that he shall be born in Bethlehem in Judea, of a virgin mother, of the stock of King David. And it is noteworthy that the Pharisees and rulers of the Jews, hating Christ with all the rancor of religious prejudice, and accusing Him falsely of many things, never once questioned that any one of the prophetic details was wanting to the fulfilment by Him of these great predictions—except at the first, when they still supposed Jesus to be a Galilean.

Two kinds of experience awaited the Messiah upon earth, suffering and glory (Luke 24: 25-27).[22] Both of these aspects of His manifestation the prophets saw and foretold. But the way in which these experiences would be related to each other they did not see, for the New Testament church was not in the vision of the Old Testament prophet (Eph. 3: 1-10).[23] That the prophets were exercised by the seeming utter contradiction of the two revelations concerning Messiah we are assured by an inspired apostle (1 Pet. 1: 19, 11).[24] For how could

---

[22] Then he said unto them, O fools, and slow of heart to believe all that the prophets have spoken:
Ought not Christ to have suffered these things, and to enter into his glory?
And beginning at Moses and all the prophets, he expounded unto them in all the scriptures the things concerning himself. —*Luke 24: 25-27.*

[23] For this cause I Paul, the prisoner of Jesus Christ for you Gentiles,
If ye have heard of the dispensation of the grace of God which is given me to you-ward:
How that by revelation he made known unto me the mystery; (as I wrote afore in few words,
Whereby, when ye read, ye may understand my knowledge in the mystery of Christ)
Which in other ages was not made known unto the sons of men, as it is now revealed unto his holy apostles and prophets by the Spirit;
That the Gentiles should be fellowheirs, and of the same body, and partakers of his promise in Christ by the gospel:
Whereof I was made a minister, according to the gift of the grace of God given unto me by the effectual working of his power.
Unto me, who am less than the least of all saints, is this grace given, that I should preach among the Gentiles the unsearchable riches of Christ;
And to make all *men* see what *is* the fellowship of the mystery, which from the beginning of the world hath been hid in God, who created all things by Jesus Christ:
To the intent that now unto the principalities and powers in heavenly *places* might be known by the church the manifold wisdom of God.—*Eph. 3: 1-10.*

[24] But with the precious blood of Christ, as of a lamb without

the Christ be a man of sorrows and acquainted with grief, despised and rejected of men, and also a king, reigning as the heir to the throne of David in the fulness of His divine power and glory? How could Isaiah 53 be reconciled with Isaiah 11 and 66? And this most natural perplexity of the prophets was quieted, not answered. It was revealed to them that the things to which they bore witness were for a distant fulfilment. "Unto whom it was revealed, that not unto themselves but unto us did they minister."

This apparent contradiction, completely reconciled as the two advents come into view,—the advent to suffer, and the advent to rule,—illustrates the fact that very much of the Higher Criticism is due to ignorance of prophecy. An instance in point is the hypothesis of two Isaiahs,—that is, the higher critical theory that the book of Isaiah as we now have it must have been written by two different men, one before the captivity, the other seventy years later. As every student of prophecy knows, the first 39 chapters of Isaiah have to do with the sins of Israel and the impending captivities. Beginning with chapter 40 the prophet's vision sweeps on to the day of Israel's restoration from a world-wide dispersion, conversion, and establishment in Palestine, never again to be moved. It is Isaiah's vision of the kingdom. What wonder that his style rises from sternness to triumph? Washington's messages to Congress, while President of a free nation, differ in style from his letter to Congress from Valley Forge; but no one but a higher critic would infer two Washingtons.

Not until Messiah had appeared and had been rejected by the Jews was any adequate explanation given of the paradox in which the prophetic testimony was left, that David's mighty Heir should also be the man on the cross of the Twenty-second Psalm, the iniquity-bearer of Isaiah Fifty-three. That explanation came from the lips of

---

blemish and without spot.—*1 Pet. 1: 19.*

Searching what, or what manner of time the Spirit of Christ which was in them did signify, when it testified beforehand the sufferings of Christ, and the glory that should follow.—*1 Pet. 1: 11.*

the Messiah himself. In the parables recorded in Matthew 13 there is the foreview of an age intervening between the sufferings and the glory—the long period of time in which we live. During this age are to be accomplished certain "mysteries" of the kingdom which had not been revealed to the Old Testament prophets (Matt. 13:17).[25] These accomplished, the Old Testament predictions are again to be taken up, and Messiah revealed in His glory in the kingdom age which follows the "Mysteries." These things will appear clearly when we come to the greater messages of the New Testament prophets.

The prophetic testimony to the humiliation and suffering of Messiah is especially voiced through David and Isaiah. The Twenty-second Psalm is a vivid picture of death by crucifixion. The bones out of joint (v. 14),[26] the profuse perspiration caused by intense suffering (v. 14),[27] strength exhausted and intense thirst (v. 15),[28] the hands and feet pierced (v. 16),[29] are all incidental to death by crucifixion. The desolate cry, "My God, my God, why hast thou forsaken me?" uttered by our Lord from the cross is taken from this Psalm. If there were no other proof of prophetic inspiration this Psalm alone would be conclusive.

Another prediction of the sufferings of Messiah is the familiar Fifty-third of Isaiah. Like the Twenty-second Psalm this great vision also closes with the note of triumph and victory. This willing Sufferer shall see of the birth-pangs of His soul and shall be satisfied (v. 11)[30]; just as in the Psalm of crucifixion the cry from the very

---

[25] For verily I say unto you, That many prophets and righteous *men* have desired to see *those things* which ye see, and have not seen *them;* and to hear *those things* which ye hear, and have not heard *them.*—*Matt. 13: 17.*

[26],[27] I am poured out like water, and all my bones are out of joint: my heart is like wax; it is melted in the midst of my bowels.—*Psalm 22:14.*

[28] My strength is dried up like a potsherd; and my tongue cleaveth to my jaws; and thou hast brought me into the dust of death.—*Psalm 22:15.*

[29] For dogs have compassed me: the assembly of the wicked have inclosed me: they pierced my hands and my feet.—*Psalm 22:16.*

[30] He shall see of the travail of his soul, *and* shall be satisfied: by his knowledge shall my righteous servant justify many; for he shall bear their iniquities. —*Isa. 53:11.*

mouth of the lion is, "I will declare thy name unto my brethren: in the midst of the congregation will I praise thee" (v. 22), and triumph is in the declaration, "For the kingdom is the Lord's: and he is the governor among the nations" (v. 28).

There is, it may be added, a clear prophetic testimony to the meaning of the sufferings of Messiah. "He was wounded for our transgressions, he was bruised for our iniquities." Nor do the prophets leave room for modern dilutions of the doctrine. If it be urged, as it sometimes is, that the true meaning is: "He suffered *on account* of our transgressions," the answer of the prophet is, "The Lord hath laid on him the iniquity of us all." And the prophetic testimony is at one with the apostolic. "Who his own self bare our sins in his own body on the tree, that we, being dead to sins, should live unto righteousness, by whose stripes ye were healed" (1 Pet. 2:24).

By far the larger part of the prophetic testimony to the coming One has to do with His manifestation in glory on the earth during the kingdom age. His heavenly glory from before the foundation of the earth (John 17:5)[31] is not the theme of the prophets, though His deity is fully recognized (for example, Isa. 9:6, 7).[32] His glory is that of the incarnate God, reigning in full manifestation of His divine glory over the kingdom covenanted to David (Isa. 9:6, 7; 11:1-12; Jer. 23:5, 6; 33:14-17; Amos 9:11; Micah 5:2; Zech. 14:9).[33]

---

[31] And now, O Father, glorify thou me with thine own self with the glory which I had with thee before the world was.—*John 17: 5.*

[32],[33] For unto us a child is born, unto us a son is given: and the government shall be upon his shoulder: and his name shall be called Wonderful, Counsellor, The mighty God, The everlasting Father, The Prince of Peace.

Of the increase of *his* government and peace *there shall be* no end, upon the throne of David, and upon his kingdom, to order it, and to establish it with judgment and with justice from henceforth even for ever. The zeal of the Lord of hosts will perform this.—*Isa. 9:6,7.*

[33] And there shall come forth a rod out of the stem of Jesse, and a Branch shall grow out of his roots:

And the spirit of the Lord shall rest upon him, the spirit of wisdom and understanding, the spirit of counsel and might, the spirit of knowledge and of the fear of the Lord;

And shall make him of quick understanding in the fear of the Lord: and he shall not judge after the sight of his eyes, neither reprove after the hearing of his ears:

THE MESSIAH

To Zechariah is given the revelation of both advents of Messiah, His advent to suffer and His advent to reign.

"Rejoice greatly, O daughter of Zion; shout, O daughter of Jerusalem: behold thy King cometh unto thee: he is just, and having salvation; lowly, and riding upon an

But with righteousness shall he judge the poor, and reprove with equity for the meek of the earth: and he shall smite the earth with the rod of his mouth, and with the breath of his lips shall he slay the wicked.

And righteousness shall be the girdle of his loins, and faithfulness the girdle of his reins.

The wolf also shall dwell with the lamb, and the leopard shall lie down with the kid; and the calf and the young lion and the fatling together; and a little child shall lead them.

And the cow and the bear shall feed; their young ones shall lie down together: and the lion shall eat straw like the ox.

And the sucking child shall play on the hole of the asp, and the weaned child shall put his hand on the cockatrice' den.

They shall not hurt nor destroy in all my holy mountain: for the earth shall be full of the knowledge of the Lord, as the waters cover the sea.

And in that day there shall be a root of Jesse, which shall stand for an ensign of the people; to it shall the Gentiles seek: and his rest shall be glorious.

And it shall come to pass in that day, *that* the Lord shall set his hand again the second time to recover the remnant of his people, which shall be left, from Assyria, and from Egypt, and from Pathros, and from Cush, and from Elam, and from Shinar, and from Hamath, and from the islands of the sea.

And he shall set up an ensign for the nations, and shall assemble the outcasts of Israel, and gather together the dispersed of Judah from the four corners of the earth.—*Isa. 11: 1-12.*

Behold, the days come, saith the Lord, that I will raise unto David a righteous Branch, and a King shall reign and prosper, and shall execute judgment and justice in the earth.

In his days Judah shall be saved, and Israel shall dwell safely: and this *is* his name whereby he shall be called, THE LORD OUR RIGHTEOUSNESS.—*Jer. 23: 5, 6.*

Behold, the days come, saith the Lord, that I will perform that good thing which I have promised unto the house of Israel and to the house of Judah.

In those days, and at that time, will I cause the Branch of righteousness to grow up unto David; and he shall execute judgment and righteousness in the land.

In those days shall Judah be saved, and Jerusalem shall dwell safely: and this *is the name* wherewith she shall be called, The Lord our righteousness.

For thus saith the Lord: David shall never want a man to sit upon the throne of the house of Israel.—*Jer. 33: 14-17.*

In that day will I raise up the tabernacle of David that is fallen, and close up the breaches thereof: and I will raise up his ruins, and I will build it as in the days of old.—*Amos 9: 11.*

But thou, Beth-lehem Ephratah, *though* thou be little among the thousands of Judah, *yet* out of thee shall he come forth unto me *that is* to be ruler in Israel; whose goings forth *have been* from of old, from everlasting.—*Micah 5: 2.*

And the Lord shall be king over all the earth: in that day shall there be one Lord, and his name one.—*Zech. 14: 9.*

ass, and upon a colt the foal of an ass" (Zech. 9:9). It is impossible to "spiritualize" away the literal meaning of this prophecy, because it was fulfilled with absolute literalness at the first advent (Matt. 21:1-11; with parallel accounts in Mark 11:1-10; Luke 19:29-38).[34]

But how marked the contrast in Zechariah's vision of the second advent. It introduces the "great and dreadful day of the Lord" (Mal. 4:5), and every detail speaks, not of meekness and lowliness, but of resistless power.

"And his feet shall stand in that day upon the mount of Olives, which is before Jerusalem on the east, and the mount of Olives shall cleave in the midst thereof toward the east and toward the west, and there shall be a very great valley; and half of the mountain shall remove toward the north, and half of it toward the south, . . . and the Lord my God shall come, and all the saints with thee. . . . And the Lord shall be king over all the earth: in that day shall there be one Lord. . . . And it shall come to pass, that every one that is left of all the nations which came against Jerusalem shall even go up from year to year to worship the King, the Lord of hosts" (Zech. 14:4, 5, 9, 16).

Amos also testifies to the exaltation of Messiah at his second advent:

---

[34] And when they drew nigh unto Jerusalem, and were come to Bethphage, unto the mount of Olives, then sent Jesus two disciples,

Saying unto them, Go into the village over against you, and straightway ye shall find an ass tied, and a colt with her: loose *them,* and bring *them* unto me.

And if any *man* say aught unto you, ye shall say, The Lord hath need of them; and straightway he will send them.

All this was done, that it might be fulfilled which was spoken by the prophet, saying,

Tell ye the daughter of Sion, Behold, thy King cometh unto thee, meek, and sitting upon an ass, and a colt the foal of an ass.

And the disciples went, and did as Jesus commanded them,

And brought the ass, and the colt, and put on them their clothes, and they set *him* thereon.

And a very great multitude spread their garments in the way; others cut down branches from the trees, and strawed *them* in the way.

And the multitudes that went before, and that followed, cried, saying, Hosanna to the son of David: Blessed *is* he that cometh in the name of the Lord; Hosanna in the highest.

And when he was come into Jerusalem, all the city was moved, saying, Who is this?

And the multitude said, This is Jesus the prophet of Nazareth of Galilee.—*Matt. 21:1-11.*

THE MESSIAH

"In that day will I raise up the tabernacle of David that is fallen, and close up the breaches thereof; and I will raise up his ruins, and I will build it as in the days of old" (Amos 9:11). And here, as in the prophecy of Zechariah, there is no possibility of giving the words a figurative interpretation, for the passage is quoted in the New Testament and applied to the return of the Lord (Acts 15:13-18).[35]

The Messianic Message of the Prophets—surely their greatest message—may be thus summarized: They foresaw and foretold a coming One who should be both Son of God and Son of David (Isa. 7:13, 14; 9:6, 7).[36] At His first advent, born in the city of David, Bethlehem; coming to Israel "meek and lowly"; rejected by the rulers of His nation; He fulfils the Abrahamic covenant of redemption (Gen. 12:3; Gal. 3:16)[37] by enduring the cross, being wounded for our transgressions, a vicarious sacrifice for us.

---

[35] And after they had held their peace, James answered, saying, Men *and* brethren, hearken unto me:

Simeon hath declared how God at the first did visit the Gentiles, to take out of them a people for his name.

And to this agree the words of the prophets; as it is written,

After this I will return, and will build again the tabernacle of David, which is fallen down; and I will build again the ruins thereof, and I will set it up:

That the residue of men might seek after the Lord, and all the Gentiles, upon whom my name is called, saith the Lord, who doeth all these things.

Known unto God are all his works from the beginning of the world.—*Acts 15: 13-18.*

[36] And he said, Hear ye now, O house of David; *Is it* a small thing for you to weary men, but will ye weary my God also?

Therefore the Lord himself shall give you a sign; Behold, a virgin shall conceive, and bear a son, and shall call his name Immanuel—*Isa. 7: 13, 14.*

For unto us a child is born, unto us a son is given: and the government shall be upon his shoulder: and his name shall be called Wonderful, Counsellor, The mighty God, The everlasting Father, The Prince of Peace.

Of the increase of *his* government and peace *there shall be* no end, upon the throne of David, and upon his kingdom; to order it, and to establish it with judgment and with justice from henceforth even for ever. The zeal of the Lord of hosts will perform this.—*Isa. 9: 6, 7.*

[37] And I will bless them that bless thee, and curse him that curseth thee: and in thee shall all families of the earth be blessed.—*Gen. 12: 3.*

Now to Abraham and his seed were the promises made. He saith not, And to seeds, as of many; but as of one, And to thy seed, which is Christ.—*Gal. 3: 16.*

At His second advent, appearing in divine glory (Zech. 14:4; Matt. 24:27, 30),[38] He regathers and converts dispersed Israel (Ezek. 20:35-44),[39] and, upon the throne of David, with Jerusalem as the capital, reigns over the

---

[38] And his feet shall stand in that day upon the mount of Olives, which *is* before Jerusalem on the east, and the mount of Olives shall cleave in the midst thereof toward the east and toward the west, *and there shall be* a very great valley; and half of the mountain shall remove toward the north, and half of it toward the south.—*Zech. 14:4.*

For as the lightning cometh out of the east, and shineth even unto the west; so shall also the coming of the Son of man be.

And then shall appear the sign of the Son of man in heaven: and then shall all the tribes of the earth mourn, and they shall see the Son of man coming in the clouds of heaven with power and great glory.—*Matt. 24:27, 30.*

[39] And I will bring you into the wilderness of the people, and there will I plead with you face to face.

Like as I pleaded with your fathers in the wilderness of the land of Egypt, so will I plead with you, saith the Lord God.

And I will cause you to pass under the rod, and I will bring you into the bond of the covenant:

And I will purge out from among you the rebels, and them that transgress against me: I will bring them forth out of the country where they sojourn, and they shall not enter into the land of Israel: and ye shall know that I *am* the Lord.

As for you, O house of Israel, thus saith the Lord God; Go ye, serve ye every one his idols, and hereafter *also,* if ye will not hearken unto me: but pollute ye my holy name no more with your gifts, and with your idols.

For in mine holy mountain, in the mountain of the height of Israel, saith the Lord God, there shall all the house of Israel, all of them in the land, serve me: there will I accept them, and there will I require your offerings, and the firstfruits of your oblations, with all your holy things.

I will accept you with your sweet savour, when I bring you out from the people, and gather you out of the countries wherein ye have been scattered; and I will be sanctified in you before the heathen.

And ye shall know that I *am* the Lord, when I shall bring you into the land of Israel, into the country *for* the which I lifted up mine hand to give it to your fathers.

And there shall ye remember your ways, and all your doings, wherein ye have been defiled; and ye shall lothe yourselves in your own sight for all your evils that ye have committed.

And ye shall know that I *am* the Lord, when I have wrought with you for my name's sake, not according to your wicked ways, nor according to your corrupt doings, O ye house of Israel, saith the Lord God.—*Ezek. 20:35-44.*

THE MESSIAH

earth in the kingdom (Isa. 9:7; 11:1-12; 2:1-4; Matt. 25:31).[40]

---

[40] Of the increase of *his* government and peace *there shall be* no end, upon the throne of David, and upon his kingdom, to order it, and to establish it with judgment and with justice from henceforth even for ever. The zeal of the Lord of hosts will perform this.—*Isa. 9:7.*

And there shall come forth a rod out of the stem of Jesse, and a Branch shall grow out of his roots:

And the spirit of the Lord shall rest upon him, the spirit of wisdom and understanding, the spirit of counsel and might, the spirit of knowledge and of the fear of the Lord.

And shall make him of quick understanding in the fear of the Lord: and he shall not judge after the sight of his eyes, neither reprove after the hearing of his ears:

But with righteousness shall he judge the poor, and reprove with equity for the meek of the earth: and he shall smite the earth with the rod of his mouth, and with the breath of his lips shall he slay the wicked.

And righteousness shall be the girdle of his loins, and faithfulness the girdle of his reins.

The wolf also shall dwell with the lamb, and the leopard shall lie down with the kid; and the calf and the young lion and the fatling together; and a little child shall lead them.

And the cow and the bear shall feed; their young ones shall lie down together: and the lion shall eat straw like the ox.

And the sucking child shall play on the hole of the asp, and the weaned child shall put his hand on the cockatrice' den.

They shall not hurt nor destroy in all my holy mountain: for the earth shall be full of the knowledge of the Lord, as the waters cover the sea.

And in that day there shall be a root of Jesse, which shall stand for an ensign of the people; to it shall the Gentiles seek: and his rest shall be glorious.

And it shall come to pass in that day, *that* the Lord shall set his hand again the second time to recover the remnant of his people, which shall be left, from Assyria, and from Egypt, and from Pathros, and from Cush, and from Elam, and from Shinar, and from Hamath, and from the islands of the sea.

And he shall set up an ensign for the nations, and shall assemble the outcasts of Israel, and gather together the dispersed of Judah from the four corners of the earth.—*Isa. 11:1-12.*

The word that Isaiah the son of Amoz saw concerning Judah and Jerusalem.

And it shall come to pass in the last days, *that* the mountain of the Lord's house shall be established in the top of the mountains, and shall be exalted above the hills; and all nations shall flow unto it.

And many people shall go and say, Come ye, and let us go up to the mountain of the Lord, to the house of the God of Jacob; and he will teach us of his ways, and we will walk in his paths: for out of Zion shall go forth the law, and the word of the Lord from Jerusalem.

And he shall judge among the nations, and shall rebuke many people: and they shall beat their swords into plowshares, and their spears into pruninghooks: nation shall not lift up sword against nation, neither shall they learn war any more.—*Isa. 2: 1-4.*

When the Son of man shall come in his glory, and all the holy angels with him, then shall he sit upon the throne of his glory.—*Matt. 25:31.*

The New Testament carries the foreview of the kingdom of Messiah to its glorious consummation in the restoration of humanity and the earth to the kingdom of God, even the Father (1 Cor. 15: 24-28).[41] The kingdom of the Son of David does not end, for it becomes one with the universal rule of God.

---

[41] Then *cometh* the end, when he shall have delivered up the kingdom to God, even the Father; when he shall have put down all rule and all authority and power.

For he must reign, till he hath put all enemies under his feet.

The last enemy *that* shall be destroyed *is* death.

For he hath put all things under his feet. But when he saith, All things are put under *him, it is* manifest that he is excepted, which did put all things under him.

And when all things shall be subdued unto him, then shall the Son also himself be subject unto him that put all things under him, that God may be all in all.—*1 Cor. 15: 24-28.*

V. THE VISION OF THE KINGDOM

TWO forms of the Divine rule over the earth are to be distinguished in Scripture, the kingdom of heaven, and the kingdom of God. The first is Messiah's kingdom; the kingdom of David's son (2 Sam. 7: 10-17; Psa. 89: 3, 4, 20-36; Matt. 1:1; Luke 1: 31-33; Acts 15: 13-17).[1] Its sphere is the earth (Isa.

---

[1] Moreover I will appoint a place for my people Israel, and will plant them, that they may dwell in a place of their own, and move no more; neither shall the children of wickedness afflict them any more, as beforetime,

And as since the time that I commanded judges *to be* over my people Israel, and have caused thee to rest from all thine enemies. Also the Lord telleth thee that he will make thee an house.

And when thy days be fulfilled, and thou shalt sleep with thy fathers, I will set up thy seed after thee, which shall proceed out of thy bowels, and I will establish his kingdom.

He shall build an house for my name, and I will stablish the throne of his kingdom for ever.

I will be his father, and he shall be my son. If he commit iniquity, I will chasten him with the rod of men, and with the stripes of the children of men:

But my mercy shall not depart away from him, as I took *it* from Saul, whom I put away before thee.

And thine house and thy kingdom shall be established for ever before thee: thy throne shall be established for ever.

According to all these words, and according to all this vision, so did Nathan speak unto David. —*2 Sam. 7: 10-17.*

I have made a covenant with my chosen, I have sworn unto David my servant,

Thy seed will I establish for ever, and build up thy throne to all generations. Selah.—*Psalm 89: 3, 4.*

I have found David my servant; with my holy oil have I anointed him:

With whom my hand shall be established: mine arm also shall strengthen him.

The enemy shall not exact upon him; nor the son of wickedness afflict him.

And I will beat down his foes before his face, and plague them that hate him.

But my faithfulness and my mercy *shall be* with him: and in my name shall his horn be exalted.

I will set his hand also in the sea, and his right hand in the rivers.

He shall cry unto me, Thou art my father, my God, and the rock of my salvation.

Also I will make him *my* first born, higher than the kings of the earth.

My mercy will I keep for him for evermore, and my covenant shall stand fast with him.

11:9; Jer. 23:5-8; Matt. 6:10).[2] The kingdom of God is the great inclusive kingdom, and may be defined as the rule of God (Father, Son, and Holy Spirit) over the universe, the sphere of nature, and especially over all moral intelligences, angelic or human.

His seed also will I make *to endure* for ever, and his throne as the days of heaven.
If his children forsake my law, and walk not in my judgments;
If they break my statutes, and keep not my commandments;
Then will I visit their transgression with the rod, and their iniquity with stripes.
Nevertheless my lovingkindness will I not utterly take from him, nor suffer my faithfulness to fail.
My covenant will I not break, nor alter the thing that is gone out of my lips.
Once have I sworn by my holiness that I will not lie unto David.
His seed shall endure for ever, and his throne as the sun before me.—*Psalm 89: 20-36.*
The book of the generation of Jesus Christ, the son of David, the son of Abraham.—*Matt. 1:1.*
And, behold, thou shalt conceive in thy womb, and bring forth a son, and shalt call his name JESUS.
He shall be great, and shall be called the son of the Highest: and the Lord God shall give unto him the throne of his father David:
And he shall reign over the house of Jacob for ever; and of his kingdom there shall be no end.—*Luke 1: 31-33.*
And after they had held their peace, James answered, saying, Men *and* brethren, hearken unto me:
Simeon hath declared how God at the first did visit the Gentiles, to take out of them a people for his name.

And to this agree the words of the prophets; as it is written,
After this I will return, and will build again the tabernacle of David, which is fallen down; and I will build again the ruins thereof, and I will set it up:
That the residue of men might seek after the Lord, and all the Gentiles, upon whom my name is called, saith the Lord, who doeth all these things.—*Acts 15: 13-17.*

[2] They shall not hurt nor destroy in all my holy mountain: for the earth shall be full of the knowledge of the Lord, as the waters cover the sea. —*Isa. 11: 9.*

Behold, the days come, saith the Lord, that I will raise unto David a righteous Branch, and a King shall reign and prosper, and shall execute judgment and justice in the earth.
In his days Judah shall be saved, and Israel shall dwell safely: and this *is* his name whereby he shall be called, THE LORD OUR RIGHTEOUSNESS.
Therefore, behold, the days come, saith the Lord, that they shall no more say, The Lord liveth, which brought up the children of Israel out of the land of Egypt;
But, The Lord liveth, which brought up and which led the seed of the house of Israel out of the north country, and from all countries whither I had driven them; and they shall dwell in their own land.—*Jer. 23: 5-8.*
Thy kingdom come. Thy will be done in earth, as *it is* in heaven.—*Matt. 6: 10.*

THE VISION OF THE KINGDOM

The kingdom of God "comes not with outward show" (Luke 17:20), but is chiefly that which is inward and spiritual (Rom. 14:17)[3]; whereas the kingdom of heaven is organic, and is to be manifested in glory on the earth (Matt. 25:31; 19:28).[4] Since the kingdom of heaven is the earthly sphere of the kingdom of God (Matt. 6:10)[5] the two have much in common, and hence many parables are spoken of the kingdom of heaven in Matthew, and of the kingdom of God in Mark and Luke. It is the *omissions* which are significant. In the kingdom of God there are neither tares (Matt. 13:24-30, 36-43)[6] nor

---

[3] For the kingdom of God is not meat and drink; but righteousness, and peace, and joy in the Holy Ghost.—*Rom. 14:17.*

[4] When the Son of man shall come in his glory, and all the holy angels with him, then shall he sit upon the throne of his glory.—*Matt. 25:31.*

And Jesus said unto them, Verily I say unto you, That ye which have followed me, in the regeneration when the Son of man shall sit in the throne of his glory, ye also shall sit upon twelve thrones, judging the twelve tribes of Israel.—*Matt. 19:28.*

[5] Thy kingdom come. Thy will be done in earth, as *it is* in heaven.—*Matt. 6:10.*

[6] Another parable put he forth unto them, saying, The kingdom of heaven is likened unto a man which sowed good seed in his field:

But while men slept, his enemy came and sowed tares among the wheat, and went his way.

But when the blade was sprung up, and brought forth fruit, then appeared the tares also.

So the servants of the householder came and said unto him, Sir, didst not thou sow good seed in thy field? from whence then hath it tares?

He said unto them, An enemy hath done this. The servants said unto him, Wilt thou then that we go and gather them up?

But he said, Nay; lest while ye gather up the tares, ye root up also the wheat with them.

Let both grow together until the harvest: and in the time of harvest I will say to the reapers, Gather ye together first the tares, and bind them in bundles to burn them: but gather the wheat into my barn.—*Matt. 13:24-30.*

Then Jesus sent the multitude away, and went into the house: and his disciples came unto him, saying, Declare unto us the parable of the tares of the field.

He answered and said unto them, He that soweth the good seed is the Son of man;

The field is the world; the good seed are the children of the kingdom; but the tares are the children of the wicked *one;*

The enemy that sowed them is the devil; the harvest is the end of the world: and the reapers are the angels.

As therefore the tares are gathered and burned in the fire; so shall it be in the end of this world.

The Son of man shall send forth his angels, and they shall gather out of his kingdom all things that offend, and them which do iniquity;

And shall cast them into a furnace of fire: there shall be wailing and gnashing of teeth.

Then shall the righteous shine forth as the sun in the kingdom of their Father. Who hath ears

bad fish (Matt. 13:47-50).[7] On the other hand the citizens of the kingdom of God are not perfected till they shall "see him as he is" (1 John 3:2) and therefore the parable of the leaven is spoken of both kingdoms (Matt. 13:33; Luke 13:20, 21).[8] There can be neither tares nor bad fish in the kingdom of God, while both are in the kingdom of heaven in its present, or mystery, form. No other of the many confusions of things that differ has wrought so disastrously in Biblical interpretation as making of one meaning all passages in which the "kingdom of God," the "kingdom of heaven," and the "church" occur.

We must remember also that "the kingdom of heaven" is used both of the millennial kingdom of the Messiah, to be ushered in by His personal coming and of the sphere of Christian profession as described in the parables of Matthew 13.

And even in the millennial kingdom on earth, when Christ is reigning with a rod of iron, not all men will be His willing subjects. There cannot in that age be any "unbelievers" on earth, for Christ will be manifested in glory, and unbelief therefore will be impossible. But there will be those who, hating God, sullenly obey Christ the King. Those referred to in Revelation 20:7-9[9] are

to hear, let him hear.—*Matt. 13: 36-43.*

[7] Again, the kingdom of heaven is like unto a net, that was cast into the sea, and gathered of every kind:

Which, when it was full, they drew to shore, and sat down, and gathered the good into vessels, but cast the bad away.

So shall it be at the end of the world: the angels shall come forth, and sever the wicked from among the just,

And shall cast them into the furnace of fire: there shall be wailing and gnashing of teeth.—*Matt. 13:47-50.*

[8] Another parable spake he unto them; The kingdom of heaven is like unto leaven, which a woman took, and hid in three measures of meal, till the whole was leavened.—*Matt. 13:33.*

And again he said, Whereunto shall I liken the kingdom of God?

It is like leaven, which a woman took and hid in three measures of meal, till the whole was leavened.—*Luke 13:20, 21.*

[9] And when the thousand years are expired, Satan shall be loosed out of his prison,

And shall go out to deceive the nations which are in the four quarters of the earth, Gog and Magog, to gather them together to battle: the number of whom *is* as the sand of the sea.

And they went up on the breadth of the earth, and compassed the camp of the saints about, and the beloved city: and fire came down from God out of heaven, and devoured them.—*Rev. 20:7-9.*

THE VISION OF THE KINGDOM

simply God-haters. They will yield an outward obedience, for disobedience will then be instantly judged.

Earth may be considered as a revolted province of the great kingdom of God, and the kingdom of heaven as the appointed means for the restoration of the divine authority in the earth. This purpose is thus definitely defined:

"Then cometh the end, when he [Christ] shall have delivered up the kingdom to God, even the Father; when he shall have put down all rule and all authority and power. For he must reign, till he hath put all enemies under his feet . . . and when all things shall be subdued unto him [Christ], then shall the Son also himself be subject unto him that put all things under him, that God may be all in all" (1 Cor. 15: 24, 25, 28).

That is the ultimate *terminus* toward which all kingdom truth moves. The dominion over the earthly creation, lost by the "first man Adam," is restored in and by the "last Adam."

The great theme of the Old Testament prophets is the kingdom of Christ, the Son of David. Except the evangelic messages of Isaiah (Isa. 53),[10] and Zechariah

---

[10] Who hath believed our report? and to whom is the arm of the Lord revealed?

For he shall grow up before him as a tender plant, and as a root out of a dry ground: he hath no form nor comeliness: and when we shall see him, *there is* no beauty that we should desire him.

He is despised and rejected of men; a man of sorrows, and acquainted with grief: and we hid as it were *our* faces from him; he was despised, and we esteemed him not.

Surely he hath borne our griefs, and carried our sorrows: yet we did esteem him stricken, smitten of God, and afflicted.

But he *was* wounded for our transgressions, he *was* bruised for our iniquities: the chastisement of our peace *was* upon him; and with his stripes we are healed.

All we like sheep have gone astray; we have turned every one to his own way; and the Lord hath laid on him the iniquity of us all.

He was oppressed, and he was afflicted, yet he opened not his mouth: he is brought as a lamb to the slaughter, and as a sheep before her shearers is dumb, so he openeth not his mouth.

He was taken from prison and from judgment: and who shall declare his generation? for he was cut off out of the land of the living: for the transgression of my people was he stricken.

And he made his grave with the wicked, and with the rich in his death; because he had done no violence, neither *was any* deceit in his mouth.

Yet it pleased the Lord to bruise him; he hath put *him* to grief; when thou shalt make his soul an offering for sin, he

(Zech. 3 : 8; 4: 6; 12: 10; 13: 1),[11] the prophetic vision of Messiah is usually of a great King. The King and His earth kingdom fill the scene. The Messiah, though "Immanuel"—God with us, is also born of a virgin of the "house of David" (Isa. 7: 13, 14).

In Isaiah 9: 6 and 7, a declaration concerning the Coming One is at once so explicit and so inclusive of His Deity, of His humanity through a natural birth, and of His kingship as to exclude any possible attempt to interpret it in a so-called "spiritual" or allegorical sense.

"For unto us a child is born, unto us a son is given: and the government shall be upon his shoulder: and his name shall be called Wonderful, Counsellor, The mighty God, The everlasting Father, The Prince of Peace. Of the increase of his government and peace there shall be no end, upon the throne of David, and upon his kingdom, to order it, and to establish it with judgment and with justice from henceforth even for ever. The zeal of the Lord of hosts will perform this."

The expression, "Throne of David," is as severely historical and geographical as "throne of the Cæsars."

This great passage may be taken as the norm of the Old Testament prophetic teaching concerning the king-

---

shall see *his* seed, he shall prolong *his* days, and the pleasure of the Lord shall prosper in his hand.

He shall see of the travail of his soul, *and* shall be satisfied: by his knowledge shall my righteous servant justify many; for he shall bear their iniquities.

Therefore will I divide him *a portion* with the great, and he shall divide the spoil with the strong; because he hath poured out his soul unto death: and he was numbered with the transgressors, and he bare the sin of many, and made intercession for the transgressors.—*Isa. 53.*

[11] Hear now, O Joshua the high priest, thou, and thy fellows that sit before thee: for they *are* men wondered at: for, behold, I will bring forth my servant the BRANCH.—*Zech. 3: 8.*

Then he answered and spake unto me, saying, This *is* the word of the Lord unto Zerubbabel, saying, Not by might, nor by power, but by my spirit, saith the Lord of hosts.—*Zech. 4: 6.*

And I will pour upon the house of David, and upon the inhabitants of Jerusalem, the spirit of grace and of supplications: and they shall look upon me whom they have pierced, and they shall mourn for him, as one mourneth for *his* only *son,* and shall be in bitterness for him as one that is in bitterness for *his* firstborn.—*Zech. 12: 10.*

In that day there shall be a fountain opened to the house of David and to the inhabitants of Jerusalem for sin and for uncleanness.—*Zech. 13: 1.*

THE VISION OF THE KINGDOM

dom of Christ. The *child* is "born"; the *Son* is "given." What exquisite accuracy! There was a point in time when the *child* began to be; the *Son* is eternal, and could be "given," but not "born."

And the passage is also typical of all the prophetic teaching about Messiah and His kingdom in that, while asserting both the Deity and humanity of the King, it links His kingdom with earth, with Israel, and with the Davidic Covenant. What is added elsewhere is detail. But it is detail of such intense interest, and so essential to any comprehensive view of the kingdom of heaven, that it must be here summarized.

The Davidic Covenant (2 Sam. 7: 16, 17, and preceding),[12] which is the foundation declaration of kingdom truth, is specific as to five things: David is to have a "house," that is, a posterity; a "throne," the symbol of royal authority; a "kingdom" or sphere of rule, *and this in perpetuity;* and all this with one condition: disobedience in the Davidic family is to be visited with chastisement, but not by the annulment of the Covenant (Psa. 89: 30-36).[13] The Eighty-ninth Psalm is the Divine confirmation of the Davidic Covenant by the oath of Jehovah.

It is most interesting to see, and of vital moment to the right interpretation of the prophetic testimony, that the Davidic Covenant, as conditioning the kingdom foretold by them, *enters the New Testament unchanged.* The angelic annunciation to Mary, the virgin of the house of

---

[12] And thine house and thy kingdom shall be established for ever before thee: thy throne shall be established for ever.

According to all these words, and according to all this vision, so did Nathan speak unto David. —*2 Sam. 7: 16, 17.*

[13] If his children forsake my law, and walk not in my judgments;

If they break my statutes, and keep not my commandments;

Then will I visit their transgression with the rod, and their iniquity with stripes.

Nevertheless my lovingkindness will I not utterly take from him, nor suffer my faithfulness to fail.

My covenant will I not break, nor alter the thing that is gone out of my lips.

Once have I sworn by my holiness that I will not lie unto David.

His seed shall endure for ever, and his throne as the sun before me.—*Psalm 89: 30-36.*

David, appointed to be mother of the "Child" (Isa. 9: 6),[14] is an explicit confirmation of that covenant.

"And, behold, thou shalt conceive in thy womb, and bring forth a son, and shalt call his name Jesus. He shall be great, and shall be called the Son of the Highest: and the Lord God shall give unto him the throne of his father David: and he shall reign over the house of Jacob for ever, and of his kingdom there shall be no end" (Luke 1: 31-33).

The eleventh chapter of Isaiah is one of the descriptive passages into which a kind of summary of all the prophetic kingdom testimony is gathered. It follows a description (Isa. 10: 20-34)[15] of the events immediately

---

[14] For unto us a child is born, unto us a son is given: and the government shall be upon his shoulder: and his name shall be called Wonderful, Counsellor, The mighty God, The everlasting Father, The Prince of Peace.—*Isa. 9: 6.*

[15] And it shall come to pass in that day, *that* the remnant of Israel, and such as are escaped of the house of Jacob, shall no more again stay upon him that smote them; but shall stay upon the Lord, the Holy One of Israel, in truth.

The remnant shall return, *even* the remnant of Jacob, unto the mighty God.

For though thy people Israel be as the sand of the sea, *yet* a remnant of them shall return: the consumption decreed shall overflow with righteousness.

For the Lord God of hosts shall make a consumption, even determined, in the midst of all the land.

Therefore thus saith the Lord God of hosts, O my people that dwellest in Zion, be not afraid of the Assyrian: he shall smite thee with a rod, and shall lift up his staff against thee, after the manner of Egypt.

For yet a very little while, and the indignation shall cease, and mine anger in their destruction.

And the Lord of hosts shall stir up a scourge for him according to the slaughter of Midian at the rock of Oreb: and *as* his rod *was* upon the sea, so shall he lift it up after the manner of Egypt.

And it shall come to pass in that day, *that* his burden shall be taken away from off thy shoulder, and his yoke from off thy neck, and the yoke shall be destroyed because of the anointing.

He is come to Aiath, he is passed to Migron; at Michmash he hath laid up his carriages;

They are gone over the passage; they have taken up their lodging at Geba; Ramah is afraid; Gibeah of Saul is fled.

Lift up thy voice, O daughter of Gallim: cause it to be heard unto Laish, O poor Anathoth.

Madmenah is removed; the inhabitants of Gebim gather themselves to flee.

As yet shall he remain at Nob that day: he shall shake his hand *against* the mount of the daughter of Zion, the hill of Jerusalem.

Behold, the Lord, the Lord of hosts, shall lop the bough with terror: and the high ones of stature *shall be* hewn down, and the haughty shall be humbled.

And he shall cut down the

THE VISION OF THE KINGDOM

preceding the coming in glory of the Branch of Jesse. Those events are more particularly described by Daniel in his seventh chapter,[16] and in Revelation 19: 11-21.[17]

thickets of the forest with iron, and Lebanon shall fall by a mighty one.—*Isa. 10:20-34*.

[16] In the first year of Belshazzar king of Babylon Daniel had a dream and visions of his head upon his bed: then he wrote the dream, *and* told the sum of the matters.

Daniel spake and said, I saw in my vision by night, and, behold, the four winds of the heaven strode upon the great sea.

And four great beasts came up from the sea, diverse one from another.

The first *was* like a lion, and had eagle's wings: I beheld till the wings thereof were plucked, and it was lifted up from the earth, and made stand upon the feet as a man, and a man's heart was given to it.

And behold another beast, a second, like to a bear, and it raised up itself on one side, and *it had* three ribs in the mouth of it between the teeth of it: and they said thus unto it, Arise, devour much flesh.

After this I beheld, and lo another, like a leopard, which had upon the back of it four wings of a fowl; the beast had also four heads; and dominion was given to it.

After this I saw in the night visions, and behold a fourth beast, dreadful and terrible, and strong exceedingly; and it had great iron teeth: it devoured and brake in pieces, and stamped the residue with the feet of it: and it *was* diverse from all the beasts that *were* before it; and it had ten horns.

I considered the horns, and, behold, there came up among them another little horn, before whom there were three of the first horns plucked up by the roots: and, behold, in this horn *were* eyes like the eyes of man, and a mouth speaking great things.

I beheld till the thrones were cast down, and the Ancient of days did sit, whose garment *was* white as snow, and the hair of his head like the pure wool: his throne *was like* the fiery flame, *and* his wheels *as* burning fire.

A fiery stream issued and came forth from before him: thousand thousands ministered unto him, and ten thousand times ten thousand stood before him: the judgment was set, and the books were opened.

I beheld then because of the voice of the great words which the horn spake: I beheld *even* till the beast was slain, and his body destroyed, and given to the burning flame.

As concerning the rest of the beasts, they had their dominion taken away: yet their lives were prolonged for a season and time.

I saw in the night visions, and, behold, *one* like the Son of man came with the clouds of heaven, and came to the Ancient of days, and they brought him near before him.

And there was given him dominion, and glory, and a kingdom, that all people, nations, and languages, should serve him: his dominion *is* an everlasting dominion, which shall not pass away, and his kingdom *that* which shall not be destroyed.

I Daniel was grieved in my spirit in the midst of *my* body, and the visions of my head troubled me.

I came near unto one of them that stood by, and asked him the truth of all this. So he told me, and made me know the interpretation of the things.

These great beasts, which are four, *are* four kings, *which* shall arise out of the earth.

But the saints of the most High shall take the kingdom, and possess the kingdom for ever, even for ever and ever.

Then I would know the truth of the fourth beast, which was diverse from all the others, exceeding dreadful, whose teeth *were of* iron, and his nails *of* brass; *which* devoured, brake in pieces, and stamped the residue with his feet;

And of the ten horns that *were* in his head, and *of* the other which came up, and before whom three fell; even *of* that horn that had eyes, and a mouth that spake very great things, whose look *was* more stout than his fellows.

I beheld, and the same horn made war with the saints, and prevailed against them;

Until the Ancient of days came, and judgment was given to the saints of the most High; and the time came that the saints possessed the kingdom.

Thus he said, The fourth beast shall be the fourth kingdom upon earth, which shall be diverse from all kingdoms, and shall devour the whole earth, and shall tread it down, and break it in pieces.

And the ten horns out of this kingdom *are* ten kings *that* shall arise: and another shall rise after them; and he shall be diverse from the first, and he shall subdue three kings.

And he shall speak *great* words against the most High, and shall wear out the saints of the most High, and think to change times and laws: and they shall be given into his hand until a time and times and the dividing of time.

But the judgment shall sit, and they shall take away his dominion, to consume and to destroy *it* unto the end.

And the kingdom and dominion, and the greatness of the kingdom under the whole heaven, shall be given to the people of the saints of the most High, whose kingdom *is* an everlasting kingdom, and all dominions shall serve and obey him.

Hitherto *is* the end of the matter. As for me Daniel, my cogitations much troubled me, and my countenance changed in me: but I kept the matter in my heart.—*Dan. 7.*

[17] And I saw heaven opened, and behold a white horse; and he that sat upon him *was* called Faithful and True, and in righteousness he doth judge and make war.

His eyes *were* as a flame of fire, and on his head *were* many crowns; and he had a name written, that no man knew, but he himself.

And he *was* clothed with a vesture dipped in blood: and his name is called The Word of God.

And the armies *which were* in heaven followed him upon white horses, clothed in fine linen, white and clean.

And out of his mouth goeth a sharp sword, that with it he should smite the nations: and he shall rule them with a rod of iron: and he treadeth the winepress of the fierceness and wrath of Almighty God.

And he hath on *his* vesture and on his thigh a name written, KING OF KINGS, AND LORD OF LORDS.

And I saw an angel standing in the sun; and he cried with a loud voice, saying to all the fowls that fly in the midst of heaven, Come and gather yourselves together unto the supper of the great God;

That ye may eat the flesh of kings, and the flesh of captains, and the flesh of mighty men, and the flesh of horses, and of them that sit on them, and the flesh of all *men, both* free and bond, both small and great.

And I saw the beast, and the kings of the earth, and their armies, gathered together to make war against him that sat

THE VISION OF THE KINGDOM

The Remnant of Israel turns to the Lord, the battle of Armageddon follows, and then the kingdom is set up.

In the kingdom description of Isaiah 11,[18] let it be noted that:

---

on the horse, and against his army.

And the beast was taken, and with him the false prophet that wrought miracles before him, with which he deceived them that had received the mark of the beast, and them that worshipped his image. These both were cast alive into a lake of fire burning with brimstone.

And the remnant were slain with the sword of him that sat upon the horse, which *sword* proceeded out of his mouth: and all the fowls were filled with their flesh.—*Rev. 19: 11-21.*

[18] And there shall come forth a rod out of the stem of Jesse, and a Branch shall grow out of his roots:

And the spirit of the Lord shall rest upon him, the spirit of wisdom and understanding, the spirit of counsel and might, the spirit of knowledge and of the fear of the Lord;

And shall make him of quick understanding in the fear of the Lord: and he shall not judge after the sight of his eyes, neither reprove after the hearing of his ears:

But with righteousness shall he judge the poor, and reprove with equity for the meek of the earth: and he shall smite the earth with the rod of his mouth, and with the breath of his lips shall he slay the wicked.

And righteousness shall be the girdle of his loins, and faithfulness the girdle of his reins.

The wolf also shall dwell with the lamb, and the leopard shall lie down with the kid; and the calf and the young lion and the fatling together; and a little child shall lead them.

And the cow and the bear shall feed; their young ones shall lie down together; and the lion shall eat straw like the ox.

And the sucking child shall play on the hole of the asp, and the weaned child shall put his hand on the cockatrice' den.

They shall not hurt nor destroy in all my holy mountain: for the earth shall be full of the knowledge of the Lord, as the waters cover the sea.

And in that day there shall be a root of Jesse, which shall stand for an ensign of the people; to it shall the Gentiles seek: and his rest shall be glorious.

And it shall come to pass in that day, *that* the Lord shall set his hand again the second time to recover the remnant of his people, which shall be left, from Assyria, and from Egypt, and from Pathros, and from Cush, and from Elam, and from Shinar, and from Hamath, and from the islands of the sea.

And he shall set up an ensign for the nations, and shall assemble the outcasts of Israel, and gather together the dispersed of Judah from the four corners of the earth.

The envy also of Ephraim shall depart, and the adversaries of Judah shall be cut off: Ephraim shall not envy Judah, and Judah shall not vex Ephraim.

But they shall fly upon the shoulders of the Philistines toward the west; they shall spoil them of the east together: they shall lay their hand upon Edom and Moab; and the children of Ammon shall obey them.

And the Lord shall utterly destroy the tongue of the Egyptian sea; and with his mighty wind shall he shake his hand over the river, and shall smite it in the seven streams, and make *men* go over dryshod.

(1) The King is Davidic (v. 1); (2) His power is the seven-fold fulness of the Spirit (v. 2); (3) the keyword of the kingdom reign is righteousness (vs. 3-5); (4) the result of the reign of righteousness is peace (vs. 6-9, for these are eternally related as cause and effect (Isa. 32:17)[19]; (5) the extent of the kingdom is "the earth" (v. 9); (6) Israel is restored to the land (vs 10-12); (7) the divided nation becomes one (v. 13).

And this is also the order of events in Jeremiah's predictions concerning the kingdom:

"I will gather the remnant of my flock out of all countries whither I have driven them, and will bring them again to their folds; and they shall be fruitful and increase . . . and they shall fear no more, nor be dismayed, neither shall they be lacking, saith the Lord. Behold, the days come, saith the Lord, that I will raise unto David a righteous Branch, and a King shall reign and prosper, and shall execute judgment and justice in the earth. In his days Judah shall be saved, and Israel shall dwell safely: and this is his name whereby he shall be called, The Lord our righteousness" (Jer. 23:3-6).

Verses 7 and 8 [20] describe the regathering of the nation announced in verse 3. And the restoration of Israel to the land in connection with the establishment of Messiah's kingdom is a great and constant theme of the Prophets (Isa. 49:8-13; 52:1-12; Jer. 31:7-25; Ezek. 36:16-38).[21]

And there shall be an highway for the remnant of his people, which shall be left, from Assyria; like as it was to Israel in the day that he came up out of the land of Egypt.—*Isa. 11.*

[19] And the work of righteousness shall be peace; and the effect of righteousness quietness and assurance for ever.—*Isa. 32:17.*

[20] Therefore, behold, the days come, saith the Lord, that they shall no more say, The Lord liveth, which brought up the children of Israel out of the land of Egypt.

But, The Lord liveth, which brought up and which led the seed of the house of Israel out of the north country, and from all countries whither I had driven them; and they shall dwell in their own land.—*Jer. 23:7, 8.*

[21] Thus saith the Lord, In an acceptable time have I heard thee, and in a day of salvation have I helped thee: and I will preserve thee, and give thee for a covenant of the people, to establish the earth, to cause to inherit the desolate heritages;

That thou mayest say to the prisoners, Go forth; to them that *are* in darkness. Shew yourselves. They shall feed in the

THE VISION OF THE KINGDOM

ways, and their pastures *shall be* in all high places.

They shall not hunger nor thirst; neither shall the heat nor sun smite them: for he that hath mercy on them shall lead them, even by the springs of water shall he guide them.

And I will make all my mountains a way, and my highways shall be exalted.

Behold, these shall come from far: and, lo, these from the north and from the west; and these from the land of Sinim.

Sing, O heavens; and be joyful, O earth; and break forth into singing, O mountains: for the Lord hath comforted his people, and will have mercy upon his afflicted.—*Isa. 49:8-13.*

Awake, awake; put on thy strength, O Zion; put on thy beautiful garments, O Jerusalem, the holy city: for henceforth there shall no more come into thee the uncircumcised and the unclean.

Shake thyself from the dust; arise, *and* sit down, O Jerusalem: loose thyself from the bands of thy neck, O captive daughter of Zion. Etc.—*Isa. 52: 1-12.*

For thus saith the Lord; Sing with gladness for Jacob, and shout among the chief of the nations: publish ye, praise ye, and say, O Lord, save thy people, the remnant of Israel.

Behold, I will bring them from the north country, and gather them from the coasts of the earth, *and* with them the blind and the lame, the woman with child and her that travaileth with child together: a great company shall return thither.

They shall come with weeping, and with supplications will I lead them: I will cause them to walk by the rivers of waters in a straight way, wherein they shall not stumble: for I am a father to Israel, and Ephraim *is* my firstborn.

Hear the word of the Lord, O ye nations, and declare *it* in the isles afar off, and say, He that scattered Israel will gather him, and keep him, as a shepherd *doth* his flock.

For the Lord hath redeemed Jacob, and ransomed him from the hand of *him that was* stronger than he.

Therefore they shall come and sing in the height of Zion, and shall flow together to the goodness of the Lord, for wheat, and for wine, and for oil, and for the young of the flock and of the herd: and their soul shall be as a watered garden; and they shall not sorrow any more at all. . . .

And there is hope in thine end, saith the Lord, that thy children shall come again to their own border. . . .

Set thee up waymarks, make thee high heaps: set thine heart toward the highway, *even* the way *which* thou wentest: turn again, O virgin of Israel, turn again to these thy cities. . . .

Thus saith the Lord of hosts, the God of Israel; As yet they shall use this speech in the land of Judah and in the cities thereof, when I shall bring again their captivity; The Lord bless thee, O habitation of justice, *and* mountain of holiness.

And there shall dwell in Judah itself, and in all the cities thereof together, husbandmen, and they *that* go forth with flocks.

For I have satiated the weary soul, and I have replenished every sorrowful soul.—*Jer. 31: 7-25.*

. . . For I will take you from among the heathen, and gather you out of all countries, and will bring you into your own land.

Then will I sprinkle clean water upon you, and ye shall be clean: from all your filthiness, and from all your idols, will I cleanse you.

A new heart also will I give you, and a new spirit will I put within you: and I will take away the stony heart out of your flesh,

It is obvious that *none of these events took place* at the first advent of Christ—the advent to suffer. Dispersed Israel was not regathered; the nation then in Palestine refused to recognize Christ as the promised king; they refused no less emphatically to give Him the name, "Our Righteousness" (Rom. 10:3); nor has Israel "dwelt safely" in the land.

The same order of events is again repeated in Jeremiah 33:1-17,[22] the word of the Lord which was given to comfort and assure the Prophet in his imprisonment; the King sets up His kingdom and Israel is regathered.

---

and I will give you an heart of flesh.

And I will put my spirit within you, and cause you to walk in my statutes, and ye shall keep my judgments, and do *them*.

And ye shall dwell in the land that I gave to your fathers; and ye shall be my people, and I will be your God. Etc.—*Ezek. 36: 16-38.*

[22] Moreover the word of the Lord came unto Jeremiah the second time, while he was yet shut up in the court of the prison, saying, . . .

And I will cause the captivity of Judah and the captivity of Israel to return, and will build them, as at the first. . . .

Thus saith the Lord; Again there shall be heard in this place, which ye say *shall be* desolate without man and without beast, *even* in the cities of Judah, and in the streets of Jerusalem, that are desolate, without man, and without inhabitant, and without beast,

The voice of joy, and the voice of gladness, the voice of the bridegroom, and the voice of the bride, the voice of them that shall say, Praise the Lord of hosts: for the Lord *is* good; for his mercy *endureth* for ever: *and* of them that shall bring the sacrifice of praise into the house of the Lord. For I will cause to return the captivity of the land, as at the first, saith the Lord.

Thus saith the Lord of hosts; Again in this place, which is desolate without man and without beast, and in all the cities thereof, shall be an habitation of shepherds causing *their* flocks to lie down.

In the cities of the mountains, in the cities of the vale, and in the cities of the south, and in the land of Benjamin, and in the places about Jerusalem, and in the cities of Judah, shall the flocks pass again under the hands of him that telleth *them,* saith the Lord.

Behold, the days come, saith the Lord, that I will perform that good thing which I have promised unto the house of Israel and to the house of Judah.

In those days, and at that time, will I cause the Branch of righteousness to grow up unto David; and he shall execute judgment and righteousness in the land.

In those days shall Judah be saved, and Jerusalem shall dwell safely: and this *is the name* wherewith she shall be called, The Lord our righteousness.

For thus saith the Lord: David shall never want a man to sit upon the throne of the house of Israel.—*Jer. 33: 1-17.*

THE VISION OF THE KINGDOM

Ezekiel again and again repeats the order of events which accompany the establishment of the kingdom (Ezek. 28:25, 26; 34:11-31; 36:1-12, 24-38; 37:1-28; 39:25-29).[23]

[23] Thus saith the Lord God: When I shall have gathered the house of Israel from the people among whom they are scattered, and shall be sanctified in them in the sight of the heathen, then shall they dwell in their land that I have given to my servant Jacob.

And they shall dwell safely therein, and shall build houses, and plant vineyards; yea, they shall dwell with confidence, when I have executed judgments upon all those that despise them. —*Ezek. 28:25, 26.*

For thus saith the Lord God; Behold, I, *even* I, will both search my sheep, and seek them out.

As a shepherd seeketh out his flock in the day that he is among his sheep *that are* scattered; so will I seek out my sheep, and will deliver them out of all places where they have been scattered in the cloudy and dark day.

And I will bring them out from the people, and gather them from the countries, and will bring them to their own land, and feed them upon the mountains of Israel by the rivers, and in all the inhabited places of the country. . . .

And I will set up one shepherd over them, and he shall feed them, *even* my servant David; he shall feed them, and he shall be their shepherd.

And I the Lord will be their God, and my servant David a prince among them; I the Lord have spoken *it.* . . . —*Ezek. 34: 11-31.*

Also, thou son of man, prophesy unto the mountains of Israel, and say, Ye mountains of Israel, hear the word of the Lord:

Thus saith the Lord God; Because the enemy hath said against you, Aha, even the ancient high places are ours in possession: . . .

For, behold, I *am* for you, and I will turn unto you, and ye shall be tilled and sown:

And I will multiply men upon you, all the house of Israel, *even* all of it: and the cities shall be inhabited, and the wastes shall be builded:

And I will multiply upon you man and beast; and they shall increase and bring fruit: and I will settle you after your old estates, and will do better *unto you* than at your beginnings: and ye shall know that I *am* the Lord.

Yea, I will cause men to walk upon you, *even* my people Israel; and they shall possess thee, and thou shalt be their inheritance, and thou shalt no more henceforth bereave them of men.—*Ezek. 36: 1-12.*

For I will take you from among the heathen, and gather you out of all countries, and will bring you into your own land.

Then will I sprinkle clean water upon you, and ye shall be clean: from all your filthiness, and from all your idols, will I cleanse you.

A new heart also will I give you, and a new spirit will I put within you: and I will take away the stony heart out of your flesh, and I will give you an heart of flesh.

And I will put my spirit within you, and cause you to walk in my statutes, and ye shall keep my judgments, and do *them.*

And ye shall dwell in the land that I gave to your fathers;

and ye shall be my people, and I will be your God . . .

And the desolate land shall be tilled, whereas it lay desolate in the sight of all that passed by.

And they shall say, This land that was desolate is become like the garden of Eden, and the waste and desolate and ruined cities *are become* fenced, *and* are inhabited.

Then the heathen that are left round about you shall know that I the Lord build the ruined *places, and* plant that that was desolate: I the Lord have spoken *it,* and I will do *it*. . . .—*Ezek. 36: 24-38.*

The hand of the Lord was upon me, and carried me out in the spirit of the Lord, and set me down in the midst of the valley which *was* full of bones.

And caused me to pass by them round about: and, behold, *there were* very many in the open valley; and, lo, *they were* very dry.

And he said unto me, Son of man, can these bones live? And I answered, O Lord God, thou knowest. . . .

Then he said unto me, Son of man, these bones are the whole house of Israel: behold, they say, Our bones are dried, and our hope is lost: we are cut off for our parts.

Therefore prophesy and say unto them, Thus saith the Lord God; Behold, O my people, I will open your graves, and cause you to come up out of your graves, and bring you into the land of Israel.

And ye shall know that I *am* the Lord, when I have opened your graves, O my people, and brought you up out of your graves. . . .

And say unto them, Thus saith the Lord God; Behold, I will take the children of Israel from among the heathen, whither they be gone, and will gather them on every side, and bring them into their own land:

And I will make them one nation in the land upon the mountains of Israel; and one king shall be king to them all: and they shall be no more two nations, neither shall they be divided into two kingdoms any more at all:

Neither shall they defile themselves any more with their idols, nor with their detestable things, nor with any of their transgressions: but I will save them out of all their dwelling places, wherein they have sinned, and will cleanse them: so shall they be my people, and I will be their God.

And David my servant *shall be* king over them; and they all shall have one shepherd; they shall also walk in my judgments, and observe my statutes, and do them.

And they shall dwell in the land that I have given unto Jacob my servant, wherein your fathers have dwelt; and they shall dwell therein, *even* they, and their children, and their children's children for ever: and my servant David *shall be* their prince for ever.

Moreover I will make a covenant of peace with them; it shall be an everlasting covenant with them: and I will place them, and multiply them, and will set my sanctuary in the midst of them for evermore.

My tabernacle also shall be with them: yea, I will be their God, and they shall be my people.

And the heathen shall know that I the Lord do sanctify Israel, when my sanctuary shall be in the midst of them for evermore.—*Ezek. 37: 1-28.*

Therefore thus saith the Lord God; Now will I bring again the captivity of Jacob, and have mercy upon the whole house of Israel, and will be jealous for my holy name;

After that they have borne their shame, and all their trespasses whereby they have tres-

THE VISION OF THE KINGDOM

The book of Daniel has a distinctive message covering the long period of Gentile world-rule. It is now mere history that, from the time of Nebuchadnezzar, king of Babylon, 610 B. C., to this present time, the government of the world has been in Gentile hands. To this long period of time our Lord gave a name, and a sign:

"Jerusalem shall be trodden under foot of the Gentiles, until the times of the Gentiles be fulfilled" (Luke 21:24). It is still the "times of the Gentiles," and Jerusalem is still "trodden under foot of the Gentiles."

Daniel is the prophet of "the times of the Gentiles." Carried away to Babylon, his long life extended from the reign of Nebuchadnezzar to that of Cyrus. Interpreting a dream of King Nebuchadnezzar (Dan. 2:31-45),[24]

---

passed against me, when they dwelt safely in their land, and none made *them* afraid.

When I have brought them again from the people, and gathered them out of their enemies' lands, and am sanctified in them in the sight of many nations;

Then shall they know that I *am* the Lord their God, which caused them to be led into captivity among the heathen: but I have gathered them unto their own land, and have left none of them any more there.

Neither will I hide my face any more from them: for I have poured out my spirit upon the house of Israel, saith the Lord God.—*Ezek. 39:25-29.*

[24] Thou, O king, sawest, and behold a great image. This great image, whose brightness *was* excellent, stood before thee; and the form thereof *was* terrible.

This image's head *was* of fine gold, his breast and his arms of silver, his belly and his thighs of brass,

His legs of iron, his feet part of iron and part of clay.

Thou sawest till that a stone was cut out without hands, which smote the image upon his feet *that were* of iron and clay, and brake them to pieces.

Then was the iron, the clay, the brass, the silver, and the gold, broken to pieces together, and became like the chaff of the summer threshingfloors; and the wind carried them away, that no place was found for them: and the stone that smote the image became a great mountain, and filled the whole earth.

This *is* the dream; and we will tell the interpretation thereof before the king.

Thou, O king, *art* a king of kings: for the God of heaven hath given thee a kingdom, power, and strength, and glory.

And wheresoever the children of men dwell, the beasts of the field and the fowls of the heaven hath he given into thine hand, and hath made thee ruler over them all. Thou *art* this head of gold.

And after thee shall arise another kingdom inferior to thee, and another third kingdom of brass, which shall bear rule over all the earth.

And the fourth kingdom shall be strong as iron: forasmuch as iron breaketh in pieces and subdueth all *things:* and as iron that breaketh all these, shall it break in pieces and bruise.

And whereas thou sawest the feet and toes, part of potters'

it was given to Daniel to see the entire course of Gentile world domination to the end. He saw four world empires fulfilled: in Babylon; Medo-Persia; the Greek empire of Alexander, with its division into four parts; and Rome. He saw no other Gentile world empire, and all attempts to establish one have failed, and are doomed to failure. He saw Rome divided, first into two parts and then into ten (vs. 33, 40-43).[25] The division into two was fulfilled in the Eastern Empire with its capital at Constantinople, and the Western Empire with its capital at Rome. He saw these (symbolized by the two legs of the image) deteriorate and divide—a division ultimately into ten kingdoms occupying the territory once covered by the undivided Roman Empire.

And then a startling and supernatural event swung into the prophet's ken. The ten final kingdoms of the Gentiles go down in catastrophe. A "stone cut out with-

clay, and part of iron, the kingdom shall be divided; but there shall be in it of the strength of the iron, forasmuch as thou sawest the iron mixed with miry clay.

And *as* the toes of the feet *were* part of iron, and part of clay, *so* the kingdom shall be partly strong, and partly broken.

And whereas thou sawest iron mixed with miry clay, they shall mingle themselves with the seed of men: but they shall not cleave one to another, even as iron is not mixed with clay.

And in the days of these kings shall the God of heaven set up a kingdom, which shall never be destroyed: and the kingdom shall not be left to other people, *but* it shall break in pieces and consume all these kingdoms, and it shall stand for ever.

Forasmuch as thou sawest that the stone was cut out of the mountain without hands, and that it brake in pieces the iron, the brass, the clay, the silver, and the gold; the great God hath made known to the king what shall come to pass hereafter: and the dream *is* certain, and the interpretation thereof sure.—*Dan. 2: 31-45.*

[25] His legs of iron, his feet part of iron and part of clay.

And the fourth kingdom shall be strong as iron: forasmuch as iron breaketh in pieces and subdueth all *things:* and as iron that breaketh all these, shall it break in pieces and bruise.

And whereas thou sawest the feet and toes, part of potters' clay, and part of iron, the kingdom shall be divided; but there shall be in it of the strength of the iron, forasmuch as thou sawest the iron mixed with miry clay.

And *as* the toes of the feet *were* part of iron, and part of clay, *so* the kingdom shall be partly strong, and partly broken.

And whereas thou sawest iron mixed with miry clay, they shall mingle themselves with the seed of men: but they shall not cleave one to another, even as iron is not mixed with clay.—*Dan. 2: 33, 40-43.*

THE VISION OF THE KINGDOM

out hands" smites the image into a destruction likened unto the chaff of the summer threshing-floor. There is no reconstruction of Gentile world power. But the sphere of earth government so long filled with Gentile empires and kingdoms gives place to quite another rule:

"And in the days of these kings shall the God of heaven set up a kingdom, which shall never be destroyed: and the kingdom shall not be left to other people, but it shall break in pieces and consume all these kingdoms, and it shall stand for ever."

It is from this passage that the designation "kingdom of heaven" comes.

The Prophecy of Daniel adds many most important details, especially of the time of the end of Gentile dominion, into which we cannot now enter. But Daniel's greatly important contribution to the message of the prophets concerning the kingdom is in his order of time. First, the four world empires of the Gentiles; second, the deterioration and division of the fourth world empire into two and ultimately into ten; third, the setting up of the kingdom of heaven after the catastrophic destruction of the ten.

It is certain that nothing of this came to pass at the advent of Messiah to suffer. The fourth empire, Rome, was in the zenith of its strength, and had undergone neither deterioration nor division. Gentile world-power does not change into the kingdom of the God of heaven by the transfer of individuals from one to the other, as by the gradual conversion of the Gentile world. The end of Gentile world-power is sudden, destructive, overwhelming. And this is also the testimony of Jesus Christ, and of His apostles (Luke 17:26-32; 1 Thess. 5:1-4; 2 Thess. 1:6-10).[26]

---

[26] And as it was in the days of Noe, so shall it be also in the days of the Son of man

They did eat, they drank, they married wives, they were given in marriage, until the day that Noe entered into the ark, and the flood came, and destroyed them all.

Likewise also as it was in the days of Lot; they did eat, they drank, they bought, they sold, they planted, they builded;

But the same day that Lot went out of Sodom it rained fire and brimstone from heaven, and destroyed *them* all.

Even thus shall it be in the day when the Son of man is revealed.

Passing over much of great interest in other of the prophets, note a brief mention of the kingdom prophecies of Zechariah. His twelfth chapter[27] gives a graphic picture of the final siege of Jerusalem and the battle of Armageddon (comp. Isa. 10; Rev. 19), followed by

---

In that day, he which shall be upon the housetop, and his stuff in the house, let him not come down to take it away: and he that is in the field, let him likewise not return back.
Remember Lot's wife.—*Luke 17: 26-32.*
But of the times and the seasons, brethren, ye have no need that I write unto you.
For yourselves know perfectly that the day of the Lord so cometh as a thief in the night.
For when they shall say, Peace and safety; then sudden destruction cometh upon them, as travail upon a woman with child; and they shall not escape.
But ye, brethren, are not in darkness, that that day should overtake you as a thief.—*1 Thess. 5: 1-4.*
Seeing *it is* a righteous thing with God to recompense tribulation to them that trouble you;
And to you who are troubled rest with us, when the Lord Jesus shall be revealed from heaven with his mighty angels,
In flaming fire taking vengeance on them that know not God, and that obey not the gospel of our Lord Jesus Christ:
Who shall be punished with everlasting destruction from the presence of the Lord, and from the glory of his power;
When he shall come to be glorified in his saints, and to be admired in all them that believe (because our testimony among you was believed) in that day.—*2 Thess. 1: 6-10.*
[27]The burden of the word of the LORD for Israel, saith the LORD, which stretcheth forth the heavens, and layeth the foundation of the earth, and formeth the spirit of man within him.

Behold, I will make Jerusalem a cup of trembling unto all the people round about, when they shall be in the siege both against Judah *and* against Jerusalem.
And in that day will I make Jerusalem a burdensome stone for all people: all that burden themselves with it shall be cut in pieces, though all the people of the earth be gathered together against it.
In that day, saith the LORD, I will smite every horse with astonishment, and his rider with madness: and I will open mine eyes upon the house of Judah, and will smite every horse of the people with blindness.
And the governors of Judah shall say in their heart, The inhabitants of Jerusalem *shall be* my strength in the LORD of hosts their God.
In that day will I make the governors of Judah like a hearth of fire among the wood, and like a torch of fire in a sheaf; and they shall devour all the people round about, on the right hand and on the left: and Jerusalem shall be inhabited again in her own place, *even* in Jerusalem.
The LORD also shall save the tents of Judah first, that the glory of the house of David and the glory of the inhabitants of Jerusalem do not magnify *themselves* against Judah.
In that day shall the LORD defend the inhabitants of Jerusalem; and he that is feeble among them at that day shall be as David; and the house of David *shall be* as God, as the angel of the LORD before them.
And it shall come to pass in that day, *that* I will seek to destroy all the nations that come against Jerusalem.

THE VISION OF THE KINGDOM 73

the repentance and conversion of the Jews, and this (Zech. 14) by the coming of the Lord in glory and the great declaration:

"And the Lord shall be king over all the earth ... And it shall come to pass, that every one that is left of all the nations which came against Jerusalem shall even go up from year to year to worship the King, the Lord of hosts, and to keep the feast of tabernacles ... Yea, every pot in Jerusalem and in Judah shall be holiness unto the Lord of hosts."

The kingdom of the Prophets, then, is founded upon the Davidic Covenant (2 Sam. 7: 10-17)[28]; is heavenly in origin and principles, and in the Person of the King (Dan. 2: 44)[29]; is set up on the earth, with Jerusalem

---

And I will pour upon the house of David, and upon the inhabitants of Jerusalem, the spirit of grace and of supplications: and they shall look upon me whom they have pierced, and they shall mourn for him, as one mourneth for *his* only *son*, and shall be in bitterness for him, as one that is in bitterness for *his* firstborn.

In that day shall there be a great mourning in Jerusalem, as the mourning of Hadadrimmon in the valley of Megiddon.

And the land shall mourn, every family apart; the family of the house of David apart, and their wives apart; the family of the house of Nathan apart, and their wives apart;

The family of the house of Levi apart, and their wives apart; the family of Shimei apart, and their wives apart;

All the families that remain, every family apart, and their wives apart.—*Zech. 12*.

[28] Moreover I will appoint a place for my people Israel, and will plant them, that they may dwell in a place of their own, and move no more; neither shall the children of wickedness afflict them any more, as beforetime,

And as since the time that I commanded judges *to be* over my people Israel, and have caused thee to rest from all thine enemies. Also the Lord telleth thee that he will make thee an house.

And when thy days be fulfilled, and thou shalt sleep with thy fathers, I will set up thy seed after thee, which shall proceed out of thy bowels, and I will establish his kingdom.

He shall build an house for my name, and I will stablish the throne of his kingdom for ever. I will be his father, and he shall be my son. If he commit iniquity, I will chasten him with the rod of men, and with the stripes of the children of men:

But my mercy shall not depart away from him, as I took *it* from Saul, whom I put away before thee.

And thine house and thy kingdom shall be established for ever before thee; thy throne shall be established for ever.

According to all these words, and according to all this vision, so did Nathan speak unto David.—*2 Sam. 7: 10-17*.

[29] And in the days of these kings shall the God of heaven set up a kingdom, which shall never be destroyed: and the kingdom shall not be left to other people, *but* it shall break in

as the capital (Isa. 2:1-4)[30] is first established over regathered and converted Israel, extending then over the earth; and is established by power, not persuasion (Isa. 9:7; Luke 1:32).[31]

---

pieces and consume all these kingdoms, and it shall stand for ever.—*Dan. 2:44.*

[30] The word that Isaiah the son of Amoz saw concerning Judah and Jerusalem.

And it shall come to pass in the last days, *that* the mountain of the Lord's house shall be established in the top of the mountains, and shall be exalted above the hills; and all nations shall flow unto it.

And many people shall go and say, Come ye, and let us go up to the mountain of the Lord, to the house of the God of Jacob; and he will teach us of his ways, and we will walk in his paths: for out of Zion shall go forth the law, and the word of the Lord from Jerusalem.

And he shall judge among the nations, and shall rebuke many people: and they shall beat their swords into ploughshares, and their spears into pruninghooks: nation shall not lift up sword against nation, neither shall they learn war any more.—*Isa. 2: 1-4.*

[31] Of the increase of his government and peace there shall be no end, upon the throne of David, and upon his kingdom, to order it, and to establish it with judgment and with justice from henceforth even for ever. The zeal of the Lord of hosts will perform this.—*Isa. 9:7.*

He shall be great, and shall be called the son of the Highest: and the Lord God shall give unto him the throne of his father David.—*Luke 1:32.*

VI. THE PROPHETIC MINISTRY OF JESUS CHRIST

THE Lord Jesus Christ in His incarnation is appointed to a three-fold ministry, indicated by the titles, Prophet, Priest, and King. He is the "Prophet like unto me" foretold by Moses (Deut. 18:15; Acts 7:37)[1]—that is, the Prophet who introduces a new order (John 1:17).[2] But He does not at once introduce the new order—grace. "Made of a woman, made under the law" (Gal. 4:4) He begins His prophetic ministry to a people also under law by the offer of Himself as the One to whom all the Old Testament prophets bore witness, the King "meek and lowly" (Matt. 21:4, 5) in whom the kingdom was now "at hand."

Like the Old Testament prophets Jesus Christ is first of all a forthteller, and, as with them, it is the refusal of His message by the Jews which calls out His predictive ministry. The Sermon on the Mount strikes the ethical note of the elder prophets, but lifts it to its highest potency. There is not a ray of grace in it, nor a drop of blood. Tested by the Sermon on the Mount the highest attainment of humanity in the reach after righteousness utterly fails. The Beatitudes describe the character that alone brings happiness, but not the *admirers* of poverty of spirit, meekness, spiritual hunger and thirst, mercifulness, and purity of heart, but the *possessors* of these supreme graces, are the "blessed."

In this ethical ministry the two ideas of the kingdom

---

[1] The Lord thy God will raise up unto thee a Prophet from the midst of thee, of thy brethren, like unto me, unto him ye shall hearken.—*Deut. 18:15.*

This is that Moses, which said unto the children of Israel, A prophet shall the Lord your God raise up unto you of your brethren, like unto me; him shall ye hear.—*Acts 7:37.*

[2] For the law was given by Moses, *but* grace and truth came by Jesus Christ.—*John 1:17.*

of God and of the kingdom of heaven blend. For the kingdom of heaven is to bring in the kingdom of God (1 Cor. 15: 24-28),[3] and the true subjects of the kingdom of heaven, that is, true believers in Christ, are already in the kingdom of God.

In considering the prophetic ministry of Christ it is of the last importance to bear in mind that, like the prophets of old, His ministry was primarily to Israel (Matt. 10: 5-7).[4] For it is always true that blessing to Gentiles comes through Israel (Isa. 11: 10; Rom. 11: 17, 24, 25).[5] It is so in all kingdom truth, and it is so in all Gospel truth, and the formula is ever, "To the Jew first, and also to the Gentile" (Rom. 1: 16; 2: 9, 10; Acts 13: 46).[6] Perhaps the most important passage for the guidance of the student of the Gospels is Romans 15: 8:

---

[3] Then *cometh* the end, when he shall have delivered up the kingdom to God, even the Father; when he shall have put down all rule and all authority and power.

For he must reign, till he hath put all enemies under his feet.

The last enemy *that* shall be destroyed *is* death.

For he hath put all things under his feet. But when he saith all things are put under *him, it is* manifest that he is excepted, which did put all things under him.

And when all things shall be subdued unto him, then shall the Son also himself be subject unto him that put all things under him, that God may be all in all.—*1 Cor. 15: 24-28.*

[4] These twelve Jesus sent forth, and commanded them, saying, Go not into the way of the Gentiles, and into *any* city of the Samaritans enter ye not:

But go rather to the lost sheep of the house of Israel.

And as ye go, preach, saying, The kingdom of heaven is at hand.—*Matt. 10: 5-7.*

[5] And in that day there shall be a root of Jesse, which shall stand for an ensign of the people; to it shall the Gentiles seek: and his rest shall be glorious.—*Isa. 11: 10.*

And if some of the branches be broken off, and thou, being a wild olive tree, were graffed in among them, and with them partakest of the root and fatness of the olive tree.—*Rom. 11: 17.*

For if thou wert cut out of the olive tree which is wild by nature, and wert graffed contrary to nature into a good olive tree: how much more shall these, which be the natural *branches*, be graffed into their own olive tree?

For I would not, brethren, that ye should be ignorant of this mystery, lest ye should be wise in your own conceits; that blindness in part is happened to Israel, until the fulness of the Gentiles be come in.—*Rom. 11: 24-25.*

[6] For I am not ashamed of the gospel of Christ: for it is the power of God unto salvation to every one that believeth; to the Jew first, and also to the Greek.—*Rom. 1: 16.*

Tribulation and anguish, upon every soul of man that doeth evil, of the Jew first, and also of the Gentile;

But glory, honour, and peace,

THE PROPHETIC MINISTRY OF JESUS CHRIST 77

"Now I say that Jesus Christ was a minister of the circumcision for the truth of God, to confirm the promises made unto the fathers: and that the Gentiles might glorify God for his mercy."

The Gentile position is stated in Ephesians 2: 12:

"Wherefore remember, that ye being in time past Gentiles . . . ye were without Christ, being aliens from the commonwealth of Israel, and strangers from the covenants of promise, having no hope, and without God in the world."

The Jew had (and has) "promises"; and coupled with these are prophetic declarations of mercy to the Gentiles, as Paul abundantly shows in Romans 9, 10, and 11.

To confirm the promises to Israel, and to bring in mercy to the hopeless and godless Gentile, Christ's earthly ministry was addressed. As son of David He offers the kingdom to the Jews; as son of Abraham He dies for both Jew and Gentile (Gen. 12:3; Matt. 1:1; Gal. 3: 13, 14).[7] If this distinction is firmly held the prophetic ministry of the Lord Jesus will be cleared of confusion.

He begins with the kingdom: the church is not mentioned until His rejection as King is evident.

New Testament prophecy begins with John the Baptist. His theme is the kingdom of heaven. That which the Old Testament prophet saw afar off, John announces as "at hand." That phrase "at hand" has acquired in Scripture usage a definite, almost technical, meaning. It signifies, not that the thing or event so announced must

---

to every man that worketh good, to the Jew first, and also to the Gentile.—*Rom. 2: 9, 10.*

Then Paul and Barnabas waxed bold, and said, It was necessary that the word of God should first have been spoken to you: but seeing ye put it from you, and judge yourselves unworthy of everlasting life, lo, we turn to the Gentiles.—*Acts 13: 46.*

[7] And I will bless them that bless thee, and curse him that curseth thee: and in thee shall all families of the earth be blessed.—*Gen. 12: 3.*

The book of the generation of Jesus Christ, the son of David, the son of Abraham.—*Matt. 1: 1.*

Christ hath redeemed us from the curse of the law, being made a curse for us: for it is written, Cursed *is* every one that hangeth on a tree:

That the blessing of Abraham might come on the Gentiles through Jesus Christ; that we might receive the promise of the Spirit through faith.—*Gal. 3: 13, 14.*

immediately appear, but that it is *the next thing in the revealed program.* When, for example, Paul wrote his letter to the Philippians the Lord was "at hand" (Phil. 4: 5). After nineteen hundred years He is still "at hand," for His descent into the air to receive His church (1 Cor. 15: 51, 52; 1 Thess. 4: 14-17)[8] is still the next event in the *revealed* program.

That the present Church Age would intervene before the return of the King in glory to set up the Messianic kingdom of heaven was, like the church itself, "a mystery hid in God" (Eph. 3: 1-11).[9] The true church is revealed in Scripture in an absolutely timeless way, unrelated to earthly events, because it is in the earth as a heavenly thing, pilgrim and stranger (1 Pet. 2: 11; Heb. 3: 1; Phil. 3: 20; 1 Pet. 1: 4).[10] Hid in God also were

---

[8] Behold, I shew you a mystery; We shall not all sleep, but we shall all be changed,

In a moment, in the twinkling of an eye, at the last trump: for the trumpet shall sound, and the dead shall be raised incorruptible, and we shall be changed.—*1 Cor. 15: 51, 52.*

For if we believe that Jesus died and rose again, even so them also which sleep in Jesus will God bring with him.

For this we say unto you by the word of the Lord, that we which are alive *and* remain unto the coming of the Lord shall not prevent them which are asleep.

For the Lord himself shall descend from heaven with a shout, with the voice of the archangel, and with the trump of God: and the dead in Christ shall rise first:

Then we which are alive *and* remain shall be caught up together with them in the clouds, to meet the Lord in the air: and so shall we ever be with the Lord.—*1 Thess. 4: 14-17.*

[9] How that by revelation he made known unto me the mystery; (as I wrote afore in few words,

Whereby, when ye read, ye may understand my knowledge in the mystery of Christ)

Which in other ages was not made known unto the sons of men, as it is now revealed unto his holy apostles and prophets by the Spirit;

That the Gentiles should be fellowheirs, and of the same body, and partakers of his promise in Christ by the gospel; . . .
—*Eph. 3: 1-11.*

[10] Whereas angels, which are greater in power and might, bring not railing accusation against them before the Lord.
—*1 Pet. 2: 11.*

Wherefore, holy brethren, partakers of the heavenly calling, consider the Apostle and High Priest of our profession, Christ Jesus.—*Heb. 3: 1.*

For our conversation is in heaven; from whence also we look for the Saviour, the Lord Jesus Christ.—*Phil. 3: 20.*

To an inheritance incorruptible, and undefiled, and that fadeth not away, reserved in heaven for you.—*1 Pet. 1: 4.*

THE PROPHETIC MINISTRY OF JESUS CHRIST 79

certain "mysteries of the kingdom of heaven" (Matt. 13: 11-17)[11] to be fulfilled during the church age. To the church "the Lord is at hand" every moment "till he come" (Phil. 4: 5; 1 Cor. 11: 26).[12] But the kingdom of heaven is not now "at hand" because many predicted events must be fulfilled before the return of the King in glory. Meantime the church pursues her pilgrim way, added to by those who are outcalled by the Gospel of God's free grace (Acts 15: 14; 2: 47).[13] Meantime, also, the "mysteries of the kingdom of heaven" are being fulfilled.

The present age, in other words, is a *parenthesis* in the prophetic order, and was hidden from the Old Testament prophets. They saw "the sufferings of Christ and the glories that should follow" confused in one horizon (1 Pet. 1: 10-12).[14] Christ revealed the truth of the present

---

[11] He answered and said unto them, Because it is given unto you to know the mysteries of the kingdom of heaven, but to them it is not given.

For whosoever hath, to him shall be given, and he shall have more abundance: but whosoever hath not, from him shall be taken away even that he hath.

Therefore speak I to them in parables: because they seeing see not; and hearing they hear not, neither do they understand.

And in them is fulfilled the prophecy of Esaias, which saith, By hearing ye shall hear, and shall not understand; and seeing ye shall see, and shall not perceive:

For this people's heart is waxed gross, and *their* ears are dull of hearing, and their eyes they have closed; lest at any time they should see with *their* eyes, and hear with *their* ears, and should understand with *their* heart, and should be converted, and I should heal them.

But blessed *are* your eyes, for they see: and your ears, for they hear.

For verily I say unto you, That many prophets and righteous *men* have desired to see *those things* which ye see, and have not seen *them;* and to hear *those things* which ye hear, and have not heard *them.*
—*Matt. 13: 11-17.*

[12] Let your moderation be known unto all men. The Lord is at hand.—*Phil. 4: 5.*

For as often as ye eat this bread, and drink this cup, ye do shew the Lord's death till he come.—*1 Cor. 11: 26.*

[13] Simeon hath declared how God at the first did visit the Gentiles, to take out of them a people for his name.—*Acts 15: 14.*

Praising God, and having favour with all the people. And the Lord added to the church daily such as should be saved.
—*Acts 2: 47.*

[14] Of which salvation the prophets have inquired and searched diligently, who prophesied of the grace *that should come* unto you:

Searching what, or what manner of time the Spirit of Christ which was in them did signify, when it testified beforehand the sufferings of Christ, and the glory that should follow.

age—the age of the outcalling of the church, and of the "mysteries of the kingdom of heaven"—as intervening between His sufferings and His kingdom glory.

But He did not lift the veil that hid this age until it had become evident that the nation to whom He had, in literal fulfilment of prophecy, come, had rejected Him. The turning point from the preaching of the kingdom of heaven as "at hand" to the entrance of the Lord into the sphere of predictive prophecy is recorded in Matthew 11, 12. The Twelve are warned of hatred and treachery (10: 17),[15] and the cities which had witnessed His mightiest works are appointed unto judgment (11: 20-24).[16] But what is supremely significant is that He no longer announces the kingdom as "at hand," but turns from the *nation* to the *individual* in the new message:

"Come unto me, all ye that labour and are heavy laden, and I will give you rest. Take my yoke upon you, and learn of me; for I am meek and lowly in heart: and ye shall find rest unto your souls."

It is now personal relationship with Himself that counts. The earthly blessings promised to Israel are postponed (Deut. 30: 1-10; Jer. 33: 14-26; Acts 15: 14-17).[17] There

---

Unto whom it was revealed, that not unto themselves, but unto us they did minister the things, which are now reported unto you by them that have preached the gospel unto you with the Holy Ghost sent down from heaven; which things the angels desire to look into.—*I Peter 1: 10-12.*

[15] But beware of men: for they will deliver you up to the councils, and they will scourge you in their synagogues.—*Matt. 10: 17.*

[16] Then began he to upbraid the cities wherein most of his mighty works were done, because they repented not:

Woe unto thee, Chorazin, woe unto thee, Bethsaida! for if the mighty works, which were done in you, had been done in Tyre and Sidon, they would have repented long ago in sackcloth and ashes.

But I say unto you, It shall be more tolerable for Tyre and Sidon at the day of judgment than for you.

And thou, Capernaum, which art exalted unto heaven, shalt be brought down to hell: for if the mighty works, which have been done in thee, had been done in Sodom, it would have remained until this day.

But I say unto you, That it shall be more tolerable for the land of Sodom in the day of judgment, than for thee.—*Matt. 11: 20-24.*

[17] And it shall come to pass, when all these things are come upon thee, the blessing and the curse, which I have set before thee, and thou shalt call *them* to mind among all the nations, whither the Lord thy God hath driven thee,

And shalt return unto the Lord thy God, and shalt obey

remained the formal offer of Himself "meek and lowly," strangely miscalled "the triumphal entry" (Matt. 21: 1-11),[18] but to His disciples the words are of His approaching death and resurrection.

---

his voice according to all that I command thee this day, thou and thy children, with all thine heart, and with all thy soul;

That then the Lord thy God will turn thy captivity, and have compassion upon thee, and will return and gather thee from all the nations, whither the Lord thy God hath scattered thee.

If *any* of thine be driven out unto the outmost *parts* of heaven, from thence will the Lord thy God gather thee, and from thence will he fetch thee:

And the Lord thy God will bring thee into the land which thy fathers possessed, and thou shalt possess it; and he will do thee good, and multiply thee above thy fathers.

And the Lord thy God will circumcise thine heart, and the heart of thy seed, to love the Lord thy God with all thine heart, and with all thy soul, that thou mayest live.

And the Lord thy God will put all these curses upon thine enemies, and on them that hate thee, which persecuted thee.

And thou shalt return and obey the voice of the Lord, and do all his commandments which I command thee this day.

And the Lord thy God will make thee plenteous in every work of thine hand, in the fruit of thy body, and in the fruit of thy cattle, and in the fruit of thy land, for good: for the Lord will again rejoice over thee for good, as he rejoiced over thy fathers:

If thou shalt hearken unto the voice of the Lord thy God, to keep his commandments and his statutes which are written in this book of the law, *and* if thou turn unto the Lord thy God with all thine heart, and with all thy soul.—*Deut. 30: 1-10.*

Behold, the days come, saith the Lord, that I will perform that good thing which I have promised unto the house of Israel and to the house of Judah.

In those days, and at that time, will I cause the Branch of righteousness to grow up unto David; and he shall execute judgment and righteousness in the land.

In those days shall Judah be saved, and Jerusalem shall dwell safely: and this *is the name* wherewith she shall be called, The Lord our righteousness. . . . —*Jer. 33: 14-26.*

Simeon hath declared how God at the first did visit the Gentiles, to take out of them a people for his name.

And to this agree the words of the prophets: as it is written,

After this I will return, and will build again the tabernacle of David, which is fallen down; and I will build again the ruins thereof, and I will set it up:

That the residue of men might seek after the Lord, and all the Gentiles, upon whom my name is called, saith the Lord, who doeth all these things.—*Acts 15: 14-17.*

[18] . . . And a very great multitude spread their garments in the way; others cut down branches from the trees, and strawed *them* in the way.

And the multitudes that went before, and that followed, cried, saying, Hosanna to the Son of David: Blessed *is* he that cometh in the name of the Lord; Hosanna in the highest.

And when he was come into Jerusalem, all the city was moved, saying, Who is this?

And the multitude said, This is Jesus the prophet of Nazareth of Galilee.—*Matt. 21: 1-11.*

The subjects of the predictions uttered by the Christ are (chiefly) concerning the kingdom of heaven during the interval between the rejection of the King and His return in glory; His own death and resurrection; judgment; the church; the Holy Spirit; and, especially, the great prophetic message which we call the Olivet Discourse (Matt. 24:1-51; 25:1-46; Luke 21:5-36).[19]

---

[19] And Jesus went out, and departed from the temple: and his disciples came to *him* for to shew him the buildings of the temple.

And Jesus said unto them, See ye not all these things? verily I say unto you, There shall not be left here one stone upon another, that shall not be thrown down.

And as he sat upon the mount of Olives, the disciples came unto him privately, saying, Tell us, when shall these things be? and what *shall be* the sign of thy coming, and of the end of the world?

And Jesus answered and said unto them, Take heed that no man deceive you.

For many shall come in my name, saying, I am Christ; and shall deceive many.

And ye shall hear of wars and rumours of wars: see that ye be not troubled: for all *these things* must come to pass, but the end is not yet.

For nation shall rise against nation, and kingdom against kingdom: and there shall be famines, and pestilences, and earthquakes, in divers places.

All these *are* the beginning of sorrows.

Then shall they deliver you up to be afflicted, and shall kill you: and ye shall be hated of all nations for my name's sake.

And then shall many be offended, and shall betray one another, and shall hate one another.

And many false prophets shall rise, and shall deceive many.

And because iniquity shall abound, the love of many shall wax cold.

But he that shall endure unto the end, the same shall be saved.

And this gospel of the kingdom shall be preached in all the world for a witness unto all nations; and then shall the end come.

When ye therefore shall see the abomination of desolation, spoken of by Daniel the prophet, stand in the holy place (whoso readeth, let him understand:)

Then let them which be in Judæa flee into the mountains:

Let him which is on the housetop not come down to take any thing out of his house:

Neither let him which is in the field return back to take his clothes.

And woe unto them that are with child, and to them that give suck in those days!

But pray ye that your flight be not in the winter, neither on the sabbath day:

For then shall be great tribulation, such as was not since the beginning of the world to this time, nor ever shall be.

And except those days should be shortened, there should no flesh be saved: but for the elect's sake those days shall be shortened.

Then if any man shall say unto you, Lo, here *is* Christ, or there; believe *it* not.

For there shall arise false Christs, and false prophets, and shall shew great signs and wonders: insomuch that, if *it were* possible, they shall deceive the very elect.

Behold, I have told you before.

Wherefore if they shall say unto you, Behold, he is in the desert; go not forth: behold, *he is* in the secret chambers; believe *it* not.

For as the lightning cometh out of the east, and shineth even unto the west; so shall also the coming of the Son of man be.

For wheresoever the carcase is, there will the eagles be gathered together.

Immediately after the tribulation of those days shall the sun be darkened, and the moon shall not give her light, and the stars shall fall from heaven, and the powers of the heavens shall be shaken:

And then shall appear the sign of the Son of man in heaven: and then shall all the tribes of the earth mourn, and they shall see the Son of man coming in the clouds of heaven with power and great glory.

And he shall send his angels with a great sound of a trumpet, and they shall gather together his elect from the four winds, from one end of heaven to the other.

Now learn a parable of the fig tree; When his branch is yet tender, and putteth forth leaves, ye know that summer *is* nigh:

So likewise ye, when ye shall see all these things, know that it is near, *even* at the doors.

Verily I say unto you, This generation shall not pass, till all these things be fulfilled.

Heaven and earth shall pass away, but my words shall not pass away.

But of that day and hour knoweth no *man*, no, not the angels of heaven, but my Father only.

But as the days of Noe *were,* so shall also the coming of the Son of man be.

For as in the days that were before the flood they were eating and drinking, marrying, and giving in marriage, until the day that Noe entered into the ark,

And knew not until the flood came, and took them all away; so shall also the coming of the Son of man be.

Then shall two be in the field; the one shall be taken, and the other left.

Two *women shall be* grinding at the mill; the one shall be taken, and the other left.

Watch therefore: for ye know not what hour your Lord doth come.

But know this, that if the goodman of the house had known in what watch the thief would come, he would have watched, and would not have suffered his house to be broken up.

Therefore be ye also ready: for in such an hour as ye think not the Son of man cometh.

Who then is a faithful and wise servant, whom his lord hath made ruler over his household, to give them meat in due season?

Blessed *is* that servant, whom his lord when he cometh shall find so doing.

Verily I say unto you, That he shall make him ruler over all his goods.

But and if that evil servant shall say in his heart, My lord delayeth his coming;

And shall begin to smite *his* fellowservants, and to eat and drink with the drunken;

The lord of that servant shall come in a day when he looketh not for *him,* and in an hour that he is not aware of,

And shall cut him asunder, and appoint *him* his portion with the hypocrites: there shall be weeping and gnashing of teeth.—*Matt. 24: 1-51.*

Then shall the kingdom of heaven be likened unto ten virgins, which took their lamps, and went forth to meet the bridegroom.

And five of them were wise, and five *were* foolish.

They that *were* foolish took their lamps, and took no oil with them:

But the wise took oil in their vessels with their lamps.

While the bridegroom tarried, they all slumbered and slept.

And at midnight there was a cry made, Behold, the bridegroom cometh; go ye out to meet him.

Then all those virgins arose, and trimmed their lamps.

And the foolish said unto the wise, Give us of your oil; for our lamps are gone out.

But the wise answered, saying, *Not so;* lest there be not enough for us and you: but go ye rather to them that sell, and buy for yourselves.

And while they went to buy, the bridegroom came; and they that were ready went in with him to the marriage: and the door was shut.

Afterward came also the other virgins, saying, Lord, Lord, open to us.

But he answered and said, Verily I say unto you, I know you not.

Watch therefore, for ye know neither the day nor the hour wherein the Son of man cometh.

For *the kingdom of heaven is* as a man travelling into a far country, *who* called his own servants, and delivered unto them his goods.

And unto one he gave five talents, to another two, and to another one; to every man according to his several ability; and straightway took his journey.

Then he that had received the five talents went and traded with the same, and made *them* other five talents.

And likewise he that *had received* two, he also gained other two.

But he that had received one went and digged in the earth, and hid his lord's money.

After a long time the lord of those servants cometh, and reckoneth with them.

And so he that had received five talents came and brought other five talents, saying, Lord, thou deliveredst unto me five talents: behold, I have gained beside them five talents more.

His lord said unto him, Well done, *thou* good and faithful servant: thou hast been faithful over a few things, I will make thee ruler over many things: enter thou into the joy of thy lord.

He also that had received two talents came and said, Lord, thou deliveredst unto me two talents: behold, I have gained two other talents beside them.

His lord said unto him, Well done, good and faithful servant: thou hast been faithful over a few things, I will make thee ruler over many things: enter thou into the joy of thy lord.

Then he which had received the one talent came and said, Lord, I knew thee that thou art an hard man, reaping where thou hast not sown, and gathering where thou hast not strawed:

And I was afraid, and went and hid thy talent in the earth: lo, *there* thou hast *that is* thine.

His lord answered and said unto him, *Thou* wicked and slothful servant, thou knewest that I reap where I sowed not, and gather where I have not strawed:

Thou oughtest therefore to have put my money to the exchangers, and *then* at my coming I should have received mine own with usury.

Take therefore the talent from him, and give *it* unto him which hath ten talents.

For unto every one that hath shall be given, and he shall have abundance: but from him

THE PROPHETIC MINISTRY OF JESUS CHRIST

that hath not shall be taken away even that which he hath.

And cast ye the unprofitable servant into outer darkness: there shall be weeping and gnashing of teeth.

When the Son of man shall come in his glory, and all the holy angels with him, then shall he sit upon the throne of his glory:

And before him shall be gathered all nations: and he shall separate them one from another, as a shepherd divideth *his* sheep from the goats:

And he shall set the sheep on his right hand, but the goats on the left.

Then shall the King say unto them on his right hand, Come, ye blessed of my Father, inherit the kingdom prepared for you from the foundation of the world:

For I was an hungred, and ye gave me meat: I was thirsty, and ye gave me drink: I was a stranger, and ye took me in:

Naked, and ye clothed me: I was sick, and ye visited me: I was in prison, and ye came unto me.

Then shall the righteous answer him, saying, Lord, when saw we thee an hungred, and fed *thee?* or thirsty, and gave *thee* drink?

When saw we thee a stranger, and took *thee* in? or naked, and clothed *thee?*

Or when saw we thee sick, or in prison, and came unto thee?

And the King shall answer and say unto them, Verily I say unto you, Inasmuch as ye have done *it* unto one of the least of these my brethren, ye have done *it* unto me.

Then shall he say also unto them on the left hand, Depart from me, ye cursed, into everlasting fire, prepared for the devil and his angels:

For I was an hungred, and ye gave me no meat: I was thirsty, and ye gave me no drink:

I was a stranger, and ye took me not in: naked, and ye clothed me not: sick, and in prison, and ye visited me not.

Then shall they also answer him, saying, Lord, when saw we thee an hungred, or athirst, or a stranger, or naked, or sick, or in prison, and did not minister unto thee?

Then shall he answer them, saying, Verily I say unto you, Inasmuch as ye did *it* not to one of the least of these, ye did *it* not to me.

And these shall go away into everlasting punishment: but the righteous into life eternal.—*Matt. 25: 1-46.*

And as some spake of the temple, how it was adorned with goodly stones and gifts, he said,

As for these things which ye behold, the days will come, in the which there shall not be left one stone upon another, that shall not be thrown down.

And they asked him, saying, Master, but when shall these things be? and what sign *will there be* when these things shall come to pass?

And he said, Take heed that ye be not deceived: for many shall come in my name, saying, I am *Christ;* and the time draweth near: go ye not therefore after them.

But when ye shall hear of wars and commotions, be not terrified: for these things must first come to pass; but the end *is* not by and by.

Then said he unto them, Nation shall rise against nation, and kingdom against kingdom:

And great earthquakes shall be in divers places, and famines, and pestilences; and fearful sights and great signs shall there be from heaven.

But before all these, they shall lay their hands on you, and persecute *you,* delivering *you* up to the synagogues, and into prisons, being brought before kings and rulers for my name's sake.

1. Consequent upon the rejection of the King, the kingdom of heaven, which had been announced by John the Baptist (Matt. 3:2),[20] by Christ (Matt. 4:17),[21] and

---

And it shall turn to you for a testimony.
Settle *it* therefore in your hearts, not to meditate before what ye shall answer:
For I will give you a mouth and wisdom, which all your adversaries shall not be able to gainsay nor resist.
And ye shall be betrayed both by parents, and brethren, and kinsfolks, and friends; and *some* of you shall they cause to be put to death.
And ye shall be hated of all *men* for my name's sake..
But there shall not an hair of your head perish.
In your patience possess ye your souls.
And when ye shall see Jerusalem compassed with armies, then know that the desolation thereof is nigh.
Then let them which are in Judæa flee to the mountains; and let them which are in the midst of it depart out; and let not them that are in the countries enter thereinto.
For these be the days of vengeance, that all things which are written may be fulfilled.
But woe unto them that are with child, and to them that give suck, in those days! for there shall be great distress in the land, and wrath upon this people.
And they shall fall by the edge of the sword, and shall be led away captive into all nations: and Jerusalem shall be trodden down of the Gentiles, until the times of the Gentiles be fulfilled.
And there shall be signs in the sun, and in the moon, and in the stars; and upon the earth distress of nations, with perplexity; the sea and the waves roaring;

Men's hearts failing them for fear, and for looking after those things which are coming on the earth: for the powers of heaven shall be shaken.
And then shall they see the Son of man coming in a cloud with power and great glory.
And when these things begin to come to pass, then look up, and lift up your heads; for your redemption draweth nigh.
And he spake to them a parable; Behold the fig tree, and all the trees;
When they now shoot forth, ye see and know of your own selves that summer is now nigh at hand.
So likewise ye, when ye see these things come to pass, know ye that the kingdom of God is nigh at hand.
Verily I say unto you, This generation shall not pass away, till all be fulfilled.
Heaven and earth shall pass away: but my words shall not pass away.
And take heed to yourselves, lest at any time your hearts be overcharged with surfeiting, and drunkenness, and cares of this life, and *so* that day come upon you unawares.
For as a snare shall it come on all them that dwell on the face of the whole earth.
Watch ye therefore, and pray always, that ye may be accounted worthy to escape all these things that shall come to pass, and to stand before the Son of man.—*Luke 21: 5-36.*

[20] And saying, Repent ye: for the kingdom of heaven is at hand.—*Matt. 3:2.*
[21] From that time Jesus began to preach, and to say, Repent: for the kingdom of heaven is at hand.—*Matt. 4:17.*

by the twelve (Matt. 10:7),[22] as "at hand," enters the period during which certain "mysteries" of the kingdom of heaven are to be fulfilled. These are described in seven parables gathered into Matthew 13. A "mystery" in Scripture is a divine purpose hitherto hidden, but now revealed.

The seven parables of Matthew 13, called by our Lord "mysteries of the kingdom of heaven," taken together, describe the result of the presence of the Gospel in the world during the present age, that is the time of seed sowing which began with our Lord's personal ministry, and ends with the "harvest" (Matt. 13:40-43).[23] Briefly, that result is the mingling of tares and wheat, good fish and bad, children of the kingdom and children of the evil one, in the sphere of Christian profession. It is that which we have been calling "Christendom." True. "children of the kingdom" are there, but mingled with them, and so closely resembling them that the "servants" cannot be trusted to distinguish them, are mere professors. So great is the danger to souls involved in mere profession that our Lord's teaching now abounds in solemn warnings (Matt. 7:22; 20:16; 21:28-31; 23:13-38).[24]

[22] And as ye go, preach, saying, The kingdom of heaven is at hand.—*Matt. 10:7.*

[23] As therefore the tares are gathered and burned in the fire, so shall it be in the end of this world.
The Son of man shall send forth his angels, and they shall gather out of his kingdom all things that offend, and them which do iniquity;
And shall cast them into a furnace of fire: there shall be wailing and gnashing of teeth.
Then shall the righteous shine forth as the sun in the kingdom of their Father. Who hath ears to hear, let him hear—*Matt. 13:40-43.*

[24] Many will say to me in that day, Lord, Lord, have we not prophesied in thy name? and in thy name have cast out devils? and in thy name done many wonderful works?—*Matt. 7:22.*

So the last shall be first, and the first last: for many be called, but few chosen.—*Matt. 20:16.*
But what think ye? A *certain* man had two sons; and he came to the first, and said, Son, go work to-day in my vineyard.
He answered and said, I will not: but afterward he repented, and went.
And he came to the second, and said likewise. And he answered and said, I *go*, sir: and went not.
Whether of them twain did the will of *his* father? They say unto him, The first. Jesus saith unto them, Verily I say unto you, That the publicans and the harlots go into the kingdom of God before you. —*Matt. 21:28-31.*
But woe unto you, scribes and Pharisees, hypocrites! for ye shut up the kingdom of heaven against men: for ye neither go

2. The Lord predicted His own death at the hands of wicked men, and His resurrection after three days (Matt. 12: 38-40; 17: 22, 23; 20: 17-19).[25]

3. The Lord predicted judgment upon persons (Matt. 25: 46)[26]; cities (Matt. 11: 22-24; 23: 37-39; Luke 21: 20-24)[27]; and nations (Matt. 25: 31-46).[28]

---

in *yourselves,* neither suffer ye them that are entering to go in.

Woe unto you, scribes and Pharisees, hypocrites! for ye devour widows' houses, and for a pretence make long prayer: therefore ye shall receive the greater damnation.

Woe unto you, scribes and Pharisees, hypocrites! for ye compass sea and land to make one proselyte, and when he is made, ye make him twofold more the child of hell than yourselves. . . .

O Jerusalem, Jerusalem, *thou* that killest the prophets, and stonest them which are sent unto thee, how often would I have gathered thy children together, even as a hen gathereth her chickens under *her* wings, and ye would not!

Behold, your house is left unto you desolate.—*Matt. 23: 13-38.*

[25] Then certain of the scribes and of the Pharisees answered, saying, Master, we would see a sign from thee.

But he answered and said unto them, An evil and adulterous generation seeketh after a sign: and there shall no sign be given to it, but the sign of the prophet Jonas:

For as Jonas was three days and three nights in the whale's belly; so shall the Son of man be three days and three nights in the heart of the earth.—*Matt. 12: 38-40.*

And while they abode in Galilee, Jesus said unto them, The Son of man shall be betrayed into the hands of men:

And they shall kill him, and the third day he shall be raised again. And they were exceeding sorry.—*Matt. 17: 22, 23.*

And Jesus going up to Jerusalem took the twelve disciples apart in the way, and said unto them,

Behold, we go up to Jerusalem; and the Son of man shall be betrayed unto the chief priests and unto the scribes, and they shall condemn him to death,

And shall deliver him to the Gentiles to mock, and to scourge, and to crucify *him:* and the third day he shall rise again.—*Matt. 20: 17-19.*

[26] And these shall go away into everlasting punishment: but the righteous into life eternal.—*Matt. 25: 46.*

[27] But I say unto you, It shall be more tolerable for Tyre and Sidon at the day of judgment than for you.

And thou, Capernaum, which art exalted unto heaven, shalt be brought down to hell: for if the mighty works, which have been done in thee, had been done in Sodom, it would have remained until this day.

But I say unto you, That it shall be more tolerable for the land of Sodom in the day of judgment, than for thee.—*Matt. 11: 22-24.*

O Jerusalem, Jerusalem, *thou* that killest the prophets, and stonest them which are sent unto thee, how often would I have gathered thy children together, even as a hen gathereth her chickens under *her* wings, ye would not!

Behold, your house is left unto you desolate.

For I say unto you, Ye shall

4. The Lord predicted the church (Matt. 16: 13-18)[29] as being yet in the future: "I will build my church."

not see me henceforth, till ye shall say, Blessed *is* he that cometh in the name of the Lord. —*Matt. 23: 37-39.*

And when ye shall see Jerusalem compassed with armies, then know that the desolation thereof is nigh.

Then let them which are in Judæa flee to the mountains; and let them which are in the midst of it depart out; and let not them that are in the countries enter thereinto.

For these be the days of vengeance, that all things which are written may be fulfilled.

But woe unto them that are with child, and to them that give suck, in those days! for there shall be great distress in the land, and wrath upon this people.

And they shall fall by the edge of the sword, and shall be led away captive into all nations: and Jerusalem shall be trodden down of the Gentiles, until the times of the Gentiles be fulfilled.—*Luke 21: 20-24.*

[28] When the Son of man shall come in his glory, and all the holy angels with him, then shall he sit upon the throne of his glory:

And before him shall be gathered all nations: and he shall separate them one from another, as a shepherd divideth *his* sheep from the goats:

And he shall set the sheep on his right hand, but the goats on the left.

Then shall the King say unto them on his right hand, Come, ye blessed of my Father, inherit the kingdom prepared for you from the foundation of the world:

For I was an hungred, and ye gave me meat: I was thirsty, and ye gave me drink: I was a stranger, and ye took me in:

Naked, and ye clothed me: I was sick, and ye visited me: I was in prison, and ye came unto me.

Then shall the righteous answer him, saying, Lord, when saw we thee an hungred, and fed *thee?* or thirsty, and gave *thee* drink?

When saw we thee a stranger, and took *thee* in? or naked, and clothed *thee?*

Or when saw we thee sick, or in prison, and came unto thee?

And the King shall answer and say unto them, Verily I say unto you, Inasmuch as ye have done *it* unto one of the least of these my brethren, ye have done *it* unto me.

Then shall he say also unto them on the left hand, Depart from me, ye cursed, into everlasting fire, prepared for the devil and his angels:

For I was an hungred, and ye gave me no meat: I was thirsty, and ye gave me no drink:

I was a stranger, and ye took me not in: naked, and ye clothed me not: sick, and in prison, and ye visited me not.

Then shall they also answer him, saying, Lord, when saw we thee an hungred, or athirst, or a stranger, or naked, or sick, or in prison, and did not minister unto thee?

Then shall he answer them, saying, Verily I say unto you, Inasmuch as ye did *it* not to one of the least of these, ye did *it* not to me.

And these shall go away into everlasting punishment: but the righteous into life eternal.— *Matt. 25: 31-46.*

[29] When Jesus came into the coasts of Cæsarea Philippi, he asked his disciples, saying, Whom do men say that I the Son of man am?

Only once more, and that in respect of discipline, does Christ refer to this new purpose.

He uses a word for this new thing, *ecclesia*="that which is called out," which, in itself, may be applied to any called out assembly. It is used of Israel in the wilderness (Acts 7:38),[30] and also of the tumultuous town meeting in Ephesus (Acts 19:32, translated "assembly").[31] But our Lord went no farther than the announcement of a purpose. All else concerning this new thing was another "mystery hid in God" and revealed through the apostle Paul (Eph. 3:1-11).[32]

5. Jesus Christ predicted the course and end of this age. As to the latter His testimony was clear and uniform, the age ends in catastrophe. To illustrate this our Lord goes back to the two catastrophic judgments of the flood, and of the destruction of the cities of the plain (Luke 17:26-37).[33]

And they said, Some *say that thou art* John the Baptist: some, Elias; and others, Jeremias, or one of the prophets.

He saith unto them, But whom say ye that I am?

And Simon Peter answered and said, Thou art the Christ, the Son of the living God.

And Jesus answered and said unto him, Blessed art thou, Simon Bar-jona: for flesh and blood hath not revealed *it* unto thee, but my Father which is in heaven.

And I say also unto thee, That thou art Peter, and upon this rock I will build my church; and the gates of hell shall not prevail against it.—*Matt. 16: 13-18.*

[30] This is he, that was in the church in the wilderness with the angel which spake to him in the mount Sina, and *with* our fathers: who received the lively oracles to give unto us.—*Acts 7: 38.*

[31] Some therefore cried one thing, and some another: for the assembly was confused; and the more part knew not wherefore they were come together.—*Acts 19: 32.*

[32] See footnote on page 78 of this chapter for the Scripture.

[33] And as it was in the days of Noe, so shall it be also in the days of the Son of man.

They did eat, they drank, they married wives, they were given in marriage, until the day that Noe entered into the ark, and the flood came, and destroyed them all.

Likewise also as it was in the days of Lot; they did eat, they drank, they bought, they sold, they planted, they builded;

But the same day that Lot went out of Sodom it rained fire and brimstone from heaven, and destroyed *them* all.

Even thus shall it be in the day when the Son of man is revealed.

In that day, he which shall be upon the housetop, and his stuff in the house, let him not come down to take it away: and he that is in the field, let him likewise not return back.

Remember Lot's wife.

Whosoever shall seek to save his life shall lose it; and whosoever shall lose his life shall preserve it.

In the great Olivet Discourse (Matt. 24:35; Luke 21:5-36)[34] our Lord enters into detail, especially with reference to the ruin and catastrophe of the end time. The question of the disciples which drew out the prophecy, the circumstances and places which environed our Lord's answer, and the form of the answer all combine to mark the discourse as a part of Christ's ministry to Israel as "a minister of the circumcision for the truth of God, to confirm the promises made unto the fathers." The whole atmosphere of the discourse is Jewish.

It is obvious that a confirmation of the promises to the fathers concerning the establishment of the kingdom according to the Davidic Covenant (2 Sam. 7:4-16),[35] confirmed by the oath of Jehovah (Psa. 89:3-6, 20-37),[36] and by the angel Gabriel (Luke 1:32, 33),[37] was necessary, for Christ had announced His approaching death. He was going back to heaven without having regathered dispersed Israel, and without re-establishing the theocracy over Israel. It must be borne in mind that the disciples gathered by our Lord during His earth-ministry were

---

I tell you, in that night there shall be two *men* in one bed; the one shall be taken, and the other shall be left.

Two *women* shall be grinding together; the one shall be taken, and the other left.

Two *men* shall be in the field; the one shall be taken, and the other left.

And they answered and said unto him, Where, Lord? And he said unto them, Wheresoever the body *is*, thither will the eagles be gathered together.—*Luke 17:26-37.*

[34] See footnote on page 85 of this chapter for the Scripture.

[35] . . .Moreover I will appoint a place for my people Israel, and will plant them, that they may dwell in a place of their own, and move no more; neither shall the children of wickedness afflict them any more, as beforetime. . . .

And when thy days be fulfilled, and thou shalt sleep with thy fathers, I will set up thy seed after thee, which shall proceed out of thy bowels, and I will establish his kingdom.

He shall build an house for my name, and I will stablish the throne of his kingdom for ever. . . .

And thine house and thy kingdom shall be established for ever before thee: thy throne shall be established for ever.—*2 Sam. 7:4-16.*

[36] I have made a covenant with my chosen, I have sworn unto David my servant,

Thy seed will I establish for ever, and build up thy throne to all generations. Selah. . . .—*Psalm 89:3-6, 20-37.*

[37] He shall be great, and shall be called the Son of the Highest: and the Lord God shall give unto him the throne of his father David:

And he shall reign over the house of Jacob for ever; and of his kingdom there shall be no end.—*Luke 1:32, 33.*

Jews who had received Him as the Messiah: "Thou art the Christ, the Son of the living God" had been Peter's confession of faith approved by the Master (Matt. 16: 16).[38] That He should go through death and resurrection back to the Father leaving that tremendous body of promises unfulfilled was staggering enough in itself; that He should leave it unconfirmed, unrenewed, would have been the death of Jewish faith in Him.

Leaving the temple for the last time, and predicting its destruction, He went to the mount of Olives. As the temple stood for the past of Israel, so the mount of Olives stood for the nation's future. For Zechariah in his vision of the second coming of Messiah and the establishment of the kingdom (Zech. 12, 13, 14) had said, "And his feet shall stand in that day upon the mount of Olives. . . . And the Lord shall be king over all the earth in that day" (Zech. 14: 4-21).[39] The very localities confirm the Jewish interpretation of the Discourse, if such confirmation were required where all is so evidently Jewish (Matt. 24: 15-31).[40]

---

[38] And Simon Peter answered and said, Thou art the Christ, the Son of the living God.—*Matt. 16:16*.

[39] And his feet shall stand in that day upon the mount of Olives, which *is* before Jerusalem on the east, and the mount of Olives shall cleave in the midst thereof toward the east and toward the west, *and there shall be* a very great valley; and half of the mountain shall remove toward the north, and half of it toward the south.

And ye shall flee *to* the valley of the mountains; for the valley of the mountains shall reach unto Azal: yea, ye shall flee, like as ye fled from before the earthquake in the days of Uzziah king of Judah; and the Lord my God shall come, *and* all the saints with thee. . . .

And the Lord shall be king over all the earth: in that day shall there be one Lord, and his name one. . . .—*Zech. 14: 4-21*.

[40] When ye therefore shall see the abomination of desolation, spoken of by Daniel the prophet, stand in the holy place, (whoso readeth, let him understand:)

Then let them which be in Judæa flee into the mountains:

Let him which is on the housetop not come down to take any thing out of his house;

Neither let him which is in the field return back to take his clothes.

And woe unto them that are with child, and to them that give suck in those days!

But pray ye that your flight be not in the winter, neither on the sabbath day:

For then shall be great tribulation, such as was not since the beginning of the world to this time, no, nor ever shall be.

And except those days should be shortened, there should no flesh be saved; but for the elect's sake those days shall be shortened.

Briefly, Jesus said that the age should be one of wars, famines, pestilences, and it should end in the reign of the beast, the abomination predicted by Daniel the prophet, and in the great tribulation. But immediately after the great tribulation He, the Lord, would return in power and great glory and *then* would He sit upon the throne of His glory. *Then* the dispersed elect nation should be regathered. His Jewish disciples, who had been promised judgships over the twelve tribes (Matt. 19:27, 28)[41] in the kingdom-time had not been deceived; all should be fulfilled (compare Acts 15:14-17).[42]

But these very Jewish disciples were to have new relationships, to Himself and to humanity, in quite another and different body of believers, to whom He had referred

---

Then if any man shall say unto you, Lo, here *is* Christ, or there; believe *it* not.

For there shall arise false Christs, and false prophets, and shall shew great signs and wonders; insomuch that, if it *were* possible, they shall deceive the very elect.

Behold, I have told you before.

Wherefore if they shall say unto you, Behold, he is in the desert; go not forth: behold, *he is* in the secret chambers; believe *it* not.

For as the lightning cometh out of the east, and shineth even unto the west; so shall also the coming of the Son of man be.

For wheresoever the carcase is, there will the eagles be gathered together.

Immediately after the tribulation of those days shall the sun be darkened, and the moon shall not give her light, and the stars shall fall from heaven, and the powers of the heavens shall be shaken:

And then shall appear the sign of the Son of man in heaven; and then shall all the tribes of the earth mourn, and they shall see the Son of man coming in the clouds of heaven with power and great glory.

And he shall send his angels with a great sound of a trumpet, and they shall gather together his elect from the four winds, from one end of heaven to the other.—*Matt. 24:15-31.*

[41] Then answered Peter and said unto him, Behold, we have forsaken all, and followed thee; what shall we have therefore?

And Jesus said unto them, Verily I say unto you, That ye which have followed me, in the regeneration when the Son of man shall sit in the throne of his glory, ye also shall sit upon twelve thrones, judging the twelve tribes of Israel—*Matt. 19:27, 28.*

[42] Simeon hath declared how God at the first did visit the Gentiles, to take out of them a people for his name.

And to this agree the words of the prophets; as it is written,

After this I will return, and will build again the tabernacle of David, which is fallen down; and I will build again the ruins thereof, and I will set it up:

That the residue of men might seek after the Lord, and all the Gentiles, upon whom my name is called, saith the Lord, who doeth all these things.—*Acts 15:14-17.*

as "my church." In the future *kingdom* the Twelve are to be judges over the restored tribes of Israel (Matt. 19:27, 28)[43]: In the *Church* they are foundation stones, Christ Himself being the chief corner stone (Eph. 2:20; 1 Pet. 2:4-7).[44] The time had not come to unveil that mystery. The cross must be endured and redemption accomplished before the new dispensation of grace could come in. Nay, more, the Holy Spirit must come to inaugurate that dispensation, to unite the redeemed into one body, and to explain the new order. All this was near, but belonged to the "many things" which Jesus would fain have said, only the disciples "could not bear" them yet (John 16:12, 13).[45]

But He could and would lay the foundation of it all.

Two days after uttering the great Olivet Discourse, confirming the promises made to the fathers concerning the kingdom of heaven as to be duly fulfilled when He should return in glory (Matt. 25:31; comp. Acts 2:25-36; 15:14-17),[46] the Lord again met His disciples. But

---

[43] Then answered Peter and said unto him, Behold, we have forsaken all, and followed thee; what shall we have therefore?

And Jesus said unto them, Verily I say unto you, That ye which have followed me, in the regeneration when the Son of man shall sit in the throne of his glory, ye also shall sit upon twelve thrones, judging the twelve tribes of Israel.—*Matt. 19:27, 28.*

[44] And are built upon the foundation of the apostles and prophets, Jesus Christ himself being the chief corner *stone.—Eph. 2:20.*

To whom coming, *as unto* a living stone, disallowed indeed of men, but chosen of God, *and* precious,

Ye also, as lively stones, are built up a spiritual house, an holy priesthood, to offer up spiritual sacrifices, acceptable to God by Jesus Christ.

Wherefore also it is contained in the scripture, Behold, I lay in Sion a chief corner stone, elect, precious: and he that believeth on him shall not be confounded.

Unto you therefore which believe *he is* precious; but unto them which be disobedient, the stone which the builders disallowed, the same is made the head of the corner.—*1 Pet. 2: 4-7.*

[45] I have yet many things to say unto you, but ye cannot bear them now.

Howbeit when he, the Spirit of truth, is come, he will guide you into all truth: for he shall not speak of himself; but whatsoever he shall hear, *that* shall he speak: and he will shew you things to come.—*John 16:12, 13.*

[46] When the Son of man shall come in his glory, and all the holy angels with him, then shall he sit upon the throne of his glory.—*Matt. 25:31.*

For David speaketh concerning him, I foresaw the Lord always before my face, for he is

THE PROPHETIC MINISTRY OF JESUS CHRIST 95

not now on Jewish ground, nor in the midst of Jewish earthly things, as the temple, or on the mount of Olives. Gathering them in "an upper chamber," as it were away from earth, He ate with them the Passover; the Jewish feast which was emphatically associated, typically, with His own sacrifice as "the Lamb of God" (John 1:36; 1 Cor. 5:7),[47] and with the separation of a redeemed people from the scene about them, unto a pilgrim pathway to a promised inheritance (Exod. 12:12, 13; 11:7; 12:11, 41, 42).[48]

---

on my right hand, that I should not be moved:
Therefore did my heart rejoice, and my tongue was glad; moreover also my flesh shall rest in hope:
Because thou wilt not leave my soul in hell, neither wilt thou suffer thine Holy One to see corruption.
Thou hast made known to me the ways of life; thou shalt make me full of joy with thy countenance.
Men *and* brethren, let me freely speak unto you of the patriarch David, that he is both dead and buried, and his sepulchre is with us unto this day.
Therefore being a prophet, and knowing that God had sworn with an oath to him, that of the fruit of his loins, according to the flesh, he would raise up Christ to sit on his throne;
He seeing this before spake of the resurrection of Christ, that his soul was not left in hell, neither his flesh did see corruption.
This Jesus hath God raised up, whereof we all are witnesses.
Therefore being by the right hand of God exalted, and having received of the Father the promise of the Holy Ghost, he hath shed forth this, which ye now see and hear.
For David is not ascended into the heavens: but he saith himself, The Lord said unto my Lord, Sit thou on my right hand,
Until I make thy foes thy footstool.
Therefore let all the house of Israel know assuredly, that God hath made that same Jesus, whom ye have crucified, both Lord and Christ.—*Acts 2:25-36.*
Simeon hath declared how God at the first did visit the Gentiles, to take out of them a people for his name.
And to this agree the words of the prophets; as it is written,
After this I will return, and will build again the tabernacle of David, which is fallen down; and I will build again the ruins thereof, and I will set it up:
That the residue of men might seek after the Lord, and all the Gentiles, upon whom my name is called, saith the Lord, who doeth all these things.—*Acts 15:14-17.*

[47] And looking upon Jesus as he walked, he saith, Behold the Lamb of God!—*John 1:36.*
Purge out therefore the old leaven, that ye may be a new lump, as ye are unleavened. For even Christ our passover is sacrificed for us.—*1 Cor. 5:7.*

[48] For I will pass through the land of Egypt this night, and will smite all the firstborn in the land of Egypt, both man and beast; and against all the gods of Egypt I will execute judgment: I *am* the Lord.
And the blood shall be to you for a token upon the houses where ye *are:* and when I see

The Passover supper finished, our Lord performed an act of singular beauty and significance. Taking the Passover bread and wine He gave them to His disciples as memorials of His own sacrifice; memorials of a finished redemption. And, in thus doing, He placed Himself and them morally on this side of the cross. "Take, eat; this is my body." "This is my blood of the new covenant" (Heb. 8: 10-13). Out of the Passover which started Israel upon a pilgrim pathway, He fashioned the feast of the church which also is a pilgrim company: "strangers and pilgrims." In all that wonderful discourse in the upper chamber, as also in the high priestly prayer (John 14: 1 to 17: 26), there is not one distinctively Jewish note. He makes it clear that the end of the pathway of the new body, the church, is not the kingdom on the earth, over restored and converted Israel, and over the nations of the Gentiles, but to be received unto Himself away from the earth (John 14: 3; 1 Thess. 4: 14-16).[49] These men will, indeed, return with Him in glory to sit with Him on their twelve thrones; but meantime He is going away to prepare a "place" for the eternal home of the new pilgrim host.

---

the blood, I will pass over you, and the plague shall not be upon you to destroy *you,* when I smite the land of Egypt.—*Exod. 12: 12, 13.*

But against any of the children of Israel shall not a dog move his tongue, against man or beast: that ye may know how that the Lord doth put a difference between the Egyptians and Israel.—*Exod. 11: 7.*

And thus shall ye eat it; *with* your loins girded; your shoes on your feet, and your staff in your hand; and ye shall eat it in haste: it *is* the Lord's passover.—*Exod. 12: 11.*

And it came to pass at the end of the four hundred and thirty years, even the selfsame day it came to pass, that all the hosts of the Lord went out from the land of Egypt.

It *is* a night to be much observed unto the Lord for bringing them out of the land of Egypt: this *is* that night of the Lord to be observed of all the children of Israel in their generations.—*Exod. 12: 41, 42.*

[49] And if I go and prepare a place for you, I will come again, and receive you unto myself; that where I am, *there* ye may be also.—*John 14: 3.*

For if we believe that Jesus died and rose again, even so them also which sleep in Jesus will God bring with him.

For this we say unto you by the word of the Lord, that we which are alive *and* remain unto the coming of the Lord shall not prevent them which are asleep.

For the Lord himself shall descend from heaven with a shout, with the voice of the archangel, and with the trump of God: and the dead in Christ shall rise first. —*1 Thess. 4: 14-16.*

And then comes the new promise, of which in all Scripture before there had been no hint or intimation:

"And if I go and prepare a place for you, I will come again, and receive you unto myself; that where I am, there ye may be also" (John 14: 1-3).

A new promise, for a new body of believers, without a sign, without a time note, and unrelated to other prophetic events.

And this promise, taken up by the pen of inspiration after our Lord's departure and the coming of the Holy Spirit, becomes the "blessed hope" of the pilgrim church.

VII. THE PROPHETIC MESSAGE OF THE ACTS

THE Lord Jesus went to the Cross after having reaffirmed, in the great Olivet Discourse, the old promise to the fathers of Israel of a Messiah who should truly sit upon the throne of David, according to the covenant confirmed by the oath of Jehovah and renewed through the angel Gabriel (2 Sam. 7: 1-17; Psa. 89: 3, 4, 20-39; Luke 1: 30-33; Matt. 24: 29-31, 37-51; 25: 31)[1]; and after giving to the church so soon to be formed a wholly new promise of a coming which would not, like the coming to establish His kingdom,

---

[1] . . . Now therefore so shalt thou say unto my servant David, Thus saith the Lord of hosts, I took thee from the sheepcote, from following the sheep, to be ruler over my people, over Israel:

And I was with thee whithersoever thou wentest, and have cut off all thine enemies out of thy sight, and have made thee a great name, like unto the name of the great *men* that are in the earth.

Moreover I will appoint a place for my people Israel, and will plant them, that they may dwell in a place of their own, and move no more; neither shall the children of wickedness afflict them any more, as beforetime,

And as since the time that I commanded judges *to be* over my people Israel, and have caused thee to rest from all thine enemies. Also the Lord telleth thee that he will make thee an house.

And when thy days be fulfilled, and thou shalt sleep with thy fathers, I will set up thy seed after thee, which shall proceed out of thy bowels, and I will establish his kingdom.

He shall build an house for my name, and I will stablish the throne of his kingdom for ever.

I will be his father, and he shall be my son. If he commit iniquity, I will chasten him with the rod of men, and with the stripes of the children of men:

But my mercy shall not depart away from him, as I took *it* from Saul, whom I put away before thee.

And thine house and thy kingdom shall be established for ever before thee: thy throne shall be established for ever. . . .—*2 Sam. 7: 1-17.*

I have made a covenant with my chosen, I have sworn unto David my servant,

Thy seed will I establish for ever, and build up thy throne to all generations. Selah.—*Psalm 89: 3, 4.*

I have found David my servant; with my holy oil have I anointed him: . . .

Also I will make him *my* first born, higher than the kings of the earth.

My mercy will I keep for him for evermore, and my covenant shall stand fast with him.

His seed also will I make *to endure* for ever, and his throne as the days of heaven. . . .

Once have I sworn by my holiness that I will not lie unto David.

His seed shall endure for ever, and his throne as the sun before me.

It shall be established for ever as the moon, and *as* a faithful witness in heaven. Selah. . . .—*Psalm 89: 20-39.*

And the angel said unto her, Fear not, Mary: for thou hast found favour with God.

And, behold, thou shalt conceive in thy womb, and bring forth a son, and shalt call his name JESUS.

He shall be great, and shall be called the Son of the Highest: and the Lord God shall give unto him the throne of his father David.

And he shall reign over the house of Jacob for ever; and of his kingdom there shall be no end.—*Luke 1: 30-33.*

Immediately after the tribulation of those days shall the sun be darkened, and the moon shall not give her light, and the stars shall fall from heaven, and the powers of the heavens shall be shaken:

And then shall appear the sign of the Son of man in heaven: and then shall all the tribes of the earth mourn, and they shall see the Son of man coming in the clouds of heaven with power and great glory.

And he shall send his angels with a great sound of a trumpet, and they shall gather together his elect from the four winds, from one end of heaven to the other.—*Matt. 24: 29-31.*

But as the days of Noe *were,* so shall also the coming of the Son of man be.

For as in the days that were before the flood they were eating and drinking, marrying, and giving in marriage, until the day that Noe entered into the ark,

And knew not until the flood came, and took them all away; so shall also the coming of the Son of man be.

Then shall two be in the field; the one shall be taken, and the other left.

Two *women shall be* grinding at the mill; the one shall be taken, and the other left.

Watch therefore: for ye know not what hour your Lord doth come.

But know this, that if the goodman of the house had known in what watch the thief would come, he would have watched, and would not have suffered his house to be broken up.

Therefore be ye also ready: for in such an hour as ye think not the Son of man cometh.

Who then is a faithful and wise servant, whom his lord hath made ruler over his household, to give them meat in due season?

Blessed *is* that servant, whom his lord when he cometh shall find so doing.

Verily I say unto you, That he shall make him ruler over all his goods.

But and if that evil servant shall say in his heart, My lord delayeth his coming;

And shall begin to smite *his* fellowservants, and to eat and drink with the drunken;

The lord of that servant shall come in a day when he looketh not for *him,* and in an hour that he is not aware of,

And shall cut him asunder, and appoint *him* his portion with the hypocrites: there shall be weeping and gnashing of teeth.—*Matt. 24: 37-51.*

And he shall send his angels with a great sound of a trumpet, and they shall gather together his elect from the four winds, from one end of heaven to the other.—*Matt. 25: 31.*

bring Him to the earth, but only into the air that He might receive His church unto Himself. This new promise was not connected with the earth, but specifically with "a place" in the heavens which He was going to "prepare."

The resurrection of Jesus after three days and nights restored Him to His disciples for forty days. The events of those days, so far as they are recorded, are set forth in Matthew 28; Mark 16; Luke 24, and John 20 and 21. The twenty-first chapter of John has a relation backward and forward, connecting the discipleship which had been on Jewish ground with the new service upon which those same men would presently enter as members of His new body, the church.

It is from the Acts of the Apostles that we learn the subjects of our Lord's supplementary instructions to His disciples during the forty days of His sojourn with them until His Ascension. Those instructions concerned the doctrine of the kingdom of God, the imminent advent of another Divine Person, the Holy Spirit, and the new service under the Holy Spirit's power (Acts 1:1-8).[2] It is evident that precisely those instructions should, at just that time, be given to the men about to be entrusted with a mission which would very soon take them out of

---

[2] The former treatise have I made, O Theophilus, of all that Jesus began both to do and teach.
Until the day in which he was taken up, after that he through the Holy Ghost had given commandments unto the apostles whom he had chosen:
To whom also he shewed himself alive after his passion by many infallible proofs, being seen of them forty days, and speaking of the things pertaining to the kingdom of God:
And, being assembled together with *them*, commanded them that they should not depart from Jerusalem, but wait for the promise of the Father, which, *saith he,* ye have heard of me.

For John truly baptized with water; but ye shall be baptized with the Holy Ghost not many days hence.
When they therefore were come together, they asked of him, saying, Lord, wilt thou at this time restore again the kingdom to Israel?
And he said unto them, It is not for you to know the times or the seasons, which the Father hath put in his own power.
But ye shall receive power, after that the Holy Ghost is come upon you; and ye shall be witnesses unto me both in Jerusalem, and in all Judæa, and in Samaria, and unto the uttermost part of the earth.—*Acts 1:1-8.*

Jewish thoughts and limitations and launch them upon a world-wide evangelization.

First of all, they would need to know the wider, larger, truth of the kingdom of God. Jews, and having the Jewish hope of the kingdom of heaven—a hope just fully confirmed by the Olivet Discourse (Matt. 24 and 25; Luke 21), the instructions of the Forty Days would remind them that the kingdom of heaven, its earth work accomplished, would merge in the universal kingdom of God (1 Cor. 15:24-28).[3]

One point, and one only, was left out of these instructions of our Lord—the *time* when the kingdom of heaven would begin its work of restoring the earth to the great, inclusive, kingdom of God. This omission became, therefore, the subject of a very natural question: "Wilt thou at this time restore again the kingdom to Israel?" It is noteworthy, first, that our Lord did not rebuke this question; and, secondly, that His answer left whole and entire the Jewish hope: "It is not for you to know the times or the seasons, which the Father hath put in his own power."

One great body of truth, about to become of supreme importance from the prophetical and dispensational point of view—that concerning the church, was not a part of the instructions of the Forty Days. The church, apart from the prophetic word "I will build my church" (Matt. 16:18),[4] remained a "mystery hid in God" (Eph. 3:9, 10).[5] The unfolding of that mystery was reserved to

---

[3] Then *cometh* the end, when he shall have delivered up the kingdom to God, even the Father; when he shall have put down all rule and all authority and power.

For he must reign, till he hath put all enemies under his feet.

The last enemy *that* shall be destroyed *is* death.

For he hath put all things under his feet. But when he saith all things are put under *him, it is* manifest that he is excepted, which did put all things under him.

And when all things shall be subdued unto him, then shall the Son also himself be subject unto him that put all things under him, that God may be all in all.—*1 Cor. 15:24-28*.

[4] And I say also unto thee, That thou art Peter, and upon this rock I will build my church; and the gates of hell shall not prevail against it.—*Matt. 16:18*.

[5] And to make all men see what is the fellowship of the mystery, which from the beginning of the world hath been hid in God, who created all things by Jesus Christ:

the Apostle Paul, to whom also was entrusted the exposition of the doctrines of grace (Eph. 3: 1-10).[6]

These disciples, rich in preparation of soul through three years of close fellowship with the Lord, and now enriched in truth through the instruction of the Forty Days, must yet wait. One thing they lacked, the filling and power of the Holy Spirit, and so supremely essential was this enduement for the new ministry that all other qualifications must wait for it. What presumption, then, for any one following them in the ministry of the grace of God to suppose that a smattering of book learning will suffice! The power of the new service was to be the Holy Spirit; the method a witnessing. A witness must have first-hand knowledge of that concerning which he speaks. Hearsay will not do.

But the disciples must begin at—or "from" Jerusalem. "To the Jew first" (Rom. 1: 16; 2: 9)[7] is the Biblical order, but the Jewish ministry of the Apostles as recorded in the first nine chapters of The Acts has a still more distinctive character.

To the intent that now unto the principalities and powers in heavenly places might be known by the church the manifold wisdom of God.—*Eph. 3: 9, 10.*

[6] For this cause I Paul, the prisoner of Jesus Christ for you Gentiles, If ye have heard of the dispensation of the grace of God which is given me to youward:

How that by revelation he made known unto me the mystery; (as I wrote afore in few words,

Whereby, when ye read, ye may understand my knowledge in the mystery of Christ)

Which in other ages was not made known unto the sons of men, as it is now revealed unto his holy apostles and prophets by the Spirit;

That the Gentiles should be fellowheirs, and of the same body, and partakers of his promise in Christ by the gospel:

Wherefore I was made a minister, according to the gift of the grace of God given unto me by the effectual working of his power.

Unto me, who am less than the least of all saints, is this grace given, that I should preach among the Gentiles the unsearchable riches of Christ;

And to make all *men* see what *is* the fellowship of the mystery, which from the beginning of the world hath been hid in God, who created all things by Jesus Christ:

To the intent that now unto the principalities and powers in heavenly places might be known by the church the manifold wisdom of God.—*Eph. 3: 1-10.*

[7] For I am not ashamed of the gospel of Christ: for it is the power of God unto salvation to every one that believeth; to the Jew first, and also to the Greek.—*Rom. 1: 16.*

Tribulation and anguish, upon every soul of man that doeth evil, of the Jew first, and also of the Gentile.—*Rom. 2: 9.*

In Luke 19:12-14 [8] this special ministry is foretold in the form of a parable—one of the parables of the *postponed* kingdom. Christ, the "nobleman" of the parable, goes away to receive the investiture—the formal appointment—of a kingdom (Dan. 7:13-18; Rev. 5:1-10),[9] and is to return. But during His absence the

---

[8] He said therefore, A certain nobleman went into a far country to receive for himself a kingdom, and to return.

And he called his ten servants, and delivered them ten pounds, and said unto them, Occupy till I come.

But his citizens hated him, and sent a message after him, saying, We will not have this *man* to reign over us.—*Luke 19:12-14.*

[9] I saw in the night visions, and, behold, *one* like the Son of man came with the clouds of heaven, and came to the Ancient of days, and they brought him near before him.

And there was given him dominion, and glory, and a kingdom, that all people, nations, and languages, should serve him: his dominion *is* an everlasting dominion, which shall not pass away, and his kingdom *that* which shall not be destroyed.

I Daniel was grieved in my spirit in the midst of *my* body, and the visions of my head troubled me.

I came near unto one of them that stood by, and asked him the truth of all this. So he told me, and made me know the interpretation of the things.

These great beasts, which are four, *are* four kings, *which* shall arise out of the earth.

But the saints of the most High shall take the kingdom, and possess the kingdom for ever, even for ever and ever.—*Dan. 7:13-18.*

And I saw in the right hand of him that sat on the throne a book written within and on the backside, sealed with seven seals.

And I saw a strong angel proclaiming with a loud voice, Who is worthy to open the book, and to loose the seals thereof?

And no man in heaven, nor in earth, neither under the earth, was able to open the book, neither to look thereon.

And I wept much, because no man was found worthy to open and to read the book, neither to look thereon.

And one of the elders saith unto me, Weep not: behold, the Lion of the tribe of Juda, the Root of David, hath prevailed to open the book, and to loose the seven seals thereof.

And I beheld, and, lo, in the midst of the throne and of the four beasts, and in the midst of the elders, stood a Lamb as it had been slain, having seven horns and seven eyes, which are the seven Spirits of God sent forth into all the earth.

And he came and took the book out of the right hand of him that sat upon the throne.

And when he had taken the book, the four beasts and four *and* twenty elders fell down before the Lamb, having every one of them harps, and golden vials full of odours, which are the prayers of saints.

And they sung a new song, saying, Thou art worthy to take the book, and to open the seals thereof: for thou wast slain, and hast redeemed us to God by thy blood out of every kindred, and tongue, and people, and nation;

And hast made us unto our God kings and priests: and we shall reign on the earth.—*Rev. 5:1-10.*

"citizens" who are to be the subjects of the returning King, whom they have already rejected in the days of His flesh, send after Him still another message of rejection. This sending implies that a new appeal has been made to the "citizens" on behalf of the absent King. It is precisely that appeal and the story of its rejection which is told in the first seven chapters of Acts.

The message is not the distinctive Gospel message for this age, "Believe on the Lord Jesus Christ, and thou shalt be saved" (Acts 16:31), with its strictly individual application, but deals with the corporate guilt of the Jews in rejecting their Messiah, Jesus, appeals to corporate or national repentance, and promises that upon condition of such repentance Jesus Christ will return (Acts 3: 19-21.[10] Revised Version).

Peter in his first sermon, on the day of Pentecost, faces directly the inevitable Jewish objection that Jesus could not be the Messiah because He had not fulfilled the promises to Israel concerning the kingdom. It was the very difficulty which Jesus had answered, so far as His own disciples were concerned, in the Olivet Discourse; and Peter, addressing the Jewish multitude, gives exactly the same solution. The promises will be fulfilled by the *risen* Christ. If it were true that Israel had been *mistaken* in expecting a kingdom which, while fully spiritual, was to be also visible and material, this was the place and time to say so. But neither in this place and time, nor in any other, does a single line of inspiration say so. On the contrary, the Apostle affirms that David himself, being a prophet, foresaw that through a *resurrection,* God, who had confirmed the Davidic Covenant with an oath (2 Sam. 7:5-17; Psa. 89:3, 4, 20-37),[11] "would raise up Christ to sit on his throne."

---

[10] Repent ye therefore, and turn again, that your sins may be blotted out, that so there may come seasons of refreshing from the presence of the Lord; and that he may send the Christ who hath been appointed for you, even Jesus: whom the heaven must receive until the times of restoration of all things, whereof God spake by the mouth of his holy prophets that have been from of old. —*Acts 3: 19-21, Revised Version.*

[11] For the Scripture text, see footnote 1 on pages 99, 100.

In the second sermon, that at the Beautiful Gate, Peter adds to his former demonstration that Christ in resurrection will sit upon the throne of David (comp. Luke 1: 30-33),[12] the tremendous promise that if Israel will *then* repent the "times of restitution" will begin, and the King will again be sent (Acts 3: 19-21).[13]

It is noteworthy that along with the corporate appeal to the nation as such there is, in all this post-pentecostal preaching, the offer of mercy to the individual:

"Then said Peter unto them, Repent and be baptized *every one of you* . . . and with many other words did he testify and exhort, saying, Save yourselves from [literally, 'from among'] this untoward generation" (Acts 2: 37-41). "Unto you first God, having raised up his Son Jesus, sent him to bless you, in turning away *every one* of you from *his* iniquities" (Acts 3: 26).

But the appeal is to Israel corporately. And, alas! the answer was soon forthcoming. In the command laid upon the apostles no longer to preach in that name (Acts 4: 13-22; 5: 28-33),[14] but still more emphatically in the

---

[12] And the angel said unto her, Fear not, Mary: for thou hast found favour with God.

And, behold, thou shalt conceive in thy womb, and bring forth a son, and shalt call his name JESUS.

He shall be great, and shall be called the Son of the Highest: and the Lord God shall give unto him the throne of his father David.

And he shall reign over the house of Jacob forever; and of his kingdom there shall be no end.—*Luke 1: 30-33.*

[13] Repent ye therefore, and be converted, that your sins may be blotted out, when the times of refreshing shall come from the presence of the Lord;

And he shall send Jesus Christ, which before was preached unto you:

Whom the heaven must receive until the times of restitution of all things, which God hath spoken by the mouth of all his holy prophets since the world began.—*Acts 3: 19-21.*

[14] Now when they saw the boldness of Peter and John, and perceived that they were unlearned and ignorant men, they marvelled; and they took knowledge of them that they had been with Jesus. . . .

And they called them, and commanded them not to speak at all nor teach in the name of Jesus. . . .—*Acts 4: 13-22.*

Saying, Did not we straitly command you that ye should not teach in this name? and, behold, ye have filled Jerusalem with your doctrine, and intend to bring this man's blood upon us.

Then Peter and the *other* apostles answered and said, We ought to obey God rather than men.

The God of our fathers raised up Jesus, whom ye slew and hanged on a tree.

Him hath God exalted with his right hand *to be* a Prince

martyrdom of Stephen, the "citizens" sent after the "nobleman" the message, "We will not have this man to reign over us."

It has been beautifully suggested by F. W. Boyle, of San Jose, Costa Rica, that in this great final appeal to the Jews we are to find an answer to the cross-prayer of our Lord, "Father, forgive them; for they know not what they do" (Luke 23:34). He points out the emphasis which Peter puts upon the spiritual unconsciousness of the Jews who were guilty of the blood of Jesus: "And now, brethren, I wot that through ignorance ye did it, as did also your rulers" (Acts 3:17). This is most helpful. But that very preaching stripped away forever the excuse of ignorance. It was a second rejection of the Messiah.

In the summing up by the Apostle James of the result of the gathering at Jerusalem which has come to be called the first council, and where, certainly, not only "the apostles and elders," but also the Holy Spirit were present (Acts 15:28),[15] occurs what has been called, "dispensationally the most important passage in the New Testament."

The contention of "certain men which came down from Judæa" to Antioch, that circumcision "after the manner of Moses" was essential to salvation (Acts 15:1), a contention carried on also by "certain of the sect of the Pharisees which believed," gave occasion to the gathering at Jerusalem, the record of which we have in Acts 15. The question submitted to the council, however, went beyond the mere rite of circumcision and put in issue the whole "law of Moses" (v. 5) as related to the Christian church. Was Christianity a ritual religion, or one in which the believer, already made righteous through faith in a righteousness so perfect that nothing could be added, was "not under the law, but under grace"?

---

and a Saviour, for to give repentance to Israel, and forgiveness of sins.

And we are his witnesses of these things; and *so is* also the Holy Ghost, whom God hath given to them that obey him.

When they heard *that,* they were cut *to the heart,* and took counsel to slay them.—*Acts 5: 28-33.*

[15] For it seemed good to the Holy Ghost, and to us, to lay upon you no greater burden than these necessary things.—*Acts 15: 28.*

The decision was for liberty; and the argument against which the legalists could say nothing was that urged by Peter—the fact that God, without circumcision or any other act in addition to simple faith in Christ, had bestowed the Holy Spirit upon the Gentile converts (vs. 7-11). It is noteworthy, as against the contention of a few in this day that the new liberty was for the Gentiles only, while Jewish believers were to go on with ceremonialism, that Peter (v. 11) puts Jews upon the same ground.

But back of the legal contention lay still in the minds of many Jewish believers the old difficulty of how to believe in a Messiah who had gone back to heaven without having fulfilled the kingdom promises; and the great prophetic passage meets that difficulty precisely as our Lord had met it in the Olivet Discourse, and as Peter had met it in the Pentecostal sermon—the kingdom was *postponed,* not abandoned, nor "spiritualized" into something bearing no resemblance to the promises to the fathers. But the passage is of exceeding value in that it not only reaffirms the Davidic promise, but that it gives the relation of this age to the kingdom age which is to follow this age.

"Simeon hath declared [Acts 15: 7-11] how God at the first [literally, 'for the first time'] did visit the Gentiles, to *take out of them* a people for his name. And to this agree the words of the prophets; as it is written [Amos 9: 11-15 [16]], After this I will return, and will build again the tabernacle of David, which is fallen down; and I

---

[16] In that day will I raise up the tabernacle of David that is fallen, and close up the breaches thereof; and I will raise up his ruins, and I will build it as in the days of old:

That they may possess the remnant of Edom, and of all the heathen, which are called by my name, saith the Lord that doeth this.

Behold, the days come, saith the Lord, that the plowman shall overtake the reaper, and the treader of grapes him that soweth seed; and the mountains shall drop sweet wine, and all the hills shall melt.

And I will bring again the captivity of my people of Israel, and they shall build the waste cities, and inhabit *them;* and they shall plant vineyards, and drink the wine thereof; they shall also make gardens, and eat the fruit of them.

And I will plant them upon their land, and they shall no more be pulled up out of their land which I have given them, saith the Lord thy God.—*Amos 9: 11-15.*

will build again the ruins thereof, and I will set it up: that the residue of men might seek after the Lord, and all the Gentiles, upon whom my name is called, saith the Lord, who doeth all these things" (15:14-17).

What Peter began the church has carried on. Wherever the Gospel has been preached among the Gentiles in the power of the Holy Spirit some have believed—never, anywhere, *all*. Jerusalem was not converted, nor Rome, nor Antioch, but there a people for His name was called out. That is the Divine program for this age. When, in the thought and intent of God, that process is complete (Rom. 11:25-27),[17] Jesus Christ will return and set up the Messianic kingdom of heaven. And then, and never till then, will there be a converted world. The earth shall indeed be full of the knowledge of the Lord as the waters cover the sea, but the prophet who tells us that, tells us also *when* it shall be: "In that day" when the Branch shall be king, and Israel restored to her ancient land (Isa. 11:9-12).[18]

It is important to note that the prophetic element in The Acts concerns the reconciliation of a postponed kingdom with the promises made to Israel through the Old Testament prophets. The *church* is not the subject of the prophetic testimony of that book. *Churches* are

---

[17] For I would not, brethren, that ye should be ignorant of this mystery, lest ye should be wise in your own conceits; that blindness in part is happened to Israel, until the fulness of the Gentiles be come in.

And so all Israel shall be saved: as it is written, There shall come out of Sion the deliverer, and shall turn away ungodliness from Jacob:

For this *is* my covenant unto them, when I shall take away their sins.—*Rom. 11:25-27*.

[18] They shall not hurt nor destroy in all my holy mountain: for the earth shall be full of the knowledge of the Lord, as the waters cover the sea.

And in that day there shall be a root of Jesse, which shall stand for an ensign of the people; to it shall the Gentiles seek: and his rest shall be glorious.

And it shall come to pass in that day, *that* the Lord shall set his hand again the second time to recover the remnant of his people, which shall be left, from Assyria, and from Egypt, and from Pathros, and from Cush, and from Elam, and from Shinar, and from Hamath, and from the islands of the sea.

And he shall set up an ensign for the nations, and shall assemble the outcasts of Israel, and gather together the dispersed of Judah from the four corners of the earth.—*Isa. 11: 9-12*.

everywhere in the book, but the unfolding of the *doctrine* of the church, as also of her prophetic future, awaits the pen of the great Apostle to the Gentiles. His conversion, ministry, sufferings—the story of these, fills the second and larger part of The Acts. In the Epistles and The Revelation prophecy tells the story of the Church.

VIII. PROPHECY IN THE EPISTLES

ON THE night of His betrayal, in the upper chamber discourse, our Lord said:

"I have yet many things to say unto you, but ye cannot bear them now. Howbeit when he, the Spirit of truth, is come, he will guide you into all truth" (John 16:12).

That this promised revelation would contain a predictive element was also announced by our Lord: "Whatsoever he [the Holy Spirit] shall hear, that shall he speak: and he will shew you things to come" (John 16:13).

When we turn to the Epistles we see that the promised revelation of new truth concerns the new body, the church. In the one hundred and fourteen chapters composing the Acts and the Epistles the kingdom is mentioned but twenty-five times, and always by the larger spiritual designation of the kingdom of God; while the church is mentioned in the same chapters *eighty-nine* times. In the great Epistle to the Romans the kingdom of God is mentioned but once in the sixteen chapters. It is the church which fills the scene.

Our Lord was Himself the first Prophet of the church. After His rejection as Israel's king had become manifest, Jesus with His disciples departed into Galilee, and there uttered the first word of Scripture concerning the church: "I will build my church." In their very terms these words were prophetic and indicated a purpose to be accomplished in the future. They pointed neither to the past nor to the present. Christ did not say, "I have been building," or, "I am building," but "I will build" (Matt. 16:18)

It is most significant that, *"From that time forth* began Jesus to shew unto his disciples, how that he must go unto Jerusalem, and suffer many things of the elders and chief priests and scribes, and be killed, and be raised again the third day" (Matt. 16:18, 21). But, lest there should be any ground for the conclusion that "church" and "kingdom" were synonymous terms, or the church be taken as fulfilling the promise of the kingdom, our Lord's prediction was almost immediately followed by the kingdom-picture of the transfiguration (Matt. 17:1-13).[1] Our Lord declared it to be a showing forth of "the Son of man coming in his kingdom" (Matt. 16:28).[2]

The kingdom elements set forth by the prophets are all present in the Transfiguration: (1) the Son of man appearing in glory (Matt. 25:31),[3] accompanied by two classes of glorified saints—those who had passed into heaven through death, like Moses (1 Cor. 15:22, 23),[4]

---

[1] And after six days Jesus taketh Peter, James, and John his brother, and bringeth them up into an high mountain apart,

And was transfigured before them: and his face did shine as the sun, and his raiment was white as the light.

And, behold, there appeared unto them Moses and Elias talking with him.

Then answered Peter, and said unto Jesus, Lord, it is good for us to be here: if thou wilt, let us make here three tabernacles; one for thee, and one for Moses, and one for Elias.

While he yet spake, behold, a bright cloud overshadowed them: and behold a voice out of the cloud, which said, This is my beloved Son, in whom I am well pleased; hear ye him.

And when the disciples heard it, they fell on their face, and were sore afraid.

And Jesus came and touched them, and said, Arise, and be not afraid.

And when they had lifted up their eyes, they saw no man, save Jesus only.

And as they came down from the mountain, Jesus charged them, saying, Tell the vision to no man, until the Son of man be risen again from the dead.

And his disciples asked him, saying, Why then say the scribes that Elias must first come?

And Jesus answered and said unto them, Elias truly shall first come, and restore all things.

But I say unto you, That Elias is come already, and they knew him not, but have done unto him whatsoever they listed. Likewise shall also the Son of man suffer of them.

Then the disciples understood that he spake unto them of John the Baptist.—*Matt. 17:1-13.*

[2] Verily I say unto you, There be some standing here, which shall not taste of death, till they see the Son of man coming in his kingdom.—*Matt. 16:28.*

[3] When the Son of man shall come in his glory, and all the holy angels with him, then shall he sit upon the throne of his glory.—*Matt. 25:31.*

[4] For as in Adam all die, even so in Christ shall all be made alive.

But every man in his own order: Christ the firstfruits; afterward they that are Christ's at his coming.—*1 Cor. 15:22, 23.*

and those who had been translated without seeing death, like Elijah (1 Cor. 15:51-53; 1 Thess. 4:14-17).[5] (2) The scene is on the earth, because the kingdom is to be set up on the earth (Jer. 23:5; Zech. 9:7-15).[6] (3) Men in the flesh will form part of the kingdom as repre-

---

[5] Behold, I shew you a mystery; We shall not all sleep, but we shall all be changed,

In a moment, in the twinkling of an eye, at the last trump: for the trumpet shall sound, and the dead shall be raised incorruptible, and we shall be changed.

For this corruptible must put on incorruption, and this mortal *must* put on immortality.—*1 Cor. 15:51-53.*

For if we believe that Jesus died and rose again, even so them also which sleep in Jesus will God bring with him.

For this we say unto you by the word of the Lord, that we which are alive, *and* remain unto the coming of the Lord shall not prevent them which are asleep.

For the Lord himself shall descend from heaven with a shout, with the voice of the archangel, and with the trump of God: and the dead in Christ shall rise first:

Then we which are alive *and* remain shall be caught up together with them in the clouds, to meet the Lord in the air: and so shall we ever be with the Lord.—*1 Thess. 4:14-17.*

[6] Behold, the days come, saith the Lord, that I will raise unto David a righteous Branch, and a King shall reign and prosper, and shall execute judgment and justice in the earth.—*Jer. 23:5.*

And I will take away his blood out of his mouth, and his abominations from between his teeth: but he that remaineth, even he, *shall be* for our God, and he shall be as a governor in Judah, and Ekron as a Jebusite.

And I will encamp about mine house because of the army, because of him that passeth by, and because of him that returneth: and no oppressor shall pass through them any more: for now have I seen with mine eyes.

Rejoice greatly, O daughter of Zion; shout, O daughter of Jerusalem: behold, thy King cometh unto thee: he *is* just, and having salvation; lowly, and riding upon an ass, and upon a colt the foal of an ass.

And I will cut off the chariot from Ephraim, and the horse from Jerusalem, and the battle bow shall be cut off: and he shall speak peace unto the heathen: and his dominion *shall be* from sea *even* to sea, and from the river *even* to the ends of the earth.

As for thee also, by the blood of thy covenant I have sent forth thy prisoners out of the pit wherein *is* no water.

Turn you to the strong hold, ye prisoners of hope: even to-day do I declare *that* I will render double unto thee;

When I have bent Judah for me, filled the bow with Ephraim, and raised up thy sons, O Zion, against thy sons, O Greece, and made thee as the sword of a mighty man.

And the Lord shall be seen over them, and his arrow shall go forth as the lightning: and the Lord God shall blow the trumpet, and shall go with whirlwinds of the south.

The Lord of hosts shall defend them; and they shall devour, and subdue with sling stones; and they shall drink, *and* make a noise as through wine; and they shall be filled like bowls, *and* as the corners of the altar.—*Zech. 9:7-15.*

sented by Peter, James, and John; and, (4) the mission of the kingdom is ministry to the multitudes of earth (vs. 14-17).

But with the announcement of the future purpose, "I will build my church," and with the picture-parable of the kingdom, now postponed to the coming of the king in glory, the church was left by Christ an unexplained "mystery hid in God" (Eph. 3:1-11).[7]

It is to the Epistles that we look for the unfolding of that mystery. Distinctively, the revelation of church truth was committed to Paul (Eph. 3:1-11.)[7] Through him we learn that the church is the body of Christ, formed by the baptism of the Spirit (1 Cor. 12:12-14)[8]; a body of which Christ is the Head, and all believers, at and from Pentecost, are the members (Eph. 1:22, 23)[9]; that this body is not an organization, with Christ as pres-

---

[7] For this cause I Paul, the prisoner of Jesus Christ for you Gentiles,
If ye have heard of the dispensation of the grace of God which is given me to you-ward:
How by that revelation he made known unto me the mystery; (as I wrote afore in few words,
Whereby, when ye read, ye may understand my knowledge in the mystery of Christ)
Which in other ages was not made known unto the sons of men, as it is now revealed unto his holy apostles and prophets by the Spirit;
That the Gentiles should be fellowheirs, and of the same body, and partakers of his promise in Christ by the gospel:
Whereof I was made a minister, according to the gift of the grace of God given unto me by the effectual working of his power.
Unto me, who am less than the least of all saints, is this grace given, that I should preach among the Gentiles the unsearchable riches of Christ;
And to make all men see what is the fellowship of the mystery, which from the beginning of the world hath been hid in God, who created all things by Jesus Christ:
To the intent that now unto the principalities and powers in heavenly places might be known by the church the manifold wisdom of God.
According to the eternal purpose which he purposed in Christ Jesus our Lord.—*Eph. 3: 1-11.*

[8] For as the body is one, and hath many members, and all the members of that one body, being many, are one body: so also *is* Christ.
For by one Spirit are we all baptized into one body, whether *we be* Jews or Gentiles, whether *we be* bond or free; and have been all made to drink into one Spirit.
For the body is not one member, but many.—*1 Cor. 12: 12-14.*

[9] And hath put all *things* under his feet, and gave him *to be* the head over all *things* to the church,
Which is his body, the fulness of him that filleth all in all.—*Eph. 1: 22, 23.*

ident, or king, but an *organism,* like the human body, the "members" corresponding not to the citizens of a republic or the subjects of a kingdom, but to the hands, feet, eye, ear, of the human body, united in oneness of life (1 Cor. 12: 14-21; John 15: 1-5; 1 John 5: 11, 12)[10] to the risen Head in the glory.

In another relation, as Eve, taken from the body of Adam, became "bone of his bone, flesh of his flesh" through marriage, so the church is the destined bride of Christ, "the last Adam" (Gen. 2: 21-23; 2 Cor. 11: 1, 2; Eph. 5: 28-33).[11]

---

[10] For the body is not one member, but many.

If the foot shall say, Because I am not the hand, I am not of the body; is it therefore not of the body?

And if the ear shall say, Because I am not the eye, I am not of the body; is it therefore not of the body?

If the whole body *were* an eye, where *were* the hearing? If the whole *were* hearing, where *were* the smelling?

But now hath God set the members every one of them in the body, as it hath pleased him.

And if they were all one member, where *were* the body?

But now *are they* many members, yet but one body.

And the eye cannot say unto the hand, I have no need of thee: nor again the head to the feet, I have no need of you.—*1 Cor. 12: 14-21.*

I am the true vine, and my Father is the husbandman.

Every branch in me that beareth not fruit he taketh away: and every *branch* that beareth fruit, he purgeth it, that it may bring forth more fruit.

Now ye are clean through the word which I have spoken unto you.

Abide in me, and I in you. As the branch cannot bear fruit of itself, except it abide in the vine; no more can ye, except ye abide in me.

I am the vine, ye *are* the branches: He that abideth in me, and I in him, the same bringeth forth much fruit: for without me ye can do nothing. —*John 15: 1-5.*

And this is the record, that God hath given to us eternal life, and this life is in his Son.

He that hath the Son hath life; *and* he that hath not the Son of God hath not life.—*1 John 5: 11, 12.*

[11] And the Lord God caused a deep sleep to fall upon Adam, and he slept: and he took one of his ribs, and closed up the flesh instead thereof;

And the rib, which the Lord God had taken from man, made he a woman, and brought her unto the man.

And Adam said, This *is* now bone of my bones, and flesh of my flesh: she shall be called Woman, because she was taken out of Man.—*Gen. 2: 21-23.*

Would to God ye could bear with me a little in *my* folly: and indeed bear with me.

For I am jealous over you with godly jealousy: for I have espoused you to one husband, that I may present you as a chaste virgin to Christ.—*2 Cor. 11: 1, 2.*

So ought men to love their wives as their own bodies. He that loveth his wife loveth himself.

For no man ever yet hated his own flesh; but nourisheth

In yet another relation the church "groweth unto an holy temple in the Lord . . . for an habitation of God through the Spirit" (Eph. 2:21, 22). The first members of this body, the church, were the disciples of our Lord, gathered out of Israel by His personal ministry. These, baptized by the Spirit on the day of Pentecost (Acts 2: 1-4),[12] were the first "members," but, "the same day there were added unto them about three thousand souls." From that day to this the growth of the body has gone on, "the Lord adding to them day by day those that were [or are] being saved" (Acts 2:47, Revised Version).

In relation to the world the believers composing the church are said by our Lord to be "in," but not "of" it (John 17:11, 16).[13] It should be borne in mind that, though believers, alas! too often, fail to manifest this holy separation from the world, it is still true that, as taken out of the world and given to Christ (John 17:6, 11, 12, 16),[14] they remain His, and are not to be involved in His world-judgments. They may, and often do, lay aside for a time the pilgrim scrip and staff (1 Pet. 2:

---

and cherisheth it, even as the Lord the church:

For we are members of his body, of his flesh, and of his bones.

For this cause shall a man leave his father and mother, and shall be joined unto his wife, and they two shall be one flesh.

This is a great mystery: but I speak concerning Christ and the church.

Nevertheless let every one of you in particular so love his wife even as himself; and the wife *see* that she reverence *her* husband.—*Eph. 5:28-33.*

[12] And when the day of Pentecost was fully come, they were all with one accord in one place.

And suddenly there came a sound from heaven as of a rushing mighty wind, and it filled all the house where they were sitting.

And there appeared unto them cloven tongues like as of fire, and it sat upon each of them.

And they were all filled with the Holy Ghost, and began to speak with other tongues, as the Spirit gave them utterance.—*Acts 2:1-4.*

[13],[14] I have manifested thy name unto the men which thou gavest me out of the world: thine they were, and thou gavest them me; and they have kept thy word.—*John 17:6.*

And now I am no more in the world, but these are in the world, and I come to thee. Holy Father, keep through thine own name those whom thou hast given me, that they may be one, as we *are*.

While I was with them in the world, I kept them in thy name: those that thou gavest me I have kept, and none of them is lost, but the son of perdition; that the scripture might be fulfilled.—*John 17:11, 12.*

They are not of the world, even as I am not of the world. —*John 17:16.*

PROPHECY IN THE EPISTLES

11),[15] but still they are "strangers and pilgrims" in relation to the present world-system.

Taken out of the world and given to Christ, the believers composing the church are by Him charged with a great mission, universal in its scope, to the world out of which they were taken. That mission is to "preach the gospel to every creature" (Mark 16:15); while as "an elect race, a royal priesthood, a holy nation, a people for God's own possession," they "shew forth the excellencies of him who hath called them out of darkness into his marvellous light" (1 Pet. 2:9, 19).

It is made clear that the church belongs to the heavenly, as Israel to the earthly sphere (Eph. 1:3).[16] Her inheritance is in heaven (Eph. 1:11; 1 Pet. 1:4; John 14:2; Rom. 8:17)[17]; her citizenship is there (Phil. 3:20)[18] and her attitude is that of expectant waiting for Christ to receive her unto Himself (1 Thess. 1:9, 10; Titus 2:13; Phil. 3:20, 21; 1 Cor. 15:51, 52; 1 Thess. 4:14-17).[19]

---

[15] Dearly beloved, I beseech *you* as strangers and pilgrims, abstain from fleshly lusts, which war against the soul.—*1 Peter 2:11.*

[16] Blessed *be* the God and Father of our Lord Jesus Christ, who hath blessed us with all spiritual blessings in heavenly *places* in Christ.—*Eph. 1:3.*

[17] In whom also we have obtained an inheritance, being predestinated according to the purpose of him who worketh all things after the counsel of his own will.—*Eph. 1:11.*

To an inheritance incorruptible, and undefiled, and that fadeth not away, reserved in heaven for you.—*1 Pet. 1:4.*

In my Father's house are many mansions: if *it were* not so, I would have told you. I go to prepare a place for you.—*John 14:2.*

And if children, then heirs; heirs of God, and joint-heirs with Christ; if so be that we suffer with *him,* that we may be also glorified together.—*Rom. 8:17.*

[18] For our citizenship is in heaven; whence also we wait for a Saviour, the Lord Jesus Christ.—*Phil. 3:20, Revised Version.*

[19] For they themselves shew of us what manner of entering in we had unto you, and how ye turned to God from idols to serve the living and true God;

And to wait for his Son from heaven, whom he raised from the dead, *even* Jesus, which delivered us from the wrath to come.—*1 Thess. 1:9, 10.*

Looking for that blessed hope, and the glorious appearing of the great God and our Saviour Jesus Christ.—*Titus 2:13.*

For our citizenship is in heaven; whence also we wait for a Saviour, the Lord Jesus Christ. *Phil. 3:20, Revised Version.*

Who shall change our vile body, that it may be fashioned like unto his glorious body, according to the working whereby he is able even to subdue all things unto himself.—*Phil. 3:21.*

The Epistles distinguish the church from the churches. The body of Christ is composed of those who have really believed on Him, and are saved; the churches are composed of those who have professed to believe, or who, as children of professed believers have been baptized, and so are accounted to be Christians. This profession may be of a true faith, or may be mere church membership.

The distinction, like all distinctions between things that differ in the Word of God, is important, but it is especially important in respect of church truth. For the predictive element in the Epistles and Revelation runs in two distinct lines. One of these concerns the future of the true "church which is his body, the fulness of him that filleth all in all" (Eph. 1:23); the other concerns the mass of profession, known in common speech as "Christendom." Individually, these are so mingled now, and so outwardly alike, like the wheat and tares of the second "mystery of the kingdom of heaven" (Matt. 13:24-30, 36-43),[20] as to be for the greater part indistin-

---

Behold, I shew you a mystery; We shall not all sleep, but we shall all be changed,

In a moment, in the twinkling of an eye, at the last trump: for the trumpet shall sound, and the dead shall be raised incorruptible, and we shall be changed.—*1 Cor. 15: 51, 52.*

For if we believe that Jesus died and rose again, even so them also which sleep in Jesus will God bring with him.

For this we say unto you by the word of the Lord, that we which are alive *and* remain unto the coming of the Lord shall not prevent them which are asleep.

For the Lord himself shall descend from heaven with a shout, with the voice of the archangel, and with the trump of God: and the dead in Christ shall rise first:

Then we which are alive *and* remain shall be caught up together with them in the clouds, to meet the Lord in the air: and so shall we ever be with the Lord.—*1 Thess. 4: 14-17.*

[20] Another parable put he forth unto them, saying, The kingdom of heaven is likened unto a man which sowed good seed in his field:

But while men slept, his enemy came and sowed tares among the wheat, and went his way.

But when the blade was sprung up, and brought forth fruit, then appeared the tares also.

So the servants of the householder came and said unto him, Sir, didst not thou sow good seed in thy field? from whence then hath it tares?

He said unto them, An enemy hath done this. The servants said unto him, Wilt thou then that we go and gather them up?

But he said, Nay; lest while ye gather up the tares, ye root up also the wheat with them.

Let both grow together until the harvest: and in the time of harvest I will say to the reapers, Gather ye together first the tares, and bind them in bundles to burn them: but gather the

PROPHECY IN THE EPISTLES

guishable. Nevertheless prophecy appoints to each a future strikingly unlike. Post-tribulationism, or the theory that the true church goes through the great tribulation, is due to confusion at this point. The mass of profession does go through the great tribulation—the church which is His body does not.

The chief themes of prophecy in the Epistles are:

1. The apostasy of the professing church.
2. The "Day of Christ" and the rapture (catching up) of the true church.
3. The "day of the Lord" and revelation of the man of sin.

1. The "last days" are to witness a widespread apostasy within the professing church. This appears from many passages of which the chief are: Luke 18:8; 2 Thess. 2:3, 7-12; 1 Tim. 4:1-3; 2 Tim. 3:1-9; 2 Pet. 3: 3-7; 1 John 2:18-23; Jude 3-19; [21] and also 1 Tim. 6: 3-5; 2 Tim. 2:17, 18; 4:3, 4; 2 Pet. 2:1-22; 1 John 4: 1-5; 2 John 7-11; 3 John 9.

---

wheat into my barn.—*Matt. 13: 24-30.*

Then Jesus sent the multitude away, and went into the house: and his disciples came unto him, saying, Declare unto us the parable of the tares of the field.

He answered and said unto them, He that soweth the good seed is the Son of man;

The field is the world; the good seed are the children of the kingdom; but the tares are the children of the wicked *one;*

The enemy that sowed them is the devil; the harvest is the end of the world; and the reapers are the angels.

As therefore the tares are gathered and burned in the fire; so shall it be in the end of this world.

The Son of man shall send forth his angels, and they shall gather out of his kingdom all things that offend, and them which do iniquity;

And shall cast them into a furnace of fire: there shall be wailing and gnashing of teeth.

Then shall the righteous shine forth as the sun in the kingdom of their Father. Who hath ears to hear, let him hear.—*Matt. 13:36-43.*

[21] I tell you that he will avenge them speedily. Nevertheless when the Son of man cometh, shall he find faith on the earth? —*Luke 18:8.*

Let no man deceive you by any means: for *that day shall not come,* except there come a falling away first, and that man of sin be revealed, the son of perdition.—*2 Thess. 2:3.*

For the mystery of iniquity doth already work: only he who now letteth *will let,* until he be taken out of the way.

And then shall that Wicked be revealed, whom the Lord shall consume with the spirit of his mouth, and shall destroy with the brightness of his coming:

Even him, whose coming is after the working of Satan with all power and signs and lying wonders,

And with all deceivableness of unrighteousness in them that perish; because they received not the love of the truth, that they might be saved.

And for this cause God shall send them strong delusion, that they should believe a lie:

That they all might be damned who believed not the truth, but had pleasure in unrighteousness.—*2 Thess. 2: 7-12.*

Now the Spirit speaketh expressly, that in the latter times some shall depart from the faith, giving heed to seducing spirits, and doctrines of devils;

Speaking lies in hypocrisy; having their conscience seared with a hot iron;

Forbidding to marry, *and commanding* to abstain from meats, which God hath created be received with thanksgiving of them which believe and know the truth.—*1 Tim. 4: 1-3.*

This know also, that in the last days perilous times shall come.

For men shall be lovers of their own selves, covetous, boasters, proud, blasphemers, disobedient to parents, unthankful, unholy,

Without natural affection, truce-breakers, false accusers, incontinent, fierce, despisers of those that are good,

Traitors, heady, highminded, lovers of pleasures more than lovers of God;

Having a form of godliness, but denying the power thereof: from such turn away. . . .—*2 Tim. 3: 1-9.*

Knowing this first, that there shall come in the last days scoffers, walking after their own lusts,

And saying, Where is the promise of his coming? for since the fathers fell asleep, all things continue as *they were* from the beginning of the creation.

For this they willingly are ignorant of, that by the word of God the heavens were of old, and the earth standing out of the water and in the water:

Whereby the world that then was, being overflowed with water, perished:

But the heavens and the earth, which are now, by the same word are kept in store, reserved unto fire against the day of judgment and perdition of ungodly men.—*2 Pet. 3: 3-7.*

Little children, it is the last time: and as ye have heard that antichrist shall come, even now are there many antichrists; whereby we know that it is the last time. . . .

Who is a liar but he that denieth that Jesus is the Christ? He is antichrist, that denieth the Father and the Son.

Whosoever denieth the Son, the same hath not the Father: [*but*] he that acknowledgeth the Son hath the Father also.—*1 John 2: 18-23.*

. . . And Enoch also, the seventh from Adam, prophesied of these, saying, Behold, the Lord cometh with ten thousands of his saints,

To execute judgment upon all, and to convince all that are ungodly among them of all their ungodly deeds which they have ungodly committed, and of all their hard *speeches* which ungodly sinners have spoken against him.

These are murmurers, complainers, walking after their own lusts; and their mouth speaketh great swelling *words,* having men's persons in admiration because of advantage.

But, beloved, remember ye the words which were spoken before of the apostles of our Lord Jesus Christ;

How that they told you there should be mockers in the last time, who should walk after their own ungodly lusts.

These be they who separate themselves, sensual, having not the Spirit.—*Jude 3-19.*

Apostasy—"falling away," is disbelief of revealed truth, and is the act of professed Christians who deliberately reject revealed truth, (1) as to the deity of Jesus Christ, and, (2), redemption through His atoning sacrifice (1 John 4:1-3; Phil. 3:18; 2 Pet. 2:1).[22] Error concerning truth may be the result of ignorance (Acts 19:1-6).[23] Even heresy may be due to a snare of Satan (2 Tim. 2:25, 26)[24] in which a true believer, if careless and uninstructed, may be caught. Apostasy does not imply an openly sinful life, or a departure from the outward profession of Christianity. The apostate may be moral, cultured, kind and generous. In the warnings above cited apostasy is traced to false teachers, and their characteristics are given. They "speak great swelling words"; they "promise liberty"; they are "of the world," and "speak of the world." They have the kind of success

---

[22] Beloved, believe not every spirit, but try the spirits whether they are of God: because many false prophets are gone out into the world.

Hereby know ye the Spirit of God: Every spirit that confesseth that Jesus Christ is come in the flesh is of God:

And every spirit that confesseth not that Jesus Christ is come in the flesh is not of God: and this is that *spirit* of antichrist, whereof ye have heard that it should come; and even now already is it in the world.—*1 John 4:1-3.*

For many walk, of whom I have told you often, and now tell you even weeping, *that they are* the enemies of the cross of Christ.—*Phil. 3:18.*

Wherefore laying aside all malice, and all guile, and hypocrisies, and envies, and all evil speakings.—*2 Pet. 2:1.*

[23] And it came to pass, that, while Apollos was at Corinth, Paul having passed through the upper coasts came to Ephesus: and finding certain disciples,

He said unto them, Have ye received the Holy Ghost since ye believed? And they said unto him, We have not so much as heard whether there be any Holy Ghost.

And he said unto them, Unto what then were ye baptized? And they said, Unto John's baptism.

Then said Paul, John verily baptized with the baptism of repentance, saying unto the people, that they should believe on him which should come after him, that is, on Christ Jesus.

When they heard *this*, they were baptized in the name of the Lord Jesus.

And when Paul had laid *his* hands upon them, the Holy Ghost came on them; and they spake with tongues, and prophesied.—*Acts 19:1-6.*

[24] In meekness instructing those that oppose themselves; if God peradventure will give them repentance to the acknowledging of the truth;

And *that* they may recover themselves out of the snare of the devil, who are taken captive by him at his will.—*2 Tim. 2:25, 26.*

which they value, for "the world heareth them" (1 John 2:18, 19; 4:1-5).[25]

2. A new "day," the "day of Christ" (1 Cor. 1:8; 5:5; 2 Cor. 1:14; Phil. 1:6, 10; 2:16)[26] is revealed in connection, always, with the new promise of the return of the Lord made to the new body the church, in the upper chamber:

"I go to prepare a place for you. And if I go and prepare a place for you, I will come again, and receive you unto myself; that where I am, there ye may be also."

The fulfilment of that promise is, indeed, the great theme of prophecy in the Epistles. The "day of Christ" is in no sense a "phase" or "aspect" of the "day of the Lord," as a comparison of the respective passages will show.

According to the Epistles the new upper chamber

---

[25] Little children, it is the last time: and as ye have heard that antichrist shall come, even now are there many antichrists; whereby we know that it is the last time.

They went out from us, but they were not of us; for if they had been of us, they would *no doubt* have continued with us: but *they went out,* that they might be made manifest that they were not all of us.—*1 John 2:18, 19.*

Beloved, believe not every spirit, but try the spirits whether they are of God: because many false prophets are gone out into the world.

Hereby know ye the Spirit of God: Every spirit that confesseth that Jesus Christ is come in the flesh is of God:

And every spirit that confesseth not that Jesus Christ is come in the flesh is not of God: and this is that *spirit* of antichrist whereof ye have heard that it should come; and even now already is it in the world.

Ye are of God, little children, and have overcome them: because greater is he that is in you, than he that is in the world.

They are of the world: therefore speak they of the world, and the world heareth them.— *1 John 4:1-5.*

[26] Who shall also confirm you unto the end, *that ye may be* blameless in the day of our Lord Jesus Christ.—*1 Cor. 1:8.*

To deliver such an one unto Satan for the destruction of the flesh, that the spirit may be saved in the day of the Lord Jesus.—*1 Cor. 5:5.*

As also ye have acknowledged us in part, that we are your rejoicing, even as ye also *are* ours in the day of the Lord Jesus.—*2 Cor. 1:14.*

Being confident of this very thing, that he which hath begun a good work in you will perform *it* until the day of Jesus Christ.—*Phil. 1:6.*

That ye may approve things that are excellent; that ye may be sincere and without offence till the day of Christ.—*Phil. 1:10.*

Holding forth the word of life; that I may rejoice in the day of Christ, that I have not run in vain, neither laboured in vain.—*Phil. 2:16.*

promise of the Lord's return will be fulfilled *in connection with a resurrection,* not of all the dead, but of "they that are Christ's at his coming" (1 Cor. 15:20-23).[27]

"Behold, I shew you a mystery: We shall not all sleep, but we shall all be changed, in a moment, in the twinkling of an eye, at the last trump; for the trumpet shall sound, and the dead shall be raised incorruptible, and we shall be changed. For this corruptible must put on incorruption" (1 Cor. 15:51-53).

The Epistles reveal the *manner* of the fulfilment of the new promise, "I will receive you unto myself." "But I would not have you to be ignorant, brethren, concerning them which are asleep, that ye sorrow not, even as others which have no hope. For if we believe that Jesus died and rose again, even so them also which sleep in Jesus will God bring with him. For this we say unto you by the word of the Lord, that we which are alive and remain unto the coming of the Lord shall not precede them which are asleep. For the Lord himself shall descend from heaven with a shout, with the voice of the archangel, and with the trump of God; and the dead in Christ shall rise first: then we which are alive and remain shall be caught up together with them in the clouds, to meet the Lord in the air: and so shall we ever be with the Lord" (1 Thess. 4:13-17).

If this elaborate description of the manner of the fulfilment of the great new promise to the new body, the church, is compared with the confirmation of the old promise to Israel concerning the kingdom, as set forth in the Olivet Discourse (Matt. 24:25),[28] it will be seen that all is contrast. There His coming is preceded by

---

[27] But now is Christ risen from the dead, *and* become the firstfruits of them that slept.

For since by man *came* death, by man *came* also the resurrection of the dead.

For as in Adam all die, even so in Christ shall all be made alive.

But every man in his own order: Christ the firstfruits; afterward they that are Christ's at his coming.—*1 Cor. 15:20-23.*

[28] Behold, I have told you before.—*Matt. 24:25.*

great signs, and the formula is, "When ye shall see." Here are no signs whatever. There, He is accompanied by angels; here there is no mention of angels. There His coming is visible to "every eye"; here only the sleeping and living "in Christ" are concerned. There His coming is to the earth; here it is into "the air." There His coming is in connection with the "throne of his glory" (Matt. 25:31)[29]; here it is in connection with a "place" among the "many mansions" of the Father's house, which He has gone away to prepare—literally "make ready" for His Bride. It is by no means to be implied that the departure of the church will be a "secret rapture." It will doubtless shake humanity to its center.

And, in the Epistles, this new promise—a promise without a sign, without a single time-note, becomes the "blessed hope" (Titus 2:13)[30] of the church. The Lord is ever "at hand" (Phil. 4:5).[31]

And, too, this "blessed hope," timeless and signless, gives the true attitude of the believer, "till he come" (1 Cor. 11:26).[32] The words which describe that attitude are, "looking" (Titus 2:13; Phil. 3:20),[33] "waiting" (Rom. 8:24, 25; 1 Thess. 1:10).[34] Any interpretation, therefore, of the new promise of His coming which makes it absurd, or a mere form of words without real substance, actually to watch and wait for "his Son from heaven," is condemned by that very fact. It is, in all practical result, saying, "My Lord delayeth his coming."

---

[29] When the Son of man shall come in his glory, and all the holy angels with him, then shall he sit upon the throne of his glory.—*Matt. 25:31.*

[30] Looking for that blessed hope, and the glorious appearing of the great God and our Saviour Jesus Christ.—*Titus 2:13.*

[31] Let your moderation be known unto all men. The Lord is at hand.—*Phil. 4:5.*

[32] For as often as ye eat this bread, and drink this cup, ye do shew the Lord's death till he come.—*1 Cor. 11:26.*

[33] For our citizenship is in heaven; from whence also we wait for a Saviour, the Lord Jesus Christ.—*Phil. 3:20, Revised Version.*

[34] For we are saved by hope: but hope that is seen is not hope: for what a man seeth, why doth he yet hope for? But if we hope for that we see not, *then* do we with patience wait for *it*.—*Rom. 8:24, 25.*
And to wait for his Son from heaven, whom he raised from the dead, *even* Jesus, which delivered us from the wrath to come.—*1 Thess. 1:10.*

PROPHECY IN THE EPISTLES

3. The "day of the Lord" is mentioned in two ways: (1) in relation to the order of events in unfulfilled prophecy; (2) to assure believers that they are not "of" that day.

The "day of the Lord," described in Scripture, both in the Old Testament and the New in terms of wrath and judgment, in which it is in absolute contrast with the new "day of Christ," is mentioned in the Epistles in two ways. (1) The saints of the church are assured that they are not of "that day." That is a "day of darkness, and not light" (Amos 5:18, 20; Joel 2:2; Zeph. 1:15),[35] but the believers are assured that "Ye are all sons of light, and sons of the day: we are *not of the night,* nor of darkness" (1 Thess. 5:1-8).[36] And the "day of the Lord" is a day of wrath (Zeph. 1:15),[37] but, "God hath not appointed us to wrath" (1 Thess. 5:9),[38] And (2) the "day of the Lord" is said to be

---

[35] Woe unto you that desire the day of the Lord! to what end *is* it for you? the day of the Lord *is* darkness, and not light.—*Amos 5:18.*

Shall not the day of the Lord *be* darkness, and no brightness in it?—*Amos 5:20.*

A day of darkness and of gloominess, a day of clouds and of thick darkness, as the morning spread upon the mountains: a great people and a strong; there hath not been ever the like, neither shall be any more after it, *even* to the years of many generations.—*Joel 2:2.*

That day *is* a day of wrath, a day of trouble and distress, a day of wasteness and desolation, a day of darkness and gloominess, a day of clouds and thick darkness.—*Zeph. 1:15.*

[36] But of the times and the seasons, brethren, ye have no need that I write unto you.

For yourselves know perfectly that the day of the Lord so cometh as a thief in the night.

For when they shall say, Peace and safety; then sudden destruction cometh upon them, as travail upon a woman with child; and they shall not escape.

But ye, brethren, are not in darkness, that that day should overtake you as a thief.

Ye are all the children of light, and the children of the day: we are not of the night, nor of darkness.

Therefore let us not sleep, as *do* others; but let us watch and be sober.

For they that sleep sleep in the night; and they that be drunken are drunken in the night.

But let us, who are of the day, be sober, putting on the breastplate of faith and love; and for an helmet, the hope of salvation.—*1 Thess. 5:1-8.*

[37] That day *is* a day of wrath, a day of trouble and distress, a day of wasteness and desolation, a day of darkness and gloominess, a day of clouds and thick darkness.—*Zeph. 1:15.*

[38] For God hath not appointed us to wrath, but to obtain salvation by our Lord Jesus Christ. —*1 Thess: 5:9.*

the day of the "man of sin" (Daniel's "little horn," the "abomination of desolation" of the Olivet Discourse, the "beast out of the sea" of Rev. 13); and the signs which precede the "day of the Lord" are given.

Briefly, then, the prophetic element in the Epistles has to do with the apostasy of the professing church; "the day of Christ"; the taking away of the true church, according to the new promise (John 14:2, 3)[39]; followed by the revelation of the "man of sin" and the "day of the Lord," in which the true church has no part.

And what, in view of current discussions, is of tremendous importance, is the outstanding fact that *not once in the Epistles, written for the especial instruction, warning, and encouragement of the church, is the great tribulation so much as mentioned!*

---

[39] In my Father's house are many mansions: if *it were* not so, I would have told you. I go to prepare a place for you. And if I go and prepare a place for you, I will come again, and receive you unto myself; that where I am, *there* ye may be also.—*John 14: 2, 3.*

IX. THE REVELATION

THE REVELATION gathers up and carries on to complete fulfilment all the visions of all the prophets concerning the future, in so far as these were not fulfilled at the first advent of Jesus Christ. In addition to that which had already been in the prophetic foreview of the Epistles, the future of the church is revealed from the end of the first century to the end of the church period.

Taken in order, the predictive portions of The Revelation are as follows:

1. *"The things which are"* (Rev. 1:19),[1] or the vision of the earth-history of the visible, or professing, church.

This prophecy is told in seven messages from the risen Christ to seven selected churches then existing in the Roman province of Asia. Taken in the order in which they appear in the messages (Rev. 2 and 3), the spiritual state of those churches corresponded exactly to the average spiritual state of the whole professing church as the same would develop historically. The proof of the interpretation which finds in the messages to the seven churches a history in prophetic form of the visible church from the close of the apostolic period to the end, is unanswerable, for it consists of the history which the church has actually made. The church *has* passed through the conditions described in the seven messages.

It is not meant that the messages had, or have, no other purpose. Their primary use was to reveal to those actual churches in John's day those things in which the Lord both approved and disapproved their state. Characteristically, He mentions first the things which He could approve. But the Christ in the glory also rebukes unspar-

---

[1] Write the things which thou hast seen, and the things which are, and the things which shall be hereafter.— *Rev. 1:19.*

ingly whatever He finds wrong. In the promises to the overcomers are given mighty encouragements to those in the churches who may overcome in respect of the evils shown to exist in the church in question. A second use of the messages is that by them any local church of any age may, if it be in earnest to amend its ways, test its spiritual condition. And a third use is that these messages constitute such an unfolding of the mind of Christ about life and service as that any Christian may make the whole message personal, and test himself by it.

But these uses are secondary. The messages, first of all, give a foreview of the history of the professing church. It is the divine way to give, at the beginning of some new thing which God is doing in the earth, a prophecy covering its future. When Israel was about to enter the Land of Promise the whole future of that nation was outlined in the last chapters of Deuteronomy. It has been fulfilled to the very letter. At the beginning of the "times of the Gentiles" God gave, in the Image Vision of Daniel 2, and in the Wild Beast Vision of Daniel 7, a panorama of world-history down to an end not yet reached; and that prophecy has been fulfilled with absolute precision in the great world empires. It would, then, be strange indeed if there were no prophetic vision of church history.

Summarizing the seven messages to the seven churches in Asia, it may be said that in the first of the messages, that to Ephesus,[2] we have a description of the general or

---

[2] Unto the angel of the church of Ephesus write; These things saith he that holdeth the seven stars in his right hand, who walketh in the midst of the seven golden candlesticks;

I know thy works, and thy labour, and thy patience, and how thou canst not bear them which are evil: and thou hast tried them which say they are apostles, and are not, and hast found them liars:

And hast borne, and hast patience, and for my name's sake hast laboured, and hast not fainted.

Nevertheless I have *somewhat* against thee, because thou hast left thy first love.

Remember therefore from whence thou art fallen, and repent, and do the first works; or else I will come unto thee quickly, and will remove thy candlestick out of his place, except thou repent.

But this thou hast, that thou hatest the deeds of the Nicolaitanes, which I also hate.

He that hath an ear, let him hear what the Spirit saith unto the churches; To him that overcometh will I give to eat of the

average state of the church at large at the end of the first century. All of the apostles except John had sealed their faith in martyrdom. As to actual vigor of life the condition of the church was excellent. Good works abounded, and there was zeal for purity of doctrine (Rev. 2:2, 3). But a change had taken place which, if not repented of, would prove fatal. The church had "left" first love. The motive back of all that abundant service had insensibly changed from devotion to Christ *Himself* (comp. John 21: 15-17) to zeal for His "name" (v. 3). There was a great "cause" now—Christianity. But that which alone gives value to service is the personal devotedness of first love (John 21: 15-17).[3] And so serious is the loss of first love, that no fervency of zeal in service can take its place. "I will come unto thee quickly, and will remove thy candlestick out of his place, except thou repent."

First love has been defined as "complete satisfaction of the heart with its object." There is no outward test of it. Surely not work, nor even "labor," for these abounded still at Ephesus, while the motive was His "name's sake." The day of "denominations" with their claim upon Christian loyalty was yet in the far future. The rift in the lute that was to widen and make the music mute was still seemingly slight. It was still possible to repent, and do the "first works." This seems without doubt a reference to soul winning.

The second message, that to Smyrna (Rev. 2: 8-11),[4]

---

tree of life, which is in the midst of the Paradise of God.— *Rev. 2: 1-7.*

[3] So when they had dined, Jesus saith to Simon Peter, Simon, *son* of Jonas, lovest thou me more than these? He saith unto him, Yea, Lord; thou knowest that I love thee. He saith unto him, Feed my lambs.

He saith to him again the second time, Simon, *son* of Jonas, lovest thou me? He saith unto him, Yea, Lord; thou knowest that I love thee. He saith unto him, Feed my sheep.

He saith unto him the third time, Simon, *son* of Jonas, lovest thou me? Peter was grieved because he said unto him the third time, Lovest thou me? And he said unto him, Lord, thou knowest all things; thou knowest that I love thee. Jesus saith unto him, Feed my sheep —*John 21: 15-17.*

[4] And unto the angel of the church in Smyrna write; These things saith the first and the last, which was dead, and is alive;

I know thy works, and tribulation, and poverty, (but thou art rich) and *I know* the blas-

belongs to the period of the great systematic persecutions which followed the close of the apostolic period, and lasted during the second and third centuries. Persecution, relentless and cruel, had indeed followed the extension of Christianity throughout the Roman Empire, but such assaults upon the infant church were local, sporadic, and usually instigated by unbelieving Jews. But during the second and third centuries bitter and persistent attempts were made by the imperial authority, and in every part of the Roman Empire, to exterminate the new faith. It is touching to see that this message has only commendation. The great Head of the body would not rebuke a church in persecution.

The third message [5] has an unmistakable application to the third period of church history—the times following the alleged conversion of Constantine, under whom Christianity became the court religion. So far from profession of faith in Christ being the signal for persecution, it now became the condition of preferment. Legions of Roman soldiers were baptized with not even the pretense of conversion. The revenues of heathen temples were

---

phemy of them which say they are Jews, and are not, but *are* the synagogue of Satan.

Fear none of those things which thou shalt suffer: behold, the devil shall cast *some* of you into prison, that ye may be tried; and ye shall have tribulation ten days: be thou faithful unto death, and I will give thee a crown of life.

He that hath an ear, let him hear what the Spirit saith unto the churches; He that overcometh shall not be hurt of the second death.—*Rev. 2:8-11.*

[5] And to the angel of the church in Pergamos write; These things saith he which hath the sharp sword with two edges;

I know thy works, and where thou dwellest, *even* where Satan's seat *is:* and thou holdest fast my name, and hast not denied my faith, even in those days wherein Antipas *was* my faithful martyr, who was slain among you, where Satan dwelleth.

But I have a few things against thee, because thou hast there them that hold the doctrine of Balaam, who taught Balac to cast a stumblingblock before the children of Israel, to eat things sacrificed unto idols, and to commit fornication.

So hast thou also them that hold the doctrine of the Nicolaitanes, which thing I hate.

Repent; or else I will come unto thee quickly, and will fight against them with the sword of my mouth.

He that hath an ear, let him hear what the Spirit saith unto the churches; To him that overcometh will I give to eat of the hidden manna, and will give him a white stone, and in the stone a new name written, which no man knoweth saving he that receiveth *it.*—*Rev. 2: 9-17.*

THE REVELATION

used to endow bishoprics. Singularly enough there was great zeal for correct doctrine, along with an utter departure from the apostolic simplicity in church order. It was the period of the great creeds.

How suited the message! "I know thy works, and where thou dwellest, even where Satan's throne is . . . where Satan dwelleth." Alas! the "stranger" and "pilgrim" church had not only left her first love but, uncured by the fires of her persecution, had become an earth-dweller. Nay, worse than that, had settled down in the "world," "where Satan's throne is." Satan does not reign in hell—that is the place of his eternal punishment (Rev. 20:10).[6] He is the "prince" and "god" of this world (John 14:30; 2 Cor. 4:4).[7] It is the world-system, organized upon the Satanic principles of avarice, pride, brute force, ambition—not the "world" of men nor of nature—into which the church settled down in the fourth century.

The fourth message pictures a condition which is an inevitable consequence of the state described in the message to Pergamos. If 'Christianity as represented by the professing church is to settle down in the world it must adjust itself to worldly conditions. It must claim authority both to teach and to rule. And this is precisely what occurred historically in the centuries following the professed conversion of Constantine until the mighty voice of Luther called men back to the Bible. Thyatira has every essential mark of the Roman apostasy.[8] Conspicuous for charity and "works," and by no

---

[6] And the devil that deceived them was cast into the lake of fire and brimstone, where the beast and the false prophet are, and shall be tormented day and night for ever and ever.—*Rev. 20:10.*

[7] Hereafter I will not talk much with you: for the prince of this world cometh, and hath nothing in me.—*John 14:30.*

In whom the god of this world hath blinded the minds of them which believe not, lest the light of the glorious gospel of Christ, who is the image of God, should shine unto them.—*2 Cor. 4:4.*

[8] And unto the angel of the church in Thyatira write; These things saith the Son of God, who hath his eyes like unto a flame of fire, and his feet are like fine brass;

I know thy works, and charity, and service, and faith, and thy patience, and thy works; and the last *to be* more than the first.

Notwithstanding I have a few things against thee, because thou

means destitute of faith though denying its sufficiency for salvation, Rome has yet been a true Jezebel, bringing pagan practises into her ritual; assuming authority to teach; forming unclean alliances with the nations, and persecuting the true church (1 Kings 21:25).[9]

The message, however, recognizes in that mass of apostate profession a "rest," or remnant (v. 24) of true believers, and to this remnant the risen Christ renews the *new* promise of His coming—the upper chamber promise: "And I will give him the morning star" (v. 28). In the older promise, that to Israel, His return is likened to the rising of the sun (Mal. 4:2).[10] But in nature there is something which precedes the sun-rising; it is the morning star. In Malachi the rising of "the Sun of righteousness" ushers in the terrible "day of the Lord," "that shall burn as an oven" (Mal. 4:1),[11] but

---

sufferest that woman Jezebel, which calleth herself a prophetess, to teach and to seduce my servants to commit fornication, and to eat things sacrificed unto idols.

And I gave her space to repent of her fornication; and she repented not.

Behold, I will cast her into a bed, and them that commit adultery with her into great tribulation, except they repent of their deeds.

And I will kill her children with death; and all the churches shall know that I am he which searcheth the reins and hearts: and I will give unto every one of you according to your works.

But unto you I say, and unto the rest in Thyatira, as many as have not this doctrine, and which have not known the depths of Satan, as they speak; I will put upon you none other burden.

But that which ye have *already*, hold fast till I come.

And he that overcometh, and keepeth my works unto the end, to him will I give power over the nations:

And he shall rule them with a rod of iron; as the vessels of a potter shall they be broken to shivers: even as I received of my Father.

And I will give him the morning star.

He that hath an ear, let him hear what the Spirit saith unto the churches.—*Rev. 2: 18-29.*

[9] But there was none like unto Ahab, which did sell himself to work wickedness in the sight of the Lord, whom Jezebel his wife stirred up.—*1 Kings 21: 25.*

[10] But unto you that fear my name shall the Sun of righteousness arise with healing in his wings; and ye shall go forth, and grow up as calves of the stall.—*Mal. 4: 2.*

[11] For, behold, the day cometh, that shall burn as an oven; and all the proud, yea, and all that do wickedly, shall be stubble: and the day that cometh shall burn them up, saith the Lord of hosts, that it shall leave them neither root nor branch.—*Mal. 4: 1.*

believers are not "appointed unto wrath" (1 Thess. 5: 9),[12] and true believers, even in Thyatira, shall be given "the morning star."

The fifth message, that to Sardis (Rev. 3:1-6)[13] speaks of the Protestant Reformation, for, historically, it was that which broke the long night of the dark ages. The keyword is, "I have not found thy works perfect [literally, 'fulfilled'] before my God." There was a remarkable arrest in the progress of the Reformation movement, which has attracted the attention of the secular historians of this period. Macaulay calls attention to the "singular fact" that after having gained nearly half of Europe, the Reformation not only ceased to gain, but lost nearly half of that which it had gained. The explanation is to be found in the fact that almost immediately the movement lost unity. Following human leaders, and so dividing into sects, marked by a bitter and controversial spirit, it is small wonder that the one work committed to the church, that of world-wide evangelization, was forgotten. Forgotten, too, was the hope and expectation of the return of the Lord, until the distinctive hope of the church (John 14:1-3; 1 Thess. 4:14-17)[14] became confused with the Jewish expectation,

---

[12] For God hath not appointed us to wrath, but to obtain salvation by our Lord Jesus Christ. —*1 Thess. 5:9.*

[13] And unto the angel of the church in Sardis write; These things saith he that hath the seven Spirits of God, and the seven stars; I know thy works, that thou hast a name that thou livest, and art dead.

Be watchful, and strengthen the things which remain, that are ready to die: for I have not found thy works perfect before God.

Remember therefore how thou hast received and heard, and hold fast, and repent. If therefore thou shalt not watch, I will come on thee as a thief, and thou shalt not know what hour I will come upon thee.

Thou hast a few names even in Sardis which have not defiled their garments; and they shall walk with me in white: for they are worthy.

He that overcometh, the same shall be clothed in white raiment; and I will not blot out his name out of the book of life, but I will confess his name before my Father, and before his angels.

He that hath an ear, let him hear what the Spirit saith unto the churches.—*Rev. 3: 1-6.*

[14] Let not your heart be troubled: ye believe in God, believe also in me.

In my Father's house are many mansions: if it were not so, I would have told you. I go to prepare a place for you.

And if I go and prepare a place for you, I will come again, and receive you unto myself;

and the whole doctrine fell into neglect and then into disbelief. Hence the warning:

"If therefore thou shalt not watch, I will come on thee as a thief, and thou shalt not know what hour I will come upon thee." Significant, too, in the light of present conditions, the weakening of the old faith in the authority of the Bible, and the decay of doctrine, is the warning: "Be watchful, and strengthen the things which remain, that are ready to die . . . remember how thou hast received and heard." Protestantism, in the grace of God, had received an open Bible—always, in any state of the church, the one resource for faith.

The two remaining messages, that to Philadelphia, and the final message, to Laodicea (Rev. 3:7-13; 3:14-22),[15] evidently present the two-fold state of Prot-

---

that where I am, *there* ye may be also.—*John 14: 1-3*.

For if we believe that Jesus died and rose again, even so them also which sleep in Jesus will God bring with him.

For this we say unto you by the word of the Lord, that we which are alive *and* remain unto the coming of the Lord shall not prevent them which are asleep.

For the Lord himself shall descend from heaven with a shout, with the voice of the archangel, and with the trump of God: and the dead in Christ shall rise first:

Then we which are alive *and* remain shall be caught up together with them in the clouds, to meet the Lord in the air: and so shall we ever be with the Lord.—*1 Thess. 4: 14-17*.

[15] And to the angel of the church in Philadelphia write: These things saith he that is holy, he that is true, he that hath the key of David, he that openeth, and no man shutteth; and shutteth, and no man openeth;

I know thy works: behold, I have set before thee an open door, and no man can shut it: for thou hast a little strength, and hast kept my word, and hast not denied my name.

Behold, I will make them of the synagogue of Satan, which say they are Jews, and are not, but do lie; behold, I will make them to come and worship before thy feet, and to know that I have loved thee.

Because thou hast kept the word of my patience, I also will keep thee from the hour of temptation, which shall come upon all the world, to try them that dwell upon the earth.

Behold, I come quickly: hold that fast which thou hast, that no man take thy crown.

Him that overcometh will I make a pillar in the temple of my God, and he shall go no more out: and I will write upon him the name of my God, and the name of the city of my God, *which is* new Jerusalem, which cometh down out of heaven from my God: and *I will write upon him* my new name.

He that hath an ear, let him hear what the Spirit saith unto the churches.—*Rev. 3: 7-13*.

And unto the angel of the church of the Laodiceans write; These things saith the Amen, the faithful and true witness,

estantism at the end—a differing state found, not in any one sect, but in all the sects. In all there are Philadelphians; in all there are Laodiceans. And again the interpretation which finds in the messages to Philadelphia and to Laodicea prophetic pictures of the state of the Protestant churches at the end of the church period is confirmed by the indisputable facts. What is there prophesied has come to pass. Not merely in every denomination, but in every local church, this division into the few who pray and witness and work, and the many who do neither, exists. What proportion of the members in any church habitually attend the prayer and missionary meetings, or have ever brought a sinner to Christ?

In the message the Philadelphians are characterized by faith: "thou hast kept my word, and hast not denied my name"; and by "a little strength" (literally, "power"). To such, right up to the end, is promised an open door, for service, and exemption from the great tribulation: "Because thou hast kept the word of my patience, I also will keep thee from [literally, 'out of'] the hour of temptation, which shall come upon all the world to try them that dwell upon the earth."

It is, indeed, and quite apart from this specific promise, remarkable that any should have supposed it possible in the light of Scripture for the true church to go

---

the beginning of the creation of God;

I know thy works, that thou art neither cold nor hot: I would thou wert cold or hot.

So then because thou art lukewarm, and neither cold nor hot, I will spue thee out of my mouth.

Because thou sayest, I am rich, and increased with goods, and have need of nothing; and knowest not that thou art wretched, and miserable, and poor, and blind, and naked:

I counsel thee to buy of me gold tried in the fire, that thou mayest be rich; and white raiment, that thou mayest be clothed, and *that* the shame of thy nakedness do not appear; and anoint thine eyes with eyesalve, that thou mayest see.

As many as I love, I rebuke and chasten: be zealous therefore, and repent.

Behold, I stand at the door, and knock: if any man hear my voice, and open the door, I will come in to him, and will sup with him, and he with me.

To him that overcometh will I grant to sit with me in my throne, even as I also overcame, and am set down with my Father in his throne.

He that hath an ear, let him hear what the Spirit saith unto the churches.—*Rev. 3: 14-22.*

through the great tribulation (Matt. 24:21; Jer. 30: 4-7).[16] The church knows *much* tribulation (Acts 14: 22; 1 Pet. 4:12-19; James 5:1-9),[17] but the great tribu-

---

[16] For there shall be great tribulation, such as was not since the beginning of the world to this time, nor ever shall be.—*Matt. 24:21.*

And these *are* the words that the Lord spake concerning Israel and concerning Judah.

For thus saith the Lord; We have heard a voice of trembling, of fear, and not of peace.

Ask ye now, and see whether a man doth travail with child? wherefore do I see every man with his hands on his loins, as a woman in travail, and all faces are turned into paleness?

Alas! for that day *is* great, so that none *is* like it: *it* is even the time of Jacob's trouble; but he shall be saved out of it.—*Jer. 30:4-7.*

[17] Confirming the souls of the disciples, *and* exhorting them to continue in the faith, and that we must through much tribulation enter into the kingdom of God.—*Acts 14:22.*

Beloved, think it not strange concerning the fiery trial which is to try you, as though some strange thing happened unto you:

But rejoice, inasmuch as ye are partakers of Christ's sufferings; that, when his glory shall be revealed, ye may be glad also with exceeding joy.

If ye be reproached for the name of Christ, happy *are ye;* for the spirit of glory and of God resteth upon you: on their part he is evil spoken of, but on your part he is glorified.

But let none of you suffer as a murderer, or *as* a thief, or *as* an evildoer, or as a busybody in other men's matters.

Yet if *any man suffer* as a Christian, let him not be ashamed; but let him glorify God on this behalf.

For the time *is come* that judgment must begin at the house of God: and if *it* first *begin* at us, what shall the end *be* of them that obey not the gospel of God?

And if the righteous scarcely be saved, where shall the ungodly and the sinner appear?

Wherefore let them that suffer according to the will of God commit the keeping of their souls *to him* in well doing, as unto a faithful Creator.—*1 Pet. 4:12-19.*

Go to now, *ye* rich men, weep and howl for your miseries that shall come upon *you.*

Your riches are corrupted, and your garments are motheaten.

Your gold and silver is cankered; and the rust of them shall be a witness against you, and shall eat your flesh as it were fire. Ye have heaped treasure together for the last days.

Behold, the hire of the labourers who have reaped down your fields, which is of you kept back by fraud, crieth: and the cries of them which have reaped are entered into the ears of the Lord of sabaoth.

Ye have lived in pleasure on the earth, and been wanton; ye have nourished your hearts, as in a day of slaughter.

Ye have condemned *and* killed the just; *and* he doth not resist you.

Be patient therefore, brethren, unto the coming of the Lord. Behold, the husbandman waiteth for the precious fruit of the earth, and hath long patience for it, until he receive the early and latter rain.

Be ye also patient; stablish your hearts: for the coming of the Lord draweth nigh.

Grudge not one against another, brethren, lest ye be condemned: behold, the judge standeth before the door.—*James 5:1-9.*

THE REVELATION

lation is never once mentioned in connection with the first resurrection; never mentioned in connection with the departure of the church to meet the Lord in the air (1 Thess. 4: 14-17)[18]; never mentioned at all in the Epistles, which were written for the instruction of the church! On the contrary, the great tribulation is both judgment and wrath, and the church is promised exemption from both (Rev. 14: 15, 16; 15: 7, 8; 16: 1-21; 1 Thess. 5: 1-9; John 5: 24).[19] And perhaps still more conclusively,

---

[18] For if we believe that Jesus died and rose again, even so them also which sleep in Jesus will God bring with him.

For this we say unto you by the word of the Lord, that we which are alive and remain unto the coming of the Lord shall not prevent them which are asleep.

For the Lord himself shall descend from heaven with a shout, with the voice of the archangel, and with the trump of God: and the dead in Christ shall rise first:

Then we which are alive and remain shall be caught up together with them in the clouds, to meet the Lord in the air: and so shall we ever be with the Lord.—*1 Thess. 4: 14-17.*

[19] And another angel came out of the temple, crying with a loud voice to him that sat on the cloud, Thrust in thy sickle, and reap: for the time is come for thee to reap; for the harvest of the earth is ripe.

And he that sat on the cloud thrust in his sickle on the earth; and the earth was reaped.—*Rev. 14: 15, 16.*

And one of the four beasts gave unto the seven angels seven golden vials full of the wrath of God, who liveth for ever and ever.

And the temple was filled with smoke from the glory of God, and from his power; and no man was able to enter into the temple, till the seven plagues of the seven angels were fulfilled.—*Rev. 15: 7, 8.*

And I heard a great voice out of the temple saying to the seven angels, Go your ways, and pour out the vials of the wrath of God upon the earth.

And the first went, and poured out his vial upon the earth; and there fell a noisome and grievous sore upon the men which had the mark of the beast, and *upon* them which worshipped his image.

And the second angel poured out his vial upon the sea; and it became as the blood of a dead *man:* and every living soul died in the sea.

And the third angel poured out his vial upon the rivers and fountains of waters; and they became blood.

And I heard the angel of the waters say, Thou art righteous, O Lord, which art, and wast, and shalt be, because thou hast judged thus.

For they have shed the blood of saints and prophets, and thou hast given them blood to drink; for they are worthy.

And I heard another out of the altar say, Even so, Lord God Almighty, true and righteous *are* thy judgments.

And the fourth angel poured out his vial upon the sun; and power was given unto him to scorch men with fire.

And men were scorched with great heat, and blasphemed the name of God, which hath power over these plagues: and they repented not to give him glory.

in the portions of The Revelation which describe with curious minuteness the events which make up the great tribulation, the church is not once mentioned. The rea-

---

And the fifth angel poured out his vial upon the seat of the beast; and his kingdom was full of darkness; and they gnawed their tongues for pain.

And blasphemed the God of heaven because of their pains and their sores, and repented not of their deeds.

And the sixth angel poured out his vial upon the great river Euphrates; and the water thereof was dried up, that the way of the kings of the east might be prepared.

And I saw three unclean spirits like frogs *come* out of the mouth of the dragon, and out of the mouth of the beast, and out of the mouth of the false prophet.

For they are the spirits of devils, working miracles, *which* go forth unto the kings of the earth and of the whole world, to gather them to the battle of that great day of God Almighty.

Behold, I come as a thief. Blessed *is* he that watcheth, and keepeth his garments, lest he walk naked, and they see his shame.

And he gathered them together into a place called in the Hebrew tongue Armageddon.

And the seventh angel poured out his vial into the air; and there came a great voice out of the temple of heaven, from the throne, saying, It is done.

And there were voices, and thunders, and lightnings; and there was a great earthquake, such as was not since men were upon the earth, so mighty an earthquake, *and* so great.

And the great city was divided into three parts, and the cities of the nations fell: and great Babylon came in remembrance before God, to give unto her the cup of the wine of the fierceness of his wrath.

And every island fled away, and the mountains were not found.

And there fell upon men a great hail out of heaven, *every stone* about the weight of a talent: and men blasphemed God because of the plague of the hail; for the plague thereof was exceeding great.—*Rev. 16: 1-21.*

But of the times and the seasons, brethren, ye have no need that I write unto you.

For yourselves know perfectly that the day of the Lord so cometh as a thief in the night.

For when they shall say, Peace and safety; then sudden destruction cometh upon them, as travail upon a woman with child; and they shall not escape.

But ye, brethren, are not in darkness, that that day should overtake you as a thief.

Ye are all the children of light, and the children of the day: we are not of the night, nor of darkness.

Therefore let us not sleep, as *do* others; but let us watch and be sober.

For they that sleep sleep in the night; and they that be drunken are drunken in the night.

But let us, who are of the day, be sober, putting on the breastplate of faith and love: and for an helmet, the hope of salvation.

For God hath not appointed us to wrath, but to obtain salvation by our Lord Jesus Christ. —*1 Thess. 5: 1-9.*

Verily, verily, I say unto you, He that heareth my word, and believeth on him that sent me, hath everlasting life, and shall not come into condemnation; but is passed from death unto life.—*John 5: 24.*

son is obvious: the true church is with the Lord, and the mass of Laodicean profession, utterly apostate, is no longer even called a church, but "Babylon."

The Laodicean spirit, however, is one of boastfulness, of pride in numbers and in the outward apparent prosperity of the church. With all this groundless optimism, there is utter blindness to the real unspirituality of the mass of professing church-members. "Because thou sayest, I am rich, and increased with goods, and have need of nothing; and knowest not that thou art wretched, and miserable, and poor, and blind, and naked."

The result is lukewarmness, and the end rejection by the Lord with disgust: "So then because thou art lukewarm, and neither cold nor hot, I will spue thee out of my mouth."

Removing the real believers who have kept His word and have not denied His name before the great tribulation (Rev. 3: 10; 1 Thess. 4: 14-17),[20] the mass of Laodicean lukewarmness and mere profession is left to its horrors.

---

[20] Because thou hast kept the word of my patience, I also will keep thee from the hour of temptation, which shall come upon all the world, to try them that dwell upon the earth.—*Rev. 3: 10.*

X. THE LAST SEVEN YEARS OF THE AGE

TO the Prophet Daniel, the prophet of the "times of the Gentiles," was given through the angel Gabriel a measure of time from the first year of Darius the Mede, first king of the second or Medo-Persian world empire (538 B. C.), to the full establishment of Messiah's kingdom of heaven (Dan. 9: 1, 20-27).[1] The measure is given in a series of sevens, and of these there are to be seventy (Dan. 9: 24). The word

---

[1] In the first year of Darius the son of Ahasuerus, of the seed of the Medes, which was made king over the realm of the Chaldeans. . . .

And whiles I *was* speaking, and praying, and confessing my sin and the sin of my people Israel, and presenting my supplication before the Lord my God for the holy mountain of my God;

Yea, whiles I *was* speaking in prayer, even the man Gabriel, whom I had seen in the vision at the beginning, being caused to fly swiftly, touched me about the time of the evening oblation.

And he informed *me*, and talked with me, and said, O Daniel, I am now come forth to give thee skill and understanding.

At the beginning of thy supplications, the commandment came forth, and I am come to shew *thee*, for thou *art* greatly beloved: therefore understand the matter, and consider the vision.

Seventy weeks are determined upon thy people and upon thy holy city, to finish the transgression, and to make an end of sins, and to make reconciliation for iniquity, and to bring in everlasting righteousness, and to seal up the vision and prophecy, and to anoint the most Holy.

Know therefore and understand, *that* from the going forth of the commandment to restore and to build Jerusalem unto the Messiah the Prince *shall be* seven weeks, and threescore and two weeks: the street shall be built again, and the wall, even in troublous times.

And after threescore and two weeks shall Messiah be cut off, but not for himself: and the people of the prince that shall come shall destroy the city and the sanctuary; and the end thereof *shall be* with a flood, and unto the end of the war desolations are determined.

And he shall confirm the covenant with many for one week: and in the midst of the week he shall cause the sacrifice and the oblation to cease, and for the overspreading of abominations he shall make *it* desolate, even until the consummation, and that determined shall be poured upon the desolate.—*Dan. 9: 1, 20-27.*

"weeks" is not in the original, which speaks only of seventy sevens. But the process of fulfilment makes it sure that "weeks," that is, weeks of years—seven years to a "week" is right. In other words 490 years of the dealing of God with His chosen people were to interpose between 538 B. C. and the consummation of that dealing in the establishment of the kingdom. But the prophecy does not say, nor may it be inferred, that the divine dealing is to be continuous—that is, without interruption.

Indeed, certain divisions of the time are distinctly announced. There is, first, a period of seven sevens=49 years during which Jerusalem is to be rebuilt, and this was fulfilled as we are told by Ezra and Nehemiah. Secondly, there is to be a period of sixty-two sevens =434 years "unto the Messiah" who is to be "cut off." And this also was exactly fulfilled according to Biblical chronology. Whatever confusion has existed at that point has been due to following the Ptolemaic instead of the Biblical chronology, as Anstey in his "Romance of Biblical Chronology" (Association Press, New York City) has shown.

But there is still one final seven, or "week," to complete the "seventy sevens" or 490 years of the divine dealing with Daniel's people, "To finish the transgression, and to make an end of sins, and to make reconciliation for iniquity, and to bring in everlasting righteousness, and to seal up the vision and prophecy, and to anoint the most Holy [place]." But this consummation is Kingdom work, as we know from the abundant testimony of the Prophets.

We are, therefore, confronted with the question, Why did fulfilment of the seventy weeks' prophecy stop short with the cutting off of Messiah at the end of the sixty-ninth week? It is the question which any acceptable scheme of prophetic interpretation must answer.

The Biblical answer is to be found in our Lord's revelation concerning His departure, return, and certain "Mysteries of the kingdom of heaven" (that is, divine secrets hitherto hidden, but now revealed) which must be fulfilled during His absence. These "mysteries" are gathered into the thirteenth chapter of Matthew. From these it becomes evident that the events of Daniel's last, or seventieth "seven," that is, seven years, constitute a *postponed* dealing—the seventieth week of seven years is cut off, and separated from the sixty-nine; and the interval, already of nineteen hundred years' duration, is the period during which the two great divine secrets— the outcalling of the church, and the mysteries of the kingdom of heaven, run their course. Both seem well-nigh completed. If this is true, the seventieth week of Daniel is upon the very horizon.

It is significant that our Lord in His great prophetic discourse from the Mount of Olives, when he reaches the time of the end refers us to Daniel. It is not the way of God to discredit His prophets.

"When ye therefore shall see the abomination of desolation, spoken of by Daniel the prophet, stand in the holy place (whoso readeth let him understand,)" etc.

Turning, then, to Daniel's ninth chapter we find the following:

"And after the threescore and two weeks shall the anointed one be cut off, and shall have nothing: and the people of the prince that shall come shall destroy the city and the sanctuary; and the end thereof shall be with a flood" (v. 26, Revised Version).

Here we are still on the firm ground of fulfilled prophecy. After the cutting off of Messiah, fulfilled in the crucifixion of Christ, the Romans came against Jerusalem and destroyed city and temple, as predicted by Daniel, and by our Lord. But the passage quoted goes farther. A "prince" is to come who is to be "the Abomination." And now we know from whence he will come, for it was his "people," the Romans, who were the destroyers. He will not, therefore, be a Russian, or a German, for Rome did not then rule those regions; neither will he be a Jew.

And, having mentioned the man who bulks so large in all prophecies of the consummation of the age which follows the cutting off of Messiah, the Spirit takes Daniel straight across the centuries to the "end"—that is to say, to the events of the postponed or seventieth week.

"And even unto the end shall be war; desolations are determined" (v. 26).

The "end" in Daniel, as a careful reading of the passages will make clear, is not an instant of time, but a period of time—the seventieth "week," that is, the last seven years of this age. Unto this "end," whatever easy optimists may imagine, "shall be war." And so it has been from the date of the prophecy of the Seventy Weeks, 538 B. C. to this very year—2,454 years of war!

Having introduced "the prince that shall come" the Seventy Weeks prophecy adds a word as to his doings:

"And he shall make a firm covenant with many for one week" (seven years): "and in the midst of the week" (that is, after three and one-half years) "he shall cause the sacrifice and the oblation to cease; and upon the pinnacle of abominations [that is, 'as the summit abomination'] one that maketh desolate; and even unto the full end, and that determined, shall wrath be poured out upon the desolator" (Dan. 9:27).

This "wrath" our Lord interprets:

"For then shall be great tribulation, such as was not since the beginning of the world to this time, no, nor ever shall be" (Matt. 24:21). And the supreme, or "pinnacle" abomination of the "prince that shall come" is something which he does in "the holy place." What that pinnacle abomination is we learn from express words in 2 Thessalonians 2:1-10:

"Now we beseech you, brethren, touching the coming of our Lord Jesus Christ, and our gathering together unto him; to the end that ye be not quickly shaken from your mind, nor yet be troubled, either by spirit, or by word, or by epistle as from us, as that the day of the Lord is just at hand; let no man beguile you in any wise: for *it will not be,* except the falling away come first, and the man of sin be revealed, the son of perdition, he that opposeth and exalteth himself against all that is called God or that is worshipped; so that he sitteth in the temple of God, setting himself forth as God. Remember ye not, that, when I was yet with you, I told you these things? And now ye know that which restraineth, to the end that he may be revealed in his

THE LAST SEVEN YEARS OF THE AGE

own season. For the mystery of lawlessness doth already work: only *there is* one that restraineth now, until he be taken out of the way. And then shall be revealed the lawless one, whom the Lord Jesus shall slay with the breath of his mouth, and bring to nought by the manifestation of his coming; *even he,* whose coming is according to the working of Satan with all power and signs and lying wonders, and with all deceit of unrighteousness for them that perish; because they received not the love of the truth, that they might be saved."

Daniel's "prince that shall come," our Lord's "abomination," and Paul's "man of sin," all refer to the same person. He is a ruler, in political sovereignty over regions which include Jerusalem, for he makes a covenant with "many," who can only be unbelieving Jews in Jerusalem, permitting the restoration of the temple service ("sacrifice and oblation," Dan. 9:27)[2] for one "week." This covenant he violates in the middle of the week, and reaches the "pinnacle" of his abominations by entering the holy place of the restored temple and demanding human worship. From this time the "great tribulation" begins (Matt. 24:21)[3] and runs its awful course of three and one-half years—the last half of Daniel's seventieth "week" (Dan. 12:11; Jer. 30:7; Dan. 12:1; Matt. 24:21).[4] The last seven years of the present age, then,

---

[2] And he shall confirm the covenant with many for one week: and in the midst of the week he shall cause the sacrifice and the oblation to cease, and for the overspreading of abominations he shall make *it* desolate, even until the consummation, and that determined shall be poured upon the desolate.—*Dan. 9:27.*

[3] For then shall be great tribulation, such as was not since the beginning of the world to this time, no, nor ever shall be.—*Matt. 24:21.*

[4] And from the time *that* the daily *sacrifice* shall be taken away, and the abomination that maketh desolate set up, *there shall be* a thousand two hundred and ninety days.—*Dan. 12:11.*

Alas! for that day *is* great, so that none *is* like it: it *is* even the time of Jacob's trouble; but he shall be saved out of it.—*Jer. 30:7.*

And at that time shall Michael stand up, the great prince which standeth for the children of thy people: and there shall be a time of trouble, such as never was since there was a nation *even* to that same time: and at that time thy people shall be delivered, every one that shall be found written in the book.—*Dan. 12:1.*

For then shall be great tribulation, such as was not since the beginning of the world to this time, nor ever shall be.—*Matt. 24:21.*

witness the rise, reign, and destruction of the fearful being thus referred to.

But before the vision of the Seventy Weeks this personage has been revealed to Daniel. In the Wild Beast Vision of Daniel 7[5] he appears as the "little horn."

[5] In the first year of Belshazzar king of Babylon Daniel had a dream and visions of his head upon his bed: then he wrote the dream, *and* told the sum of the matters.

Daniel spake and said, I saw in my vision by night, and, behold, the four winds of the heaven strove upon the great sea.

And four great beasts came up from the sea, diverse one from another.

The first *was* like a lion, and had eagle's wings: I beheld till the wings thereof were plucked, and it was lifted up from the earth, and made stand upon the feet as a man, and a man's heart was given to it.

And behold another beast, a second, like to a bear, and it raised up itself on one side, and *it had* three ribs in the mouth of it between the teeth of it: and they said thus unto it, Arise, devour much flesh.

After this I beheld, and lo another, like a leopard, which had upon the back of it four wings of a fowl; the beast had also four heads; and dominion was given to it.

After this I saw in the night visions, and behold a fourth beast, dreadful and terrible, and strong exceedingly; and it had great iron teeth: it devoured and brake in pieces, and stamped the residue with the feet of it: and it *was* diverse from all the beasts that *were* before it; and it had ten horns.

I considered the horns, and, behold, there came up among them another little horn, before whom there were three of the first horns plucked up by the roots: and, behold, in this horn *were* eyes like the eyes of man, and a mouth speaking great things.

I beheld till the thrones were cast down, and the Ancient of days did sit, whose garment *was* white as snow, and the hair of his head like the pure wool: his throne *was like* the fiery flame, *and* his wheels *as* burning fire.

A fiery stream issued and came forth from before him: thousand thousands ministered unto him, and ten thousand times ten thousand stood before him: the judgment was set, and the books were opened.

I beheld then because of the voice of the great words which the horn spake: I beheld *even* till the beast was slain, and his body destroyed, and given to the burning flame.

As concerning the rest of the beasts, they had their dominion taken away: yet their lives were prolonged for a season and time.

I saw in the night visions, and, behold, *one* like the Son of man came with the clouds of heaven, and came to the Ancient of days, and they brought him near before him.

And there was given him dominion, and glory, and a kingdom, that all people, nations, and languages, should serve him: his dominion *is* an everlasting dominion, which shall not pass away, and his kingdom *that* which shall not be destroyed.

I Daniel was grieved in my spirit in the midst of *my* body, and the visions of my head troubled me.

I came near unto one of them that stood by, and asked him the truth of all this. So he told

The whole course of the "times of the Gentiles" (Luke 21:24),[6] which was shown to King Nebuchadnezzar as an imposing image, is revealed to Daniel under the similitude of four wild beasts, answering to the four world empires of the image vision, but exposing the true nature of Gentile world-rule as rapacious and insatiable. Following the four empires, but in some sense a continuation, or revival of the fourth, or Roman empire, Daniel sees ten kings (7:7, 24), "And the ten horns out of this kingdom are ten kings that shall arise." But Daniel particularly "would know the truth" concerning a "little horn before whom there were three of the first horns

---

me, and made me know the interpretation of the things.

These great beasts, which are four, *are* four kings, *which* shall arise out of the earth.

But the saints of the most High shall take the kingdom, and possess the kingdom for ever, even for ever and ever.

Then I would know the truth of the fourth beast, which was diverse from all the others, exceeding dreadful, whose teeth *were of* iron, and his nails *of* brass; *which* devoured, brake in pieces, and stamped the residue with his feet;

And of the ten horns that *were* in his head, and *of* the other which came up, and before whom three fell; even *of* that horn that had eyes, and a mouth that spake very great things, whose look *was* more stout than his fellows.

I beheld, and the same horn made war with the saints, and prevailed against them;

Until the Ancient of days came, and judgment was given to the saints of the most High; and the time came that the saints possessed the kingdom.

Thus he said, The fourth beast shall be the fourth kingdom upon earth, which shall be diverse from all kingdoms, and shall devour the whole earth, and shall tread it down, and break it in pieces.

And the ten horns out of this kingdom *are* ten kings *that* shall arise: and another shall rise after them; and he shall be diverse from the first, and he shall subdue three kings.

And he shall speak *great* words against the most High, and shall wear out the saints of the most High, and think to change times and laws: and they shall be given into his hand until a time and times and the dividing of time.

But the judgment shall sit, and they shall take away his dominion, to consume and to destroy *it* unto the end.

And the kingdom and dominion, and the greatness of the kingdom under the whole heaven, shall be given to the people of the saints of the most High, whose kingdom *is* an everlasting kingdom, and all dominions shall serve and obey him.

Hitherto is the end of the matter. As for me Daniel, my cogitations much troubled me, and my countenance changed in me: but I kept the matter in my heart.—*Dan. 7.*

[6] And they shall fall by the edge of the sword, and shall be led away captive into all nations: and Jerusalem shall be trodden down of the Gentiles, until the times of the Gentiles be fulfilled.—*Luke 21:24.*

plucked up by the roots: and, behold, in this horn were eyes like the eyes of a man [superior discernment], and a mouth speaking great things" (Dan. 7:8).

Daniel is answered that the "little horn" is a king who shall arise after the ten kings have begun to reign over the ten kingdoms into which the former Roman empire shall be divided in the time of the end, "and he shall be diverse from the first [the ten kings], and he shall subdue three kings. And he shall speak great words against the most High, and shall wear out the saints of the most High" (Jews, as that expression shows), and the vision ends in the destruction of the "little horn," and the establishment of the kingdom of heaven.

The Revelation, obediently to the command given to the Apostle John, to "Write the things which thou hast seen, and the things which are, and the things which shall be after these" (Rev. 1:19), falls into three general divisions, and these again into sub-divisions.

The first, or "the things which thou hast seen" is chapter 1. "The things which are," the churches in Asia, arranged in an order which is prophetic of the whole history of the Church on earth, is in chapters 2 and 3.

It is, however, the third division which bulks largest in The Revelation. This division is indicated in the command to "write" by the words, "the things which shall be after these," that is, after the churches. The church period ends with Thyatira (Romanism), Philadelphia (the true believers in the Protestant churches), and Laodicea (the mass of mere profession in Protestantism), in view. In Rome there is a "rest," or remnant (Rev. 2:24)[7] of true believers. These, together with the Philadelphian believers throughout the Protestant churches, are caught up to meet the Lord in the air (John 14:1-3; 1 Cor. 15:51, 52; 1 Thess. 4:14-17; Rev. 2:24-29; 4:1),[8] thus leaving on the earth to pass

---

[7] But unto you I say, and unto the rest in Thyatira, as many as have not this doctrine, and which have not known the depths of Satan, as they speak; I will put upon you none other burden. —*Rev. 2:24.*

[8] Let not your heart be troubled: ye believe in God, believe also in me.

In my Father's house are many mansions: if *it were* not *so,* I would have told you. I go to prepare a place for you.

through the great tribulation the mass of mere Christian profession, whether Roman or Protestant. Then follows (deducting certain parenthetical passages which have nothing to do with the narrative) "the things which shall be."

And these are the very things which Daniel foretold concerning the end of the "times of the Gentiles"—the end-time of this age. The essential difference is that the Patmos vision enters more into detail. The central figure is still the "prince that shall come," the "Little Horn," the "abomination," the "man of sin"; but here he is the "Beast" (Rev. 13: 1-7).[9]

And if I go and prepare a place for you, I will come again, and receive you unto myself; that where I am, *there* ye may be also.—*John 14: 1-3*.

Behold, I shew you a mystery; We shall all not sleep, but we shall all be changed,

In a moment, in the twinkling of an eye, at the last trump: for the trumpet shall sound, and the dead shall be raised incorruptible, and we shall be changed.—*1 Cor. 15:51, 52*.

For if we believe that Jesus died and rose again, even so them also which sleep in Jesus will God bring with him.

For this we say unto you by the word of the Lord, that we which are alive *and* remain unto the coming of the Lord shall not prevent them which are asleep.

For the Lord himself shall descend from heaven with a shout, with the voice of the archangel, and with the trump of God: and the dead in Christ shall rise first:

Then we which are alive *and* remain shall be caught up together with them in the clouds, to meet the Lord in the air: and so shall we ever be with the Lord.—*1 Thess. 4: 14-17*.

But unto you I say, and unto the rest in Thyatira, as many as have not this doctrine, and which have not known the depths of Satan, as they speak; I will put upon you none other burden.

But that which ye have *already* hold fast till I come.

And he that overcometh, and keepeth my works unto the end, to him will I give power over the nations:

And he shall rule them with a rod of iron; as the vessels of a potter shall they be broken to shivers: even as I received of my Father.

And I will give him the morning star.

He that hath an ear, let him hear what the Spirit saith unto the churches.—*Rev. 2: 24-29*.

[9] And I stood upon the sand of the sea, and saw a beast rise up out of the sea, having seven heads and ten horns, and upon his horns ten crowns, and upon his heads the name of blasphemy.

And the beast which I saw was like unto a leopard, and his feet were as *the feet* of a bear, and his mouth as the mouth of a lion: and the dragon gave him his power, and his seat, and great authority.

In this great prophetic picture of the end the symbols which have already appeared in Daniel, and which have there acquired definite meanings, recur. Again we have the Gentile world-power in ten kingdoms; again we have these federated into one empire which, as in Daniel 7, is itself called "beast" (comp. Dan. 7:3, 5, 7; Rev. 13:1-3),[10] and a "beast" emperor rules over the restored "beast" empire (Dan. 7:8; Rev. 13:4-8).[11] As in Dan-

---

And I saw one of his heads as it were wounded to death; and his deadly wound was healed: and all the world wondered after the beast.

And they worshipped the dragon which gave power unto the beast: and they worshipped the beast, saying, Who *is* like unto the beast? who is able to make war with him?

And there was given unto him a mouth speaking great things and blasphemies; and power was given unto him to continue forty *and* two months.

And he opened his mouth in blasphemy against God, to blaspheme his name, and his tabernacle, and them that dwell in heaven.

And it was given unto him to make war with the saints, and to overcome them: and power was given him over all kindreds, and tongues, and nations.—*Rev. 13: 1-7.*

[10] And four great beasts came up from the sea, diverse one from another.

And behold another beast, a second, like to a bear, and it raised up itself on one side, and *it had* three ribs in the mouth of it between the teeth of it: and they said thus unto it, Arise, devour much flesh.

After this I saw in the night visions, and behold a fourth beast, dreadful and terrible, and strong exceedingly; and it had great iron teeth: it devoured and brake in pieces, and stamped the residue with the feet of it: and it *was* diverse from all the beasts that *were* before it; and it had ten horns.—*Dan. 7: 3, 5, 7.*

And I stood upon the sand of the sea, and saw a beast rise up out of the sea, having seven heads and ten horns, and upon his horns ten crowns, and upon his heads the name of blasphemy.

And the beast which I saw was like unto a leopard, and his feet were as *the feet* of a bear, and his mouth as the mouth of a lion: and the dragon gave him his power, and his seat, and great authority.

And I saw one of his heads as it were wounded to death; and his deadly wound was healed: and all the world wondered after the beast. — *Rev. 13: 1-3.*

[11] I considered the horns, and, behold, there came up among them another little horn, before whom there were three of the first horns plucked up by the roots: and, behold, in this horn *were* eyes like the eyes of man, and a mouth speaking great things.—*Dan. 7: 8.*

And they worshipped the dragon which gave power unto the beast: and they worshipped the beast, saying, Who *is* like unto the beast? who is able to make war with him?

And there was given unto him a mouth speaking great things and blasphemies; and power was given unto him to continue forty *and* two months.

And he opened his mouth in blasphemy against God, to blas-

THE LAST SEVEN YEARS OF THE AGE 151

iel the duration of his full power is "forty and two months" (Dan. 7:25; Rev. 13:5).[12]

The Revelation also gives the full detail of that which makes the great tribulation to be a time of unparalleled horror. The awful tyranny of the beast, to whom has been given over the full power of Satan, and who is aided by the antichrist, the "beast" out of the earth (Rev. 13:2-17),[13] is but one element in that horror. Already

---

pheme his name, and his tabernacle, and them that dwell in heaven.

And it was given unto him to make war with the saints, and to overcome them: and power was given him over all kindreds, and tongues, and nations.

And all that dwell upon the earth shall worship him, whose names are not written in the book of life of the Lamb slain from the foundation of the world.—*Rev. 13:4-8*.

[12] And he shall speak *great* words against the most High, and shall wear out the saints of the most High, and think to change.—*Dan. 7:25*.

And there was given unto him a mouth speaking great things and blasphemies; and power was given unto him to continue forty *and* two months. — *Rev. 13:5*.

[13] And the beast which I saw was like unto a leopard, and his feet were as *the feet* of a bear, and his mouth as the mouth of a lion: and the dragon gave him his power, and his seat, and great authority.

And I saw one of his heads as it were wounded to death; and his deadly wound was healed: and all the world wondered after the beast.

And they worshipped the dragon which gave power unto the beast: and they worshipped the beast, saying, Who *is* like unto the beast? who is able to make war with him?

And there was given unto him a mouth speaking great things and blasphemies; and power was given unto him to continue forty *and* two months.

And he opened his mouth in blasphemy against God, to blaspheme his name, and his tabernacle, and them that dwell in heaven.

And it was given unto him to make war with the saints, and to overcome them: and power was given him over all kindreds, and tongues, and nations.

And all that dwell upon the earth shall worship him, whose names are not written in the book of life of the Lamb slain from the foundation of the world.

If any man have an ear, let him hear.

He that leadeth into captivity shall go into captivity: he that killeth with the sword must be killed with the sword. Here is the patience and the faith of the saints.

And I beheld another beast coming up out of the earth; and he had two horns like a lamb, and he spake as a dragon.

And he exerciseth all the power of the first beast before him, and causeth the earth and them which dwell therein to worship the first beast, whose deadly wound was healed.

And he doeth great wonders, so that he maketh fire come down from heaven on the earth in the sight of men,

And deceiveth them that dwell on the earth by *the means of* those miracles which he had power to do in the sight of the beast; saying to them that dwell on the earth, that they should

the "trumpet" judgments are in the earth, and now, at the beginning of the last half of Daniel's seventieth "week" of this age—the three and one-half years of the great tribulation—the seven "vials of the wrath of God" (Rev. 16: 1-21)[14] are poured out "upon the earth." And

make an image to the beast, which had the wound by a sword, and did live.

And he had power to give life unto the image of the beast, that the image of the beast should both speak, and cause that as many as would not worship the image of the beast should be killed.

And he causeth all, both small and great, rich and poor, free and bond, to receive a mark in their right hand, or in their foreheads:

And that no man might buy or sell, save he that had the mark, or the name of the beast, or the number of his name.—*Rev. 13: 2-17.*

[14] And I heard a great voice out of the temple saying to the seven angels, Go your ways, and pour out the vials of the wrath of God upon the earth.

And the first went, and poured out his vial upon the earth; and there fell a noisome and grievous sore upon the men which had the mark of the beast, and *upon* them which worshipped his image.

And the second angel poured out his vial upon the sea; and it became as the blood of a dead *man:* and every living soul died in the sea.

And the third angel poured out his vial upon the rivers and fountains of waters; and they became blood.

And I heard the angel of the waters say, Thou art righteous, O Lord, which art, and wast, and shalt be, because thou hast judged thus.

For they have shed the blood of saints and prophets, and thou hast given them blood to drink; for they are worthy.

And I heard another out of the altar say, Even so, Lord God Almighty, true and righteous *are* thy judgments.

And the fourth angel poured out his vial upon the sun; and power was given unto him to scorch men with fire.

And men were scorched with great heat, and blasphemed the name of God, which hath power over these plagues: and they repented not to give him glory.

And the fifth angel poured out his vial upon the seat of the beast; and his kingdom was full of darkness; and they gnawed their tongues for pain,

And blasphemed the God of heaven because of their pains and their sores, and repented not of their deeds.

And the sixth angel poured out his vial upon the great river Euphrates; and the water thereof was dried up, that the way of the kings of the east might be prepared.

And I saw three unclean spirits like frogs *come* out of the mouth of the dragon, and out of the mouth of the beast, and out of the mouth of the false prophet.

For they are the spirits of devils, working miracles, *which* go forth unto the kings of the earth and of the whole world, to gather them to the battle of that great day of God Almighty.

Behold, I come as a thief, Blessed *is* he that watcheth, and keepeth his garments, lest he walk naked, and they see his shame.

And he gathered them together into a place called in the Hebrew tongue Armageddon.

And the seventh angel poured out his vial into the air; and

in this fact alone, that the great tribulation is a manifestation of the wrath of God upon the earth, is proof conclusive that the church is no longer on earth, for the church is not "appointed unto wrath."

It must be remembered that these judgments upon the earth and the nations have nothing to do with individuals, as such. World-powers are creatures of time, as national organizations are mere human arrangements. If, therefore, they are amenable to the justice of God at all, their judgment must come, not in eternity, but in time. They fall during the great tribulation.

To all this is added "the spirits of demons, working miracles" (Rev. 16: 14; comp. 2 Thess. 2: 9, 10).[15]

A complete view of the end-time of the age must include, besides the reconstruction of the Roman empire in ten kingdoms federated under the Beast-emperor, the religious organization called in the Apocalypse, "Babylon." It will be Laodicea and Thyatira—Protestantism and Romanism after the true believers out of both have been caught up to meet the Lord in the air (1 Thess. 4: 14-17).[8] Babylon="confusion" is the mingling of both in one great world-church. Many voices of influence are pleading now for such a union—the sacrifice of truth to seeming expediency. It is the Beast and his asso-

---

there came a great voice out of the temple of heaven, from the throne, saying, It is done.

And there were voices, and thunders, and lightnings; and there was a great earthquake, such as was not since men were upon the earth, so mighty an earthquake, *and* so great.

And the great city was divided into three parts, and the cities of the nations fell: and great Babylon came in remembrance before God, to give unto her the cup of the wine of the fierceness of his wrath.

And every island fled away, and the mountains were not found.

And there fell upon men a great hail out of heaven, *every stone* about the weight of a talent: and men blasphemed God because of the plague of the hail; for the plague thereof was exceeding great.—*Rev. 16: 1-21.*

[15] For they are the spirits of devils, working miracles, *which* go forth unto the kings of the earth and of the whole world, to gather them to the battle of that great day of God Almighty. —*Rev. 16: 14.*

Even him, whose coming is after the working of Satan with all power and signs and lying wonders,

And with all deceivableness of unrighteousness in them that perish; because they received not the love of the truth, that they might be saved.—*2 Thess. 2: 9, 10.*

ciated kings who turn upon and rend "Babylon." The Beast will brook no rival worship, even though it be but a form (Rev. 17:1-18; 18:1-24).[16]

---

[16] And there came one of the seven angels which had the seven vials, and talked with me, saying unto me, Come hither; I will shew unto thee the judgment of the great whore that sitteth upon many waters:

With whom the kings of the earth have committed fornication, and the inhabitants of the earth have been made drunk with the wine of her fornication.

So he carried me away in the spirit into the wilderness: and I saw a woman sit upon a scarlet coloured beast, full of names of blasphemy, having seven heads and ten horns.

And the woman was arrayed in purple and scarlet colour, and decked with gold and precious stones and pearls, having a golden cup in her hand full of abominations and filthiness of her fornication:

And upon her forehead *was* a name written, MYSTERY, BABYLON THE GREAT, THE MOTHER OF HARLOTS AND ABOMINATIONS OF THE EARTH.

And I saw the woman drunken with the blood of the saints, and with the blood of the martyrs of Jesus: and when I saw her, I wondered with great admiration.

And the angel said unto me, Wherefore didst thou marvel? I will tell thee the mystery of the woman, and of the beast that carrieth her, which hath the seven heads and ten horns.

The beast that thou sawest was, and is not; and shall ascend out of the bottomless pit, and go into perdition: and they that dwell on the earth shall wonder, whose names were not written in the book of life from the foundation of the world, when they behold the beast that was, and is not, and yet is.

And here *is* the mind which hath wisdom. The seven heads are seven mountains, on which the woman sitteth.

And there are seven kings: five are fallen, and one is, *and* the other is not yet come; and when he cometh, he must continue a short space.

And the beast that was, and is not, even he is the eighth, and is of the seven, and goeth into perdition.

And the ten horns which thou sawest are ten kings, which have received no kingdom as yet; but receive power as kings one hour with the beast.

These have one mind, and shall give their power and strength unto the beast.

These shall make war with the Lamb, and the Lamb shall overcome them: for he is Lord of lords, and King of kings: and they that are with him *are* called, and chosen, and faithful.

And he saith unto me, The waters which thou sawest, where the whore sitteth, are peoples, and multitudes, and nations, and tongues.

And the ten horns which thou sawest upon the beast, these shall hate the whore, and shall make her desolate and naked, and shall eat her flesh, and burn her with fire.

For God hath put in their hearts to fulfil his will, and to agree, and to give their kingdom unto the beast, until the words of God shall be fulfilled.

And the woman which thou sawest is that great city, which reigneth over the kings of the earth.—*Rev. 17: 1-18.*

And after these things I saw another angel come down from heaven, having great power; and the earth was lightened with his glory.

And he cried mightily with a strong voice, saying, Babylon the great is fallen, and is become the habitation of devils, and the hold of every foul spirit, and a cage of every unclean and hateful bird.

For all nations have drunk of the wine of the wrath of her fornication, and the kings of the earth have committed fornication with her, and the merchants of the earth are waxed rich through the abundance of her delicacies.

And I heard another voice from heaven, saying, Come out of her, my people, that ye be not partakers of her sins, and that ye receive not of her plagues.

For her sins have reached unto heaven, and God hath remembered her iniquities.

Reward her even as she rewarded you, and double unto her double according to her works: in the cup which she hath filled fill to her double.

How much she hath glorified herself, and lived deliciously, so much torment and sorrow give her: for she saith in her heart, I sit a queen, and am no widow, and shall see no sorrow.

Therefore shall her plagues come in one day, death, and mourning, and famine; and she shall be utterly burned with fire: for strong *is* the Lord God who judgeth her.

And the kings of the earth, who have committed fornication and lived deliciously with her, shall bewail her, and lament for her, when they shall see the smoke of her burning.

Standing afar off for the fear of her torment, saying, Alas, alas that great city Babylon, that mighty city! for in one hour is thy judgment come.

And the merchants of the earth shall weep and mourn over her; for no man buyeth their merchandise any more:

The merchandise of gold, and silver, and precious stones, and of pearls, and fine linen, and purple, and silk, and scarlet, and all thyine wood, and all manner vessels of ivory, and all manner vessels of most precious wood, and of brass, and iron, and marble,

And cinnamon, and odours, and ointments, and frankincense, and wine, and oil, and fine flour, and wheat, and beasts, and sheep, and horses, and chariots, and slaves, and souls of men.

And the fruits that thy soul lusted after are departed from thee, and all things which were dainty and goodly are departed from thee, and thou shalt find them no more at all.

The merchants of these things, which were made rich by her, shall stand afar off for the fear of her torment, weeping and wailing,

And saying, Alas, alas that great city, that was clothed in fine linen, and purple, and scarlet, and decked with gold, and precious stones, and pearls!

For in one hour so great riches is come to nought. And every shipmaster, and all the company in ships, and sailors, and as many as trade by sea, stood afar off,

And cried when they saw the smoke of her burning, saying, What *city is* like unto this great city!

And they cast dust on their heads, and cried, weeping and wailing, saying, Alas, alas that great city wherein were made rich all that had ships in the sea by reason of her costliness! for in one hour is she made desolate.

Rejoice over her, *thou* heaven, and *ye* holy apostles and prophets; for God hath avenged you on her.

And a mighty angel took up a stone like a great millstone, and cast *it* into the sea, saying, Thus with violence shall that great city Babylon be thrown down, and shall be found no more at all.

But quite apart from "Babylon" there will be at the end-time a true testimony to God and to his Christ in the earth. These true witnesses come into view in the seventh chapter of the Revelation. A Jewish remnant is first revealed as sealed, and after that "a great multitude, which no man could number, of all nations, and kindreds, and people, and tongues," are seen. In verse 14 it is definitely stated that, "these are they which came out of the great tribulation."

The very last of the last days of this age are involved in some measure of obscurity in the prophecy. Possibly this is the appointed method of impressing our minds with the fact that the times of the Gentiles and this present age end in a whirlwind of confusion. Putting together the passages in the Old Testament prophets which evidently relate to the Great Tribulation and Armageddon (Jer. 30:4-7; Dan. 12:1; Matt. 24:21; Joel 2:11; Isa. 10:28; 29:3; Micah 1:6; Joel 3:9; Rev. 18:11-21),[17,16] and the passages in the New Testa-

And the voice of harpers, and musicians, and of pipers, and trumpeters, shall be heard no more at all in thee; and no craftsman, of whatsoever craft *he be,* shall be found any more in thee; and the sound of a millstone shall be heard no more at all in thee;

And the light of a candle shall shine no more at all in thee; and the voice of the bridegroom and of the bride shall be heard no more at all in thee: for thy merchants were the great men of the earth; for by thy sorceries were all nations deceived.

And in her was found the blood of prophets, and of saints, and of all that were slain upon the earth.—*Rev. 18: 1-24.*

[17]And these *are* the words that the Lord spake concerning Israel and concerning Judah.

For thus saith the Lord; We have heard a voice of trembling, of fear, and not of peace.

Ask ye now, and see whether a man doth travail with child? wherefore do I see every man with his hands on his loins, as a woman in travail, and all faces are turned into paleness?

Alas! for that day *is* great, so that none *is* like it: it *is* even the time of Jacob's trouble; but he shall be saved out of it. —*Jer. 30: 4-7.*

And at that time shall Michael stand up, the great prince which standeth for the children of thy people: and there shall be a time of trouble, such as never was since there was a nation *even* to that same time: and at that time thy people shall be delivered, every one that shall be found written in the book.— *Dan. 12: 1.*

For then shall be great tribulation, such as was not since the beginning of the world to this time, no, nor ever shall be. —*Matt. 24: 21.*

And the Lord shall utter his voice before his army: for his camp *is* very great: for *he is* strong that executeth his word: for the day of the Lord *is* great

THE LAST SEVEN YEARS OF THE AGE

ment covering the same ground, so much may be discerned:

"Babylon," the apostate world-church, has been destroyed by the civil power headed up in the Emperor-Beast. Life is allowed no conditions of prosperity apart from the worship of the Beast and his image (Rev. 13: 16, 17).[18] There is another ecclesiastical despotism, for all power is bestowed upon the Antichrist, the "false prophet," that all may be compelled to worship the Beast (Rev. 13:12).[19] The saints of Revelation 7, especially the Remnant sealed out of all the tribes, who have turned to Jesus as the Messiah, are terribly persecuted.

There is an invasion of the holy land from the North. The words "Gog and Magog," with geographical designations which seem to warrant that conclusion (Ezek. 38:2),[20] have been well-nigh universally held to indicate that Russia heads this invasion. It is far from impossible that Japan and perhaps China swell the invading host. The Beast and his power seem to be, at first, the objects of the invasion. The hosts approach Jerusalem

---

and very terrible; and who can abide it?—*Joel 2:11*.

He is come to Aiath, he is passed to Migron; at Michmash he hath laid up his carriages.—*Isa. 10:28*.

And I will camp against thee round about, and will lay siege against thee with a mount, and I will raise forts against thee.—*Isa. 29:3*.

Therefore I will make Samaria as an heap of the field, and as plantings of a vineyard: and I will pour down the stones thereof into the valley, and I will discover the foundations thereof.—*Micah 1:6*.

Proclaim ye this among the Gentiles; Prepare war, wake up the mighty men, let all the men of war draw near; let them come up.—*Joel 3:9*.

[18] And he causeth all, both small and great, rich and poor, free and bond, to receive a mark in their right hand, or in their foreheads:

And that no man might buy or sell, save he that had the mark, or the name of the beast, or the number of his name.—*Rev. 13:16, 17*.

[19] And he exerciseth all the power of the first beast before him, and causeth the earth and them which dwell therein to worship the first beast, whose deadly wound was healed.—*Rev. 13:12*.

[20] Son of man, set thy face against Gog, the land of Magog, the chief prince of Meshech and Tubal, and prophesy against him. —*Ezek. 38:2*.

(Isa. 10:28-34).[21] It is then that the obscurity deepens, for in the final scene the Beast and False Prophet with their armies fight with the invaders against the heavenly armies led by Messiah in glory. This is Armageddon. It is the end not only of the Beast and his system, but of all Gentile world power. It is possible that signs in the heavens impress both the invaders and the Beast, driving them into a sudden confederacy against God. As to the fact that the end of Gentile supremacy has come there is no obscurity. The earth-scene is now cleared for the Kingdom of Jesus Christ.

---

[21] He is come to Aiath, he is passed to Migron; at Michmash he hath laid up his carriages:

They are gone over the passage: they have taken up their lodging at Geba; Ramah is afraid; Gibeah of Saul is fled.

Lift up thy voice, O daughter of Gallim: cause it to be heard unto Laish, O poor Anathoth.

Madmenah is removed; the inhabitants of Gebim gather themselves to flee.

As yet shall he remain at Nob that day: he shall shake his hand *against* the mount of the daughter of Zion, the hill of Jerusalem.

Behold, the Lord, the Lord of hosts, shall lop the bough with terror: and the high ones of stature *shall be* hewn down, and the haughty shall be humbled.

And he shall cut down the thickets of the forest with iron, and Lebanon shall fall by a mighty one.—*Isa. 10:28-34*.

XI. EARTH'S GOLDEN AGE

THERE is a deathless thing in the heart of humanity. Sometimes there is with it the dull pain of disappointed expectation. A panacea for earth's ills has been tried and failed. Sometimes it finds speech: "How long, O Lord, how long!" Sometimes it is a cry out of the darkness; sometimes it glows with faith.

It is the belief that there must yet be for humanity on this earth a life, a corporate, ordered life, a life not for a few fortunate and powerful ones, but a life for all which shall be rich in truth, justice, power, and love. No dateless centuries of lies, injustice, weakness, and hate have been able to extinguish that thing in the heart of humanity.

And now and again men thoughtful and wise have striven to give form to it—to say *what* it is for which the heart of humanity aches and longs; and Plato writes his "Republic," and Campanella his "City of the Sun," and Sir Thomas More his "Utopia," and Bacon his "New Atlantis," and Harrington his "Oceana." And when they have written, time counts out the days and years and they are still as before years of war, of the ruthless reign of the strong over the weak, of the delusions of a shallow optimism which shuts its eyes to realities. Such "optimists" patter of peace when there is no peace, and will not see that the evils from which the philosophers would save us are all as old as the race.

There is absolutely no mystery about these evils. The oldest brick dug from a Mesopotamian mound bears the same record of ambition, pride, greed, which are making the history of to-day. And we turn from the beautiful dreams of Plato and the others knowing only too well how impossible they are of accomplishment, how certainly even if once established they would be doomed by the rise of the superman, or the craft of the powerful few.

And not only are the facts unchanged, but we are absolutely at the end of our resources. Every method whereby the race has sought to realize the deathless vision has been tried to the dregs, and has failed. Forms of government from despotism to democracy; education—it is the most educated of the nations which to-day are engaged in the most brutal of wars; legislation; even "religion," have left the world-factors unchanged.

The futility of the ideal commonwealths of Plato and the others is precisely the futility of all superficial optimism—the notion that for the common good men are going to give up ambition, greed, and pride. We read their Utopias with a little sadness.

The race, after all, is one; and it is a kind of corporate logic which keeps the hope of a golden age alive in the universal human mind. It is the conviction, vague and undefined but real, that the divine wisdom and power in the human experiment requires a majestic vindication—a vindication that can only come through a reign of righteousness and love in the human social order.

Why should it be thought incredible that God, who recreated the earth and set man in it with full authority over the works of His hands, should return, at the end of the immense drama of human history, to His original thought and purpose? It is forgotten too easily that there is a "second man," another and a "last Adam." Might it not be well to ask, Why a "second" man? Why another *"Adam"?* and to demand an answer in larger terms than theology has ever found—an answer of cosmic breadth and grandeur.

And this, precisely, is the answer of Scripture. Not in Plato, nor in the Vedas, as Max Muller thought, still less in Hesiod, are we to look for the true theogony of the race—the solution of the pathetic effort, ever foredoomed to tragic failure, of the race to achieve its own destiny in that which Paul magnificently calls "the liberty of the glory of the sons of God" (Rom. 8:21).[1]

---

[1] Because the creature itself also shall be delivered from the bondage of corruption into the glorious liberty of the children of God.—*Rom. 8:21*.

For that which is an intellectual ideal, an inner urge toward the perfected social order in the mind of the race, and has sought expression in the Utopias, stands boldly forth in Scripture as a revealed purpose of God. The golden age is made sure by the covenants and promises of the Almighty.

Doubtless the whole subject has been made an offense to many sincere and well-meaning students of the Bible by the too exclusively Jewish conception of the "age to come" in controversies over it.

That the coming age is to fulfil the Davidic Covenant of the earth-rule of Messiah, as explained by the Prophets and confirmed by the oath of Jehovah and the message through Gabriel, is most true. But the New Testament lifts the work and purpose of the age to come into a breadth and majesty far beyond the promises to Israel, while including—nay, resting upon, those promises. For the thought and word of God have ever an inner and vaster content than appears upon the surface. There are perpetual surprises in the interpretation of Scripture by Scripture as the student follows the progressive unfolding of the Divine will.

The Davidic Covenant is indeed to be fulfilled in the age to come, but a vastly grander thing is fulfilled—the destiny of the race.

The testimony of Scripture to this great consummation may be summarized as follows:

It is well to remember that all the answers to questions concerning an age to come must be drawn from the Scriptures. If there is to be yet another age, or period of time marked off for a special dealing of God with the human race, our only possible source of knowledge about it is the Bible.

The traditional teaching, in which Protestant theology follows that of Rome, affirms a complete conversion of the world in this present age through the preaching of the Gospel by the church, followed by the return of Christ, the resurrection of the dead, the judgment of the "great white throne," and the eternal state.

But this present age is described by our Lord in terms which absolutely exclude the possibility of a universal conversion. Wheat and tares grow together till the harvest, and the tares are not merely unsaved men in the world, but unsaved men within the very sphere of profession—"among the wheat." So like to true believers are they that the "servants" cannot be trusted to "root them up." Good fish and bad are together in the very gospel net. And it is distinctly stated that the "harvest is the end of the age" (Matt. 13:28-30, 37-43, 49, 50).[2] To the same purport is the picture of the present age and of its end in the parables of the end-time, which is likened to Sodom and Gomorrah, and to the Flood.

But especially in the Olivet discourse (Matt. 24:1-30)[3] our Lord addresses Himself to the very task of

---

[2] He said unto them, An enemy hath done this. The servants said unto him, Wilt thou then that we go and gather them up?

But he said, Nay; lest while ye gather up the tares, ye root up also the wheat with them.

Let both grow together until the harvest: and in the time of harvest I will say to the reapers, Gather ye together first the tares, and bind them in bundles to burn them: but gather the wheat into my barn.—*Matt. 13:28-30.*

He answered and said unto them, He that soweth the good seed is the Son of man;

The field is the world; the good seed are the children of the kingdom; but the tares are the children of the wicked *one;*

The enemy that sowed them is the devil; the harvest is the end of the world; and the reapers are the angels.

As therefore the tares are gathered and burned in the fire; so shall it be in the end of this world.

The Son of man shall send forth his angels, and they shall gather out of his kingdom all things that offend, and them which do iniquity;

And shall cast them into a furnace of fire: there shall be wailing and gnashing of teeth.

Then shall the righteous shine forth as the sun in the kingdom of their Father. Who hath ears to hear, let him hear.—*Matt. 13: 37-43.*

So shall it be at the end of the world: the angels shall come forth, and sever the wicked from among the just,

And shall cast them into the furnace of fire: there shall be wailing and gnashing of teeth.—*Matt. 13:49, 50.*

[3] And Jesus went out, and departed from the temple: and his disciples came to *him* for to shew him the buildings of the temple.

And Jesus said unto them, See ye not all these things? verily I say unto you, There shall not be left here one stone upon another, that shall not be thrown down.

And as he sat upon the mount of Olives, the disciples came unto him privately, saying, Tell us, when shall these things be? and what *shall be* the sign of thy coming, and of the end of the world?

And Jesus answered and said unto them, Take heed that no man deceive you.

For many shall come in my name, saying, I am Christ; and shall deceive many.

describing the age, its end, and the events following the end. Wars, pestilences, famines, false Christs, and persecutions go through the age and rise to their most awful potency in the end, which is the "great tribulation."

And ye shall hear of wars and rumours of wars: see that ye be not troubled: for all *these things* must come to pass, but the end is not yet.

For nation shall rise against nation, and kingdom against kingdom: and there shall be famines, and pestilences, and earthquakes, in divers places.

All these *are* the beginning of sorrows.

Then shall they deliver you up to be afflicted, and shall kill you: and ye shall be hated of all nations for my name's sake.

And then shall many be offended, and shall betray one another, and shall hate one another.

And many false prophets shall rise, and shall deceive many.

And because iniquity shall abound, the love of many shall wax cold.

But he that shall endure unto the end, the same shall be saved.

And this gospel of the kingdom shall be preached in all the world for a witness unto all nations; and then shall the end come.

When ye therefore shall see the abomination of desolation, spoken of by Daniel the prophet, stand in the holy place, (whoso readeth, let him understand:)

Then let them which be in Judæa flee into the mountains.

Let him which is on the housetop not come down to take anything out of his house:

Neither let him which is in the field return back to take his clothes.

And woe unto them that are with child, and to them that give suck in those days!

But pray ye that your flight be not in the winter, neither on the sabbath day:

For then shall be great tribulation, such as was not since the beginning of the world to this time, no, nor ever shall be.

And except those days should be shortened, there should no flesh be saved: but for the elect's sake those days shall be shortened.

Then if any man shall say unto you, Lo, here *is* Christ, or there; believe *it* not.

For there shall arise false Christs, and false prophets, and shall shew great signs and wonders; insomuch that, if *it were* possible, they shall deceive the very elect.

Behold, I have told you before.

Wherefore if they shall say unto you, Behold, he is in the desert; go not forth: behold, *he is* in the secret chambers; believe *it* not.

For as the lightning cometh out of the east, and shineth even unto the west; so shall also the coming of the Son of man be.

For wheresoever the carcase is, there will the eagles be gathered together.

Immediately after the tribulation of those days shall the sun be darkened, and the moon shall not give her light, and the stars shall fall from heaven, and the powers of the heavens shall be shaken:

And then shall appear the sign of the Son of man in heaven: and then shall all the tribes of the earth mourn, and they shall see the Son of man coming in the clouds of heaven with power and great glory.—*Matt. 24: 1-30.*

The agencies are indeed present in this age in the Gospel of the grace of God, and the convicting, regenerating and sanctifying power of the Holy Spirit, which, if received by faith, would save every soul of man. But faith is not compulsory, and nigh two thousand years of preaching have demonstrated that as the age began with an outcalling from among the Gentiles of "a people for his name" (Acts 15:14)[4] so it has gone on. Glorious victories have been won for Christ, but never, anywhere, have all the hearers been converted. The age ends in catastrophe, in Armageddon, in the return of the Lord in glory, in the judgment of living Gentile nations preparatory to the kingdom, in the regathering of dispersed Israel, and the re-establishment of the Davidic monarchy in the person of Jesus Christ the Son of David (Matt. 1:1; Luke 1:30-33; Acts 15:14-17).[5] The Scripture testimony concerning the age to come may be thus summarized:

1. Such an age is definitely foretold in the following Scriptures: Matthew 12:32; Mark 10:30, with Luke 18:30; Luke 20:35; Ephesians 1:21; Hebrews 6:5.[6]

---

[4] Simeon hath declared how God at the first did visit the Gentiles, to take out of them a people for his name.—*Acts 15:14.*

[5] The book of the generation of Jesus Christ, the son of David, the son of Abraham.—*Matt. 1:1.*

And the angel said unto her, Fear not, Mary: for thou hast found favour with God.

And, behold, thou shalt conceive in thy womb, and bring forth a son, and shalt call his name JESUS.

He shall be great, and shall be called the son of the Highest: and the Lord God shall give unto him the throne of his father David:

And he shall reign over the house of Jacob for ever; and of his kingdom there shall be no end.—*Luke 1:30-33.*

Simeon hath declared how God at the first did visit the Gentiles, to take out of them a people for his name.

And to this agree the words of the prophets; as it is written,

After this I will return, and will build again the tabernacle of David, which is fallen down; and I will build again the ruins thereof, and I will set it up:

That the residue of men might seek after the Lord, and all the Gentiles, upon whom my name is called, saith the Lord, who doeth all these things.—*Acts 15:14-17.*

[6] And whosoever speaketh a word against the Son of man, it shall be forgiven him: but whosoever speaketh against the Holy Ghost, it shall not be forgiven him, neither in this world, neither in the *world* to come.—*Matt. 12:32.*

But he shall receive an hundredfold now in this time, houses, and brethren, and sisters, and mothers, and children,

In all these passages the Greek *aion,* transliterated by the English word *eon,* is translated in the Authorized Version by the word "world." It never means "world," but invariably, in Scripture as in classical Greek, means "age, dispensation." So any lexicon. So, also, any authoritative English dictionary definition of *eon.* Bengel truly says: "The horologe of earth is no measure for the eonloge of heaven."

2. The age to come is introduced by the return of the Lord in power and glory. He is accompanied by the sons of God, also in glory. These sons of God are they who have "received him" during this age (John 1:12, 13),[7] and who, if sleeping were raised in bodies "like unto his glorious body" (Phil. 3:20, 21),[8] if living, "changed" into the same likeness (1 Cor. 15:51, 52)[9] and caught up "to meet the Lord in the air" (1 Thess. 4:14-17),[10] before the great tribulation, that "hour of temptation which shall come upon all the world" (Rev. 3:10). Four events mark the beginning of the age to come. (1) The taking up of the church to meet the Lord in the air (1 Thess. 4:14-17).[11] (2) The judg-

---

and lands, with persecutions; and in the world to come eternal life.—*Mark 10:30.*

Who shall not receive manifold more in this present time, and in the world to come life everlasting.—*Luke 18:30.*

But they which shall be accounted worthy to obtain that world, and the resurrection from the dead, neither marry, nor are given in marriage.—*Luke 20:35.*

Far above all principality, and power, and might, and dominion, and every name that is named, not only in this world, but also in that which is to come. —*Eph. 1:21.*

And have tasted the good word of God, and the powers of the world to come.—*Heb. 6:5.*

[7] But as many as received him, to them gave he power to become the sons of God, *even* to them that believe on his name: Which were born not of blood, nor of the will of the flesh, nor of the will of man, but of God. —*John 1:12, 13.*

[8] For our conversation is in heaven; from whence also we look for the Saviour, the Lord Jesus Christ:

Who shall change our vile body, that it may be fashioned like unto his glorious body, according to the working whereby he is able even to subdue all things unto himself.—*Phil. 3: 20, 21.*

[9] Behold, I shew you a mystery: We shall not all sleep, but we shall all be changed,

In a moment, in the twinkling of an eye, at the last trump: for the trumpet shall sound, and the dead shall be raised incorruptible, and we shall be changed. —*1 Cor. 15:51, 52.*

[10, 11] For if we believe that Jesus died and rose again, even so them also which sleep in Jesus will God bring with him.

ment of the living Gentile nations who for near thirty centuries have misgoverned the earth in greed, pride, and ceaseless war (Matt. 25:31-46).[12] (3) The regathering of God's elect people, Israel (Deut. 30:1-10; Matt. 24:30, 31).[13] (4) The conversion of Israel (Zech.

For this we say unto you by the word of the Lord, that we which are alive *and* remain unto the coming of the Lord shall not prevent them which are asleep.

For the Lord himself shall descend from heaven with a shout, with the voice of the archangel, and with the trump of God: and the dead in Christ shall rise first:

Then we which are alive *and* remain shall be caught up together with them in the clouds, to meet the Lord in the air: and so shall we ever be with the Lord.—*1 Thess. 4: 14, 17.*

[12] When the Son of man shall come in his glory, and all the holy angels with him, then shall he sit upon the throne of his glory:

And before him shall be gathered all nations: and he shall separate them one from another, as a shepherd divideth *his* sheep from the goats:

And he shall set the sheep on his right hand, but the goats on the left.

Then shall the King say unto them on his right hand, Come, ye blessed of my Father, inherit the kingdom prepared for you from the foundation of the world:

For I was an hungred, and ye gave me meat: I was thirsty, and ye gave me drink: I was a stranger, and ye took me in:

Naked, and ye clothed me: I was sick, and ye visited me: I was in prison, and ye came unto me.

Then shall the righteous answer him, saying, Lord, when saw we thee an hungred, and fed *thee?* or thirsty, and gave *thee* drink?

When saw we thee a stranger, and took *thee* in? or naked, and clothed *thee?*

Or when saw we thee sick, or in prison, and came unto thee?

And the King shall answer and say unto them, Verily I say unto you, Inasmuch as ye have done *it* unto one of the least of these my brethren, ye have done *it* unto me.

Then shall he say also unto them on the left hand, Depart from me, ye cursed, into everlasting fire, prepared for the devil and his angels:

For I was an hungred, and ye gave me no meat: I was thirsty, and ye gave me no drink:

I was a stranger, and ye took me not in: naked, and ye clothed me not: sick, and in prison, and ye visited me not.

Then shall they also answer him, saying, Lord, when saw we thee an hungred, or athirst, or a stranger, or naked, or sick, or in prison, and did not minister unto thee?

Then shall he answer them, saying, Verily I say unto you, Inasmuch as ye did *it* not to one of the least of these, ye did *it* not to me.

And these shall go away into everlasting punishment: but the righteous into life eternal.—*Matt. 25: 31-46.*

[13] And it shall come to pass, when all these things are come upon thee, the blessing and the curse, which I have set before thee, and thou shalt call *them* to mind among all the nations, whither the Lord thy God hath driven thee,

And shalt return unto the Lord thy God, and shalt obey

12:10; Ezek. 20:33-38; Rom. 11:25-27).[14] (5) The

his voice according to all that I command thee this day, thou and thy children, with all thine heart, and with all thy soul;

That then the Lord thy God will turn thy captivity, and have compassion upon thee, and will return and gather thee from all the nations, whither the Lord thy God hath scattered thee.

If *any* of thine be driven out unto the outmost *parts* of heaven, from thence will the Lord thy God gather thee, and from thence will he fetch thee:

And the Lord thy God will bring thee into the land which thy fathers possessed, and thou shalt possess it; and he will do thee good, and multiply thee above thy fathers.

And the Lord thy God will circumcise thine heart, and the heart of thy seed, to love the Lord thy God with all thine heart, and with all thy soul, that thou mayest live.

And the Lord thy God will put all these curses upon thine enemies, and on them that hate thee, which persecuted thee.

And thou shalt return and obey the voice of the Lord, and do all his commandments which I command thee this day.

And the Lord thy God will make thee plenteous in every work of thine hand, in the fruit of thy body, and in the fruit of thy cattle, and in the fruit of thy land, for good: for the Lord will again rejoice over thee for good, as he rejoiced over thy fathers:

If thou shalt hearken unto the voice of the Lord thy God, to keep his commandments and his statutes which are written in this book of the law, *and* if thou turn unto the Lord thy God with all thine heart, and with all thy soul.—*Deut. 30: 1-10.*

And then shall appear the sign of the Son of man in heaven: and then shall all the tribes of the earth mourn, and they shall see the Son of man coming in the clouds of heaven with power and great glory.

And he shall send his angels with a great sound of a trumpet, and they shall gather together his elect from the four winds, from one end of heaven to the other.—*Matt. 24: 30, 31.*

[14] And I will pour upon the house of David, and upon the inhabitants of Jerusalem, the spirit of grace and of supplications: and they shall look upon me whom they have pierced, and they shall mourn for him, as one mourneth for *his* only *son*, and shall be in bitterness for him, as one that is in bitterness for *his* firstborn.—*Zech. 12: 10.*

As I live, saith the Lord God, surely with a mighty hand, and with a stretched out arm, and with fury poured out, will I rule over you:

And I will bring you out from the people, and will gather you out of the countries wherein ye are scattered, with a mighty hand, and with a stretched out arm, and with fury poured out.

And I will bring you into the wilderness of the people, and there will I plead with you face to face.

Like as I pleaded with your fathers in the wilderness of the land of Egypt, so will I plead with you, saith the Lord God.

And I will cause you to pass under the rod, and I will bring you into the bond of the covenant:

And I will purge out from among you the rebels, and them that transgress against me: I will bring them forth out of the country where they sojourn, and they shall not enter into the land of Israel: and ye shall know that I *am* the Lord.—*Ezek. 20: 33-38.*

For I would not, brethren, that ye should be ignorant of this mystery, lest ye should be

filling of the earth with the knowledge of the glory of the Lord (Isa. 11:9; Hab. 2:14; Acts 15:16, 17).[15]

3. The "righteousness" which is the ethical keyword of the age to come is simply right *doing*. The prophetic descriptions of the age surprise one accustomed to the high *spiritual* standard of the Epistles—the "fruit of the Spirit" (Gal. 5: 22, 23).[16] The practical "righteousness" of the age to come is summarily expressed in Micah 6:8: "He hath showed thee, O man, what is good, and what doth the Lord thy God require of thee, but to do justly, and to love mercy, and to walk humbly with thy God?" (Zech. 7:9, 10; 8:15-17.)[17]

The end of wars, the protection of the poor, the widow, and the orphan (Psa. 72: 2-4, 12-15),[18] the inflex-

---

wise in your own conceits; that blindness in part is happened to Israel, until the fulness of the Gentiles be come in.

And so all Israel shall be saved: as it is written, There shall come out of Sion the Deliverer, and shall turn away ungodliness from Jacob:

For this *is* my covenant unto them, when I shall take away their sins.—*Rom. 11: 25-27.*

[15] They shall not hurt nor destroy in all my holy mountain: for the earth shall be full of the knowledge of the Lord, as the waters cover the sea.—*Isa. 11: 9.*

For the earth shall be filled with the knowledge of the glory of the Lord, as the waters cover the sea.—*Hab. 2: 14.*

After this I will return, and will build again the tabernacle of David, which is fallen down; and I will build again the ruins thereof, and I will set it up:

That the residue of men might seek after the Lord, and all the Gentiles, upon whom my name is called, saith the Lord, who doeth all these things.—*Acts 15: 16, 17.*

[16] But the fruit of the Spirit is love, joy, peace, longsuffering, gentleness, goodness, faith,
Meekness, temperance: against such there is no law.—*Gal. 5: 22, 23.*

[17] Thus speaketh the Lord of hosts, saying, Execute true judgment, and shew mercy and compassions every man to his brother:

And oppress not the widow, nor the fatherless, the stranger, nor the poor; and let none of you imagine evil against his brother in your heart.—*Zech. 7: 9, 10.*

So again have I thought in these days to do well unto Jerusalem and to the house of Judah: fear ye not.

These *are* the things that ye shall do; Speak ye every man the truth to his neighbour; execute the judgment of truth and peace in your gates:

And let none of you imagine evil in your hearts against his neighbour; and love no false oath: for all these *are things* that I hate, saith the Lord.—*Zech. 8: 15-17.*

[18] He shall judge thy people with righteousness, and thy poor with judgment.

The mountains shall bring peace to the people, and the little hills, by righteousness.

He shall judge the poor of the people, he shall save the chil-

EARTH'S GOLDEN AGE

ible demand for just dealing, will be enforced by resistless power. It is the age of the "rod of iron." Whatever the inner thought of man may be, he must *do* right or die (Isa. 11:4; Psa. 2:9; Rev. 2:27).[19] Inflexible justice, inexorably enforced: "They *shall not* hurt nor destroy in all my holy mountain."

4. The unseen powers of evil, headed up in Satan, are removed from the scene (Rev. 20:1-3)[20] during the entire period.

5. At His first advent, while preaching to Israel the kingdom as "at hand" (Matt. 4:17; 10:5-7),[21] our Lord demonstrated in seven great miracles His power to deal with all the temporal (as well as the eternal) consequences of sin. He healed leprosy, type of the loathsomeness of sin, incurable by human power; palsy, the helplessness of the sinner; fever, the restlessness of sin; stilled a tempest, showing power over nature; cast out demons; raised from the dead, and healed the blind. Manifesting in full sway these powers, the age to come

---

dren of the needy, and shall break in pieces the oppressor.—*Psalm 72: 2-4*.

For he shall deliver the needy when he crieth; the poor also, and *him* that hath no helper.

He shall spare the poor and needy, and shall save the souls of the needy.

He shall redeem their soul from deceit and violence: and precious shall their blood be in his sight.

And he shall live, and to him shall be given of the gold of Sheba: prayer also shall be made for him continually; *and* daily shall he be praised.—*Psalm 72: 12-15*.

[19] But with righteousness shall he judge the poor, and reprove with equity for the meek of the earth: and he shall smite the earth with the rod of his mouth, and with the breath of his lips shall he slay the wicked.—*Isa. 11:4*.

Thou shalt break them with a rod of iron; thou shalt dash them in pieces like a potter's vessel.—*Psalm 2:9*.

And he shall rule them with a rod of iron; as the vessels of a potter shall they be broken to shivers: even as I received of my Father.—*Rev. 2:27*.

[20] And I saw an angel come down from heaven, having the key of the bottomless pit and a great chain in his hand.

And he laid hold on the dragon, that old serpent, which is the Devil, and Satan, and bound him a thousand years,

And cast him into the bottomless pit, and shut him up, and set a seal upon him, that he should deceive the nations no more, till the thousand years should be fulfilled: and after that he must be loosed a little season.—*Rev. 20: 1-3*.

[21] From that time Jesus began to preach, and to say, Repent: for the kingdom of heaven is at hand.—*Matt. 4:17*.

These twelve Jesus sent forth, and commanded them, saying, Go not into the way of the Gen-

will be one of health and so of restored longevity (Isa. 65:18-20).[22]

6. But these are merely the foundational and administrative features of the age to come. They are largely negative—the casting out of the present causes of degeneracy and disease, but essential to that which is, constructively, the glory of the age to come. For that age is to witness the "manifestation [*apokalupsis*=unveiling] of the sons of God." The sons of God, partakers of the Divine nature through the new birth (2 Pet. 1:4),[23] and of the very eternal life of the Son of God (John 3:16; 6:47; Col. 3:4; 1 John 5:11, 12),[24] are "joint heirs" with Him who is "heir of all things" (Rom. 8:17; Col. 1:16; Heb. 1:2).[25] As He was veiled in the flesh of His humiliation so that only faith discerned

---

tiles, and into *any* city of the Samaritans enter ye not:

But go rather to the lost sheep of the house of Israel.

And as ye go, preach, saying, The kingdom of heaven is at hand.—*Matt. 10:5-7.*

[22] But be ye glad and rejoice for ever *in that* which I create: for, behold, I create Jerusalem a rejoicing, and her people a joy.

And I will rejoice in Jerusalem, and joy in my people: and the voice of weeping shall be no more heard in her, nor the voice of crying.

There shall be no more thence an infant of days, nor an old man that hath not filled his days: for the child shall die an hundred years old; but the sinner *being* an hundred years old shall be accursed.—*Isa. 65:18-20.*

[23] Whereby are given unto us exceeding great and precious promises: that by these ye might be partakers of the divine nature, having escaped the corruption that is in the world through lust.—*2 Pet. 1:4.*

[24] For God so loved the world, that he gave his only begotten Son, that whosoever believeth in him should not perish, but have everlasting life.—*John 3:16.*

Verily, verily, I say unto you, He that believeth on me hath everlasting life.—*John 6:47.*

When Christ, *who is* our life, shall appear, then shall ye also appear with him in glory.—*Col. 3:4.*

And this is the record, that God hath given to us eternal life, and this life is in his Son.

He that hath the Son hath life; *and* he that hath not the Son of God hath not life.—*1 John 5:11,12.*

[25] And if children, then heirs; heirs of God, and joint-heirs with Christ; if so be that we suffer with *him*, that we may be also glorified together.—*Rom. 8:17.*

For by him were all things created, that are in heaven, and that are in earth, visible and invisible, whether *they be* thrones, or dominions, or principalities, or powers: all things were created by him, and for him.—*Col. 1:16.*

Hath in these last days spoken unto us by *his* Son, whom he hath appointed heir of all things, by whom also he made the world. —*Heb. 1:2.*

EARTH'S GOLDEN AGE

Him as the Son of God, so the sons of God are veiled—"the world knoweth us not" (1 John 3:1).[26]

But that is not all. Creation, made for the Son and sons of God, following the fortunes of the "first man Adam" (1 Cor. 15:45)[27] has been "made subject to vanity" ("emptiness" of the real objects of creation), (Rom. 8:20; Eccl. 1:4-8).[28] From the entrance of sin to the very end of the present age, creation, made for the sons of God "waits" for the unveiling of the sons of God. Nature does not give up her greater forces to man in his avarice, his ruthless use of her powers, his unequal distribution of her benefits. We cannot reach by imagination even a conception of the reserves of nature never to be given up except to the Heir, and the joint heirs. Till they are "unveiled" and on the scene, creation "waits."

At no point does the divine revelation say so much, and yet with an impenetrable reserve, of an inconceivably wonderful age awaiting humanity as in Romans 8:18-23, with Hebrews 2:1-13.[29]

---

[26] Behold, what manner of love the Father hath bestowed upon us, that we should be called the sons of God: therefore the world knoweth us not, because it knew him not.—*1 John 3:1.*

[27] And so it is written, The first man Adam was made a living soul; the last Adam *was made* a quickening spirit.—*1 Cor. 15:45.*

[28] For the creature was made subject to vanity, not willingly, but by reason of him who hath subjected *the same* in hope.—*Rom. 8:20.*

One generation passeth away, and *another* generation cometh: but the earth abideth for ever.

The sun also ariseth, and the sun goeth down, and hasteth to his place where he arose.

The wind goeth toward the south, and turneth about unto the north; it whirleth about continually, and the wind returneth again according to his circuits.

All the rivers run into the sea; yet the sea *is* not full; unto the place from whence the rivers come, thither they return again.

All things *are* full of labour; man cannot utter *it*: the eye is not satisfied with seeing, nor the ear filled with hearing.—*Eccl. 1:4-8.*

[29] For I reckon that the sufferings of this present time *are* not worthy *to be compared* with the glory which shall be revealed in us.

For the earnest expectation of the creature waiteth for the manifestation of the sons of God.

For the creature was made subject to vanity, not willingly, but by reason of him who hath subjected *the same* in hope,

Because the creature itself also shall be delivered from the bondage of corruption into the glorious liberty of the children of God.

For we know that the whole creation groaneth and travaileth in pain together until now.

Incontestably the three "groans" of Romans 8:22-26 still continue.[30] All the discoveries and inventions of man have not silenced one of them. Creation groans under the pains of unavailing labor—the pangs that bring forth nothing; we ourselves, though we have the first fruits of the Spirit, groan in longing for the redemption

---

And not only *they*, but ourselves also, which have the firstfruits of the Spirit, even we ourselves groan within ourselves, waiting for the adoption, *to wit*, the redemption of our body.—*Rom. 8: 18-23.*

Therefore we ought to give the more earnest heed to the things which we have heard, lest at any time we should let *them* slip.

For if the word spoken by angels was stedfast, and every transgression and disobedience received a just recompence of reward;

How shall we escape, if we neglect so great salvation; which at the first began to be spoken by the Lord, and was confirmed unto us by them that heard *him;*

God also bearing *them* witness, both with signs and wonders, and with divers miracles, and gifts of the Holy Ghost, according to his own will?

For unto the angels hath he not put in subjection the world to come, whereof we speak.

But one in a certain place testified, saying, What is man, that thou art mindful of him? or the son of man, that thou visitest him?

Thou madest him a little lower than the angels; thou crownedst him with glory and honour, and didst set him over the works of thy hands:

Thou hast put all things in subjection under his feet. For in that he put all in subjection under him, he left nothing *that is* not put under him. But now we see not yet all things put under him.

But we see Jesus, who was made a little lower than the angels for the suffering of death, crowned with glory and honour; that he by the grace of God should taste death for every man.

For it became him, for whom *are* all things, and by whom *are* all things, in bringing many sons unto glory, to make the captain of their salvation perfect through sufferings.

For both he that sanctifieth and they who are sanctified *are* all of one: for which cause he is not ashamed to call them brethren,

Saying, I will declare thy name unto my brethren, in the midst of the church will I sing praise unto thee.

And again, I will put my trust in him. And again, Behold I and the children which God hath given me.—*Heb. 2: 1-13.*

[30] For we know that the whole creation groaneth and travaileth in pain together until now.

And not only *they,* but ourselves also, which have the firstfruits of the Spirit, even we ourselves groan within ourselves, waiting for the adoption, *to wit,* the redemption of our body.

For we are saved by hope: but hope that is seen is not hope: for what a man seeth, why doth he yet hope for?

But if we hope for that we see not, *then* do we with patience wait for *it.*

Likewise the Spirit also helpeth our infirmities: for we know not what we should pray for as we ought: but the Spirit itself maketh intercession for us with groanings which cannot be uttered.—*Rom. 8: 22-26.*

of the body to be wrought by the coming of the Lord for His church (Rom. 8: 22, 23; Eph. 1: 14),[31] and the Spirit within us intercedes with groanings which cannot be uttered (Rom. 8: 26).[32] In heaven, the Lord waits.

It should be remembered (1) that both the great tribulation, and the age to come which the tribulation introduces, are periods during which the Gospel wins its greatest triumphs in salvation. Out of the great tribulation comes the Jewish remnant which turns to Christ in that awful time, and "a great multitude, which no man could number, of all nations, and kindreds, and people, and tongues"—Gentiles—who have washed their robes in the blood. We number converts easily enough now; in that awful time they become innumerable (Rev. 7: 4-10).[33] And the age to come will also witness an all

---

[31] For we know that the whole creation groaneth and travaileth in pain together until now.

And not only *they,* but ourselves also, which have the firstfruits of the Spirit, even we ourselves groan within ourselves, waiting for the adoption, *to wit,* the redemption of our body.—*Rom. 8: 22, 23.*

Which is the earnest of our inheritance until the redemption of the purchased possession, unto the praise of his glory.—*Eph. 1: 14.*

[32] Likewise the Spirit also helpeth our infirmities: for we know not what we should pray for as we ought: but the Spirit itself maketh intercession for us with groanings which cannot be uttered.—*Rom. 8: 26.*

[33] And I heard the number of them which were sealed: *and there were* sealed an hundred *and* forty *and* four thousand of all the tribes of the children of Israel.

Of the tribe of Juda *were* sealed twelve thousand. Of the tribe of Reuben *were* sealed twelve thousand. Of the tribe of Gad *were* sealed twelve thousand.

Of the tribe of Aser *were* sealed twelve thousand. Of the tribe of Nepthalim *were* sealed twelve thousand. Of the tribe of Manasses *were* sealed twelve thousand.

Of the tribe of Simeon *were* sealed twelve thousand. Of the tribe of Levi *were* sealed twelve thousand. Of the tribe of Issachar *were* sealed. twelve thousand.

Of the tribe of Zabulon *were* sealed twelve thousand. Of the tribe of Joseph *were* sealed twelve thousand. Of the tribe of Benjamin *were* sealed twelve thousand.

After this I beheld, and, lo, a great multitude, which no man could number, of all nations, and kindreds, and people, and tongues, stood before the throne, and before the Lamb, clothed with white robes, and palms in their hands;

And cried with a loud voice, saying, Salvation to our God which sitteth upon the throne, and unto the Lamb.—*Rev. 7: 4-10.*

but complete conversion of the human family (Acts 15: 16, 17).[34]

But alas! an inveterately God-hating residuum of the race remains. Satan is allowed to test humanity once more, and gathers an army of these (Rev. 20:7-9).[35] The final judgment of the wicked "dead" follows, and the scene is cleared for the new heavens and the new earth.

---

[34] After this I will return, and will build again the tabernacle of David, which is fallen down; and I will build again the ruins thereof, and I will set it up:

That the residue of men might seek after the Lord, and all the Gentiles, upon whom my name is called, saith the Lord, who doeth all these things.—*Acts 15: 16, 17.*

[35] And when the thousand years are expired, Satan shall be loosed out of his prison,

And shall go out to deceive the nations which are in the four quarters of the earth, Gog and Magog, to gather them together to battle: the number of whom *is* as the sand of the sea.

And they went up on the breadth of the earth, and compassed the camp of the saints about, and the beloved city: and fire came down from God out of heaven, and devoured them.—*Rev. 20: 7-9.*